ATHEISM
&
PHILOSOPHY

Kai Nielsen

ATHEISM
&
PHILOSOPHY

With a new Preface by the Author

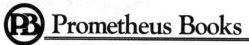

Prometheus Books

59 John Glenn Drive
Amherst, New York 14228-2197

Published 2005 by Prometheus Books

Inquiries should be addressed to
Prometheus Books
59 John Glenn Drive
Amherst, New York 14228–2197
VOICE: 716–691–0133, ext. 207
FAX: 716–564–2711
WWW.PROMETHEUSBOOKS.COM

09 08 07 06 05   5 4 3 2 1

Library of Congress Cataloging-in-Publication Data

Nielsen, Kai, 1926–.
    Atheism and philosophy / Kai Nielsen.
        p. cm.
    Originally published: Philosophy & Atheism. Buffalo, N.Y. :
Prometheus Books, 1985.
    Includes bibliographical references.
    ISBN 1–59102–298–3 (pbk. : alk. paper)
    1. Atheism. 2. Agnosticism. 3. Religion. I. Title: Atheism and
philosophy. II. Title.

BL2747.3.N49 2005
211'.8—dc22

                                                        2005047254

Printed in the United States of America on acid-free paper

CONTENTS

5

To Sidney Hook
our differences notwithstanding
and to whom I stand in intellectual debt

Preface

The essays collected together in this volume were written over a number of years for diverse audiences, on various occasions, and for a variety of purposes. "The Making of an Atheist" and "Does God Exist?: Reflections on Disbelief" were written for general audiences. There I try to be very direct and I eschew the protection of the qualifications with which philosophers, when writing principally for other philosophers, tend to hedge their bets. When philosophical essays of a more technical kind are the product of a creative and disciplined mind, such complex accounts are, in spite of the demands made on the reader, very valuable indeed; but there is also a place in our intellectual life for rather more simplified and unqualified statements. The latter, when successful, have a way of speaking directly to a diverse group of people in a way that more nuanced accounts cannot hope to achieve. I try to do this in the essays mentioned above and it might be best for an utter novice in philosophy to read these first; indeed, it might be better to read them even before turning to my introduction. However, for those with an equivalent to an introductory course in philosophy, it would be better, I believe, to read the book in the conventional manner, from beginning to end.

I would not want these remarks to be misunderstood. I have sought, throughout all the essays in this volume, to write in a relatively nontechnical, jargon free manner and to write in such a way that any reader who can follow my argument will readily come to see its underlying rationale. Whether it strikes a chord of agreement is, of course, another matter. But what I am trying to do, the point of doing it, and the argument for it should be tolerably evident. That notwithstanding, it is true that in the essays, other than the two mentioned above, I do make greater demands on my reader.

The essays in this volume were, as I remarked initially, written over a number of years and while I hope they form a coherent and integrated whole, it is the case that my views have developed, or at least in some measure changed, and between some of these essays there is, at some points, something of a tension. The place where it is most pronounced is between "Religion and Commitment" (1961), an essay written two decades ago, and a more recent essay entitled "The Burden of Proof and *The Presumption of Atheism*" (1977). "Religion and Commitment" is resolutely verificationist—too verificationist for many people's taste—while "The Burden of Proof" raises a series of issues that verificationist accounts in the philosophy of religion need to meet. I am inclined, though not without a certain ambivalence, to think that they can be met; and I am inclined to believe, as well, that such an empiricism is not incompatible with realism but, that notwithstanding, such a verificationist account would need to be more qualified than it is in "Religion and Commitment."

Again, I do not want to be misunderstood. I am not in effect disavowing the core set of claims in "Religion and Commitment," for they seem to me to press home, though sometimes in too crude a form, questions that very much need to be faced in thinking about religion. But for those who think that such verificationist medicine just won't work, "In Defense of Atheism," "Religion and Rationality," and "The Embeddedness of Atheism" show how much of the case for atheism can be conducted without reliance on verificationist assumptions.

The essays are designed to provide an unfolding integrated whole to which the introduction gives guidance as well as providing a delineation of atheism that clearly captures it as not quite the straightforward conception many have taken it to be. But it is also the case that each essay (the introductory essay apart) is self-contained and may be read in any order without reference to the others.

Conversations with many people, including generations of students, have been of considerable value to me in giving shape to these thoughts. Indeed, there are far more people who have helped me than I can even begin to mention, but I would like to acknowledge some of the individuals to whom I owe the most, namely: Angel Alcala, William Bean, Rodger Beehler, Pat Brown, Russell Cornett, Adel Daher, Joseph Epstein, Karl Frank, Joseph Gilbert, Jack Glickman, Sidney Hook, Grace Mariane Jantzen, Tziporah Kasachkopff, George Kateb, Janet Keating, William Kennick, C. B. Martin, Stanley Malinovitch, Hugo Meynell, Robert McKim, James Moulder, George Monticone, Robert Moses, Louis Navia, Elisabeth Nielsen, Terence Penelhum, Alfred Prettyman, Neil Rossman, Stanley Stein, Kenneth Stern, R. X. Ware, and Nettie Wiebe. I should also like to thank Merlette Schnell and Arlene Thomas for their cheerful and accurate typing of the manuscript and Shabbir Akhtar for his reading of the proof with such dispatch and, in doing so, saving me from some blunders.

Kai Nielsen
University of Calgary

PREFACE
TO THE
PAPERBACK EDITION

I

If I were to write this book anew, I would not write a very different book. Of course, I would put certain things differently. After all, more water has flowed over the dam. But whether it is the hardening of intellectual arteries or not, I would still basically say what I said in the original *Philosophy and Atheism*. There are, however, some places that need clarifying and filling in, and there is a need to further query some things I said or assumed. Much of the latter results from my being rooted in the increasing influence of Ludwig Wittgenstein (particularly his *On Certainty*), as well as Richard Rorty's metaphilosophical thought—his distinctive brand of pragmatism, deep contextualism, and historicism; I have also been increasingly influenced by *certain* aspects of Charles Saunders Peirce's work: his fallibilism and his subtle meshing of his critical commonsensism with his pragmatism. Perhaps by what I say in this preface those influences will not seem evident (though I hope otherwise), but they are there all the same giving a new nuance to my thinking. (It already had started in *Atheism and Philosophy* but it had not so filled itself out or taken as coherent a pattern.) If I were to write *Atheism and Philosophy* anew there would as a result of these influences have been a different *stress*. My *Naturalism and Religion* comes nearer to it. But earlier thoughts *may* be better than later ones. Others are the ones to judge that. But rereading *Atheism and Philosophy* reawakened a sense of agreement with most of what I said there.

All that perhaps opaque reference to influences and effects aside, what I want to do in this preface is generally make it harder for the believer (and not only for the simple believer) and for the atheist (and not only for the simple atheist). (See here pp. 249–56 of the text.) Here in this preface, and even more extensively in *Naturalism and Religion*, I want for we moderns (postmoderns also, if you will) to articulate religious belief, agnosticism, and atheism in their strongest forms and to ask ourselves which of these life-forms, if any, are most worthy of our allegiance or whether anything like that can even be intelligibly asked.

I will not repeat here (even in summary form) the arguments of the body of the book. I shall instead lay stress on some of the crucial strains and lacunae in the book where I think more reflection and argument are needed—where the case for atheism needs strengthening but also where it needs querying and challenging. The introduction to *Atheism and Philosophy* lays out how atheism is to be characterized; chapters 2 and 3 provide simple and I hope clearly articulated reasons for my endorsing atheism, and chapter 4 carefully distinguishes both traditional forms of agnosticism and atheism from each other, discusses some sophisticated forms of atheism and agnosticism that have emerged after the rise of linguistic philosophy, pursues agnosticism's deep rationale so articulated in the modern mode, and contrasts it with fideism. Chapter 5 and chapter 11 are arguably the centerpieces of *Atheism and Philosophy*; in chapter 5 after setting out and then facing the strongest forms of agnosticism and fideism I can muster, I argue for the superiority of atheism.

It is clear that, like Wittgenstein, J. L. Austin, Burton Dreben, the logical positivists, Richard Rorty, and, in effect, W. V. O.

Quine and Donald Davidson, that I reject metaphysics regarding it as nonsense or as Austin said, "cackle." I defend a thorough-going substantive naturalism with its corollary atheism in my *Naturalism without Foundations*, but I do not do so as a metaphysical view or as Quine says somewhat misleadingly as an ontology. (But remember, for Quine philosophy is intended to be just a part of natural science.) What he calls "ontology" is not something distinct from physics. So he should also be seen as taking an antimetaphysical stance. Where I conflict with him is over his *scientism*. I do not think that he or Russell are right in believing that what science (natural science?) cannot tell us, we cannot know. There are all sorts of common-sense knowledge and social, political, and moral knowledge that science can tell us little (if anything) about: that human beings stand in need of love, that promises are generally to be kept, that justice involves reciprocity, that respect for others is, or at least should be, a central feature in our lives, and that indifference to one's fellow humans is evil are good examples. People who have no understanding of science—who even lived before the rise of science—can understand them and know them to be justified. And things are no different for us moderns. We need not wait on science to confirm or disconfirm them and for most of them at least we have no understanding of how science could confirm or disconfirm (infirm) them. Here I stand with Wittgenstein and Georg von Wright rather than with Russell and Quine.

However, I claim that standard theism, where not grossly anthropomorphic and thus unacceptable to modern believers and nonbelievers alike, in its modern forms also makes false claims, though their meaning is sufficiently indeterminate that it is not clear whether they are false or incoherent. That makes it problematic how to classify them. But, whether false or incoherent, they are hardly strong contenders for religious acceptance. However, in both its standard and less standard forms, theism is inescapably a *metaphysical religiosity*; essential parts of such theisms (standard and less standard) have metaphysical beliefs, e.g., "God created the heavens and earth," "God has all creatures in His providential care," "God is the perfect good," "God is transcendent to the world," and "God is to be identified with no finite being." These are not empirical claims; they do not make claims open to empirical confirmation or disconfirmation, and they are not hypotheses to be tested. Moreover, believers do not regard them to be testable. Most believers just accept them as unassailable. They do not try to prove them or try to test them. However, without them their faith would be destroyed; they are, that is, the life-string for their Judeo, Christian, or Islamic beliefs (whichever they have). Without them these religions would be undermined. Without such metaphysical beliefs they would be what Richard Wollheim calls "dying religions."

However, need or not, we have very good reasons to regard Judeo-Christian-Islamic belief as containing metaphysical beliefs and as therefore, however much some believers may want to deny it, nonsense. At least the philosophers mentioned two paragraphs above have given us in various ways reasons for the rejection of metaphysics; a rejection backed up with reasons (and I provide further reasons, particularly in chapter 5) for regarding metaphysical beliefs as nonsensical. (See also part 1 of my *On Transforming Philosophy* and the postscript of my *Naturalism and Religion*.) However, as much as *some* of us think we stand in need of God's mercy and forgiveness, we also think there is no God there to answer that need. Believers' beliefs *about* their beliefs drive them to a metaphysical religiosity (Hägerström, *Philosophy and Religion*). It is not of course the whole of religious belief or attunement to their religion, but it is an inescapable part of it. Without it religious people are adrift.

Some will respond to this by trying to defend metaphysical beliefs as not being nonsensical. I will not reenter that debate here though I have done so extensively elsewhere (see, for example, the references above). However, I would like to remark that my belief is not just a hangover from logical positivism, a movement which is now dead. I would like here just to cite two claims of two eminent philosophers who I find claiming things I have felt for a long time. The first is Richard Rorty, no friend of positivism. Rorty remarks, "I am saying that the positivists were absolutely right in thinking [metaphysics] imperative to extirpate when 'metaphysics' means the attempt to give knowledge of what science cannot know" (Rorty, *Philosophy and the Mirror of Nature*, p. 384). I do not take it that Rorty is embracing scientism here (though it sounds like it). The context indicates that he is speaking of the kind of "knowledge" that has traditionally been identified with metaphysics which claims to a "metaphysical knowledge" that science cannot know, but this does not seek to extirpate Quine's ontology, something that Quine regards as part of natural science. Rorty refers to Plato's theory of the good and not to common-sense moral truisms such as truth is to be told or promises are to be kept. The metaphysics which Rorty with the logical positivists seeks to extirpate is what has traditionally classically been meant by "metaphysics." (This is also what I mean by it. See my *On Transforming Philosophy*.) And metaphysical religiosity is one of the things he thinks positivism rightly extirpates (*Philosophy and the Mirror of Nature*, p. 384). But this is not to deny that there are certain common-sense beliefs which science does not articulate and very likely cannot articulate.

The other sentence comes from the opening paragraph of Elliott Sober's presidential address to the central division of the American Philosophical Association's meetings of 1999:

> That some propositions are testable while others are not was a fundamental idea of the philosophical program known as logical empiricism (positivism). The program is now widely thought to be defunct. Quine's (1953) "Two Dogmas of Empiricism" and Hempel's (1950) "Problems and Changes in the Empiricist Criterion of Meaning" are among its most notable epitaphs. Yet, as we know from Mark Twain's comment on the obituary that he once had the pleasure of reading about himself, the report of a death can be an exaggeration. The research program that began in Vienna and Berlin continues, even though many of the specific formulations that came out of those circles are flawed and need to be replaced. (Sober, "Testability," p. 47)

Sober then proceeds, swimming against the current, to show, first, that the concept of testability is not the vestige of a bygone age, and then to state a criterion of testability, and to show it has important applications. We can see here that not all is dross that was logical positivism (empiricism), and we can come to have a sense that such purportedly factual claims as that it is a fact that God created the heavens and the earth might well do with a little attention to their possible testability. We do well to query metaphysical claims particularly in the grand robust sense that metaphysical religiosity requires.

The other way to respond to my claim that key religious utterances are nonsense is to claim that they all can be plausibly construed as nonmetaphysical. But look at the examples I gave four paragraphs back. They are paradigm and central cases of Judeo-Christian-Islamic religious claims—hinge beliefs for these religions—but they are also plainly not empirical claims, not tautologies or in other ways analytic or grammatical (in the Wittgensteinian sense). And they are not just (if at all) moral utterances. If they are not taken to be metaphysical their logical status is very obscure, though, in any case, their logical status is very obscure. But they certainly appear to be metaphysical claims though not metaphysical claims tied to any particular philosopher's metaphysical system, e.g., Plato's, Leibnitz's, Hegel's, or Whitehead's. But they are nonanalytic, nongrammatical claims which are also nonempirical but still allegedly making claims about how things are. They (1) make claims that are nontestable, and (2) refer to what is claimed to be a reality that is transcendent to the universe. These at least look like very good candidates for metaphysical statements (pseudo-statements, if you will).

There are empiricist philosophers such as Richard Braithwaite and R. M. Hare who attempt to "translate" or "interpret" these sentences as sentences used to express attitudes and ways of acting (Braithwaite, "An Empiricist's View"; Hare, "The Simple Believer"; Nielsen, *God, Scepticism and Modernity*, pp. 172–89). "God exists" becomes "Have an agapeistic attitude and associate it with a certain narrative (e.g., the Gospels) which you entertain and can either believe or not believe." "God created the heavens and the earth" means something like "Have an agapeistic attitude and view the world benignly and associate this with certain narratives which while you entertain, you may or may not believe." "To believe in God" is "To take an agapeistic attitude and to associate it with certain narratives which you entertain but may or may not believe," and so on. Here we have an utterly empirical conception all right, expressed in what Rudolf Carnap might call an "empiricist language." But taken as a reading of the religious sentences in question, it is hard not to take it as a joke even if it did come from distinguished philosophers. It certainly is a *reductio* of religious talk. In reality it is a desperate attempt by empiricist philosophers who take themselves to be Christians, to render their beliefs consistent and intelligible. They render their beliefs consistent all right but only at the expense of making them preposterous and not at all catching the needs and beliefs of religiously attuned people (Nielsen, *God, Scepticism and Modernity*, pp. 172–81).

Other attempts like Martin Buber's, John Wisdom's, and D. Z. Phillips's try to give nonmetaphysical accounts of religious discourse. But they end up giving us accounts that are so obscure that we cannot tell what they want to say (Nielsen, *God, Scepticism and Modernity*, pp. 134–59; and my exchange with D. Z. Phillips in *Wittgensteinian Fideism?*). So we can see how these two attempts to evade metaphysical religiosity fail. There are other twists and turnings of similar conceptions that are to be found in the text and still different ones in my *God, Scepticism and Modernity*.

II

Standard (ordinary) theists, as Plantinga and Mackie like to call them, and perhaps other Jews, Christians, and Moslems as well, except the most noncognitivist or symbolic ones (expressivists) believe that it's a fact that there is a God, and a further fact that he created the universe and created us as well as the other creatures and that he looks after us with his providential loving care and has endowed us with immortal souls and that we stand in need of him. These things, these believers unshakably believe, whether others believe them or not, are in fact so. They are commitments of theirs but they do not take them as just commitments ultimate or otherwise. In some way "God created the heavens and the earth" is thought to be a factual utterance and a true one at that. And without them Christianity (for example) loses its life-string.

I believe and argue in the text that none of this (the last sentence perhaps apart) is or even can be true or justifiably be believed or even taken intelligibly as an article of faith. I claim in various ways throughout *Atheism and Philosophy* (most crucially in chapters 5 and 11) that, to put it more bluntly and crudely than I put it there, though such believers believe these things and they must hold these beliefs *about* their beliefs to make sense of their faith, there are no such facts and there could be no such facts. They are *pseudo-facts* essential to sustain their belief, but utterly illusory all the same. I argue this with particular force on pages 132 to 137. I think the argumentation there is crucial and indeed, subject to a certain interpretation which I shall give in this preface, well taken, though if I were to rewrite this book I would put the matter somewhat differently than I did, particularly, as we shall see, in my talk about facts. Since the matter is crucial I should comment in some detail on it. (The reader without analytical philosophical acculturation might well skip this section until she has studied chapter 5 and in particularly pages 132 to 137. But then it is imperative to return to it.)

A reasonable, standard (ordinary) theist may well respond that here I am too positivist and empiricist. I, in effect, treat "fact" as if "an empirical fact" were a pleonasm. But it is not, for there are mathematical facts—$4 + 4 = 8$—and there are moral facts as well, including moral religious facts. Moreover, these different factual claims can be given their appropriate justification by anyone who is familiar with the appropriate way of doing things in their respective domains. If we have been taught mathematics we know that $4 + 4 = 8$, and if we have had a reasonably standard moral enculturation or can carefully reflect, we know that "promises, everything equal, should be kept" is so. Similarly if we have been enculturated into the appropriate religious language-games we believe that it is a fact that God created the heavens and the earth.

I am, the response could continue, simply confused about "fact." Facts are not events, processes, occurrences, entities, or things. You can't pack up and weigh a fact as you could a thing (say, a stone) or, time a fact's occurrence and sometimes its duration as you could an event. Facts, it is tempting to say, are what true statements state and a statement is true (trivially) if what it states is so. We need, to escape being clouded by metaphysics, to think of truth disquotationally, minimally, and deflationally. A statement "p" is true if and only if p. "The robins returned to Quebec in April" is true if and only if the robins returned to Quebec in April. "Ten plus ten equals twenty" is true if and only if $10 + 10 = 20$. "Killing is wrong" is true if and only if killing is wrong. "God loves his children" is true if and only if God loves his children. It is sentences or perhaps statements or propositions that are true. Take the quotation marks off a sentence (or the formula "p" is true if and only if p) and there, *voilà*, the truth on the righthand side is revealed. And there are many kinds of truth going with many kinds of statements made (they indicate sentences used) often for very different purposes. In speaking of truth we should not worry about correspondence, coherence, or warranted assertability. This may indeed *sound* trivial as I first (mistakenly) thought that Alfred Tarski's account was. But it is crucial in declouding our minds about "truth." Such accounts break metaphysical puzzles and in important ways show how unimportant truth is, I say here, sounding like a frivolous postmodern, though I am neither frivolous nor postmodern, though I am what Jürgen Habermas calls postmetaphysical. I will explain that seemingly outrageous remark about truth—a remark that *sounds* like I have no respect for the truth—in a moment.

However, before that, allow me first a further and connected response by my theistic retorter. (Though it is not only theists who could plausibly say what was said above.) He will point out that besides in effect treating "empirical fact" as a pleonasm my positivist danglers are further revealed in what I say (on page 133) about factual significance. I maintain that a statement (proposition, sentence) "has factual significance only if it is at least logically possible to indicate conditions or a set of conditions under which it could be to some degree confirmed or infirmed, i.e., that it is logically possible to state evidence for or against its truth." But that, as the above considerations show, is pure positivist dogma. We have seen how mathematical sentences and moral sentences can be true, can state facts, even can be usefully and credibly employed and can be true even though no coherent question about their confirmation or disconfirmation can arise.

Now for my response both to what has just been said about my criterion for factual significance and the puzzling-sounding remark—also an outrageously *sounding*, nihilistic-*sounding* remark—about truth being unimportant. Note first that we can, and perhaps should, acquiesce in the truisms that truth is what a true statement states and what it states is so and further to take to heart Rudolf Carnap's remark that truth is time independent and confirmation (testability, justification) is time dependent (Carnap, "Truth and Confirmation," pp. 119–27). A statement may be ever so well justified (confirmed, established, corroborated), justified, that is, as well as it could possibly be done at any particular time, and still be false though at that time we would have no reason to think that it was false and the best of reasons to think it true. It is something that in that situation we should *take for true*. But truth and knowledge of truth are crucially different. What we are after, and the only thing we can coherently be after, in seeking *knowledge* of what is true, is to get the best justified beliefs we can get at any particular time in any particular circumstance. But what is so justified at time t1 *may* not turn out to be justified at time t2.

We should also note that besides its disquotational function "truth" has a *cautionary* function, as Richard Rorty has well pointed out. He reminds us that no matter how well justified a belief is it may still be false. To try to escape this some pragmatist philosophers have sought to take truth to be warranted assertability or something like that. But that can't be right if the *meaning* of "truth" is what is at issue, for beliefs that are warrantedly asserted may turn out to be false. And there is no end, though perhaps there are goals, of inquiry. We will always be in the position (goals or not) where the best-laid plans of mice and men may turn out to be naught. Or nonmetaphorically put, whatever happens to be our best-justified beliefs at a given time and in a given place may be discovered at some later time to be unjustified and therefore beliefs that we should believe (when thus obtained) to be "false." We should always (or almost always) believe (take for true) what is best justified at a particular time and place while still (as I have stressed) realizing that it may still be false.[1] That is not skepticism but the fallibilism that pragmatists have taught us.

That is why we should acquiesce in (be satisfied with) justification—the fullest and best justification at any time we can get—and not try *in addition* to get truth. That is to ask for the color of heat. Once we have gained the fullest and best justification we can get that is all we can have as concerns the truth of what is at issue and all we can intelligibly want. Again metaphysical impulses may drive us to seek the Unconditional, the Absolute, the Truth. But that is something we cannot even make intelligible. Fallibilism is the name of the game. And that isn't a positivist dogma.

This makes sense of the claim that truth is not important while justification is. It also hints at giving sense to my claim about factual significance. Sure we can intelligibly speak of facts that are not empirical facts. That is simply because facts are what true statements state and there can be true statements that are not empirical statements, e.g., mathematical statements or moral and political statements. And for those, as we have noted, who play the language-games connected with mathematics or morality or politics, they can in the distinctive ways governed by these language-games corroborate these statements (or at least some of them) in their own distinctive ways.

Why cannot the same things be said for the language-games distinctive of our theistic religions? Isn't something that is good for the goose good for the gander? The stumbling block is that the language-games of these religions, as I have previously illustrated, inescapably involve blockbuster metaphysical statements with the metaphysical religiosity that goes with them.[2] And recall that facts go with truth. To use jargon, "fact" and "truth" are internally related. If we accept the kind of disquotational, minimal, and deflationist conception of truth I have advocated, then it makes perfectly good *sense* to say of any well-formed indicative sentence that it is true (or false): that the truth predicate can be appropriately applied to it. We can say of "God loves his children" or any other religious utterance in the indicative mode that, if we can intelligibly say it, we can also intelligibly say it is true or that it is false: that "true" is not being misused when we say that. But that we can say that of our or anyone's saying something (uttering of some indicative sentence) that it is true—saying, that is, that that sentence ("It is true") is intelligible—doesn't in the slightest make for or establish or justify, even with the slightest probability, that what we are saying in making that utterance is actually true. What we want to know or to be justified in believing is that we are *justified* in believing that something is true or probably true. What we want (or at least should want) is something that is as well justified as it can be. Calling it true adds nothing of justificatory interest or import (Rorty , *Philosophy and Social Hope*, pp. 23–71; "Universality and Truth"; and "Response to Habermas"). And don't say "Nielsen doesn't respect the truth" for that would be to say that I do not respect the making of those claims or holding those beliefs that are as well-justified as we can now get them. Those beliefs are in almost all circumstances what we must believe in, if we would be nonevasive.

It is perhaps considerations like those just presented that led John Dewey to try to construe truth as warranted assertability and to, when he came to see that didn't work, *replace* truth with warranted assertability (Bentley and Dewey, *Knowing and the Known*). But while truth as other than warranted assertability adds no justficatory considerations to any claim, it is indispensable in having other uses such as its cautionary one. That keeps our hubris from getting out of control.

There are those with a metaphysical itch—not uncommon among philosophers—who will seek something of which we can justifiably say coherently that it is unconditionally or absolutely true or in some not very clear sense is "unconditionally warranted." But these things we cannot get and not because of our frail capacities but because logically we can't get them as we can't have a round square. Indeed it is senseless (at least where the matter is substantive) to even try for it. There is nothing that can be established to be absolutely true or that can have an unconditional warrant. What is justifiable and what is not is time and place dependent. Carnap, no wanton postmodernist, was right (or nearly so) that truth is time independent and confirmation (justification or warrant more generally) is time dependent.

With this under our belts we can profitably return to remarking on the claim that the metaphysical religiosity inherent in our religious language-games makes problems for the intelligibility, and thus the justifiability, of religious language-games. After all we cannot possibly justify something that is unintelligible, and it could not possibly be true. We can say of the indicative sentences of mathematical and moral language-games that it makes sense to say they are true or false. There are established practices in mathematics where we can show that a claim like 10 + 10 = 20 is warranted and there are established practices in morality whereby we can justify that promises generally, but not invariably, should be kept. There is (that is) a standing presumption that if I make a promise I must keep it. If that were not so there would be no communication among us, and with that a coherent life among us would be impossible. We can in these domains give reasons which justify saying (sometimes with nearly decisive reasons) that something is true. There may be some wanton sentences (propositions) in morals and even in mathematics concerning which we do not know what to say and that even may be true of physics. But in all these practices, in all these language-games, including their very crucial parts, we have a critical mass of interconnected sentences that are plainly used to make justifiably true (warrantedly assertable here) statements. We, and more than we normally believe, also have ungrounded statements as well, some of which, as Wittgenstein stressed in *On Certainty*, that it would be insane to doubt. It would be insane to doubt that live human beings have heads, that we have never been to the sun, that in most places and at all places at some times it gets dark at night and light in the morning, that it is cold in the winter and hot or hotter in the summer, that fire burns and water is wet. It would be at least silly to go around trying to ground such beliefs but we also in science, in math, in morals have a critical mass of beliefs that we can (if pressed) justify and this includes at least some of the more fundamental ones. Sometimes justification comes to pragmatic vindication. But that is often quite appropriate.

But in religious language-games we have (at least for us moderns) nothing or at least little like this. We have as hinge or framework beliefs those metaphysical blockbusters "God created the world," "God will ensure our survival of death," "God is transcendent but still acts in the world," "God is pure spirit," "God is a person but without a body," etc., etc., etc. Framework or hinge beliefs, a la Wittgenstein or not, it is perfectly possible and reasonable to doubt whether these are, as sentences, supposedly expressive of beliefs, which are not strong candidates for being coherent. We have no idea what should or could justify them (confirm them or infirm them) or in any other way justify them. And we cannot just take them on faith or trust for we do not understand what we are to take on faith or trust (Nielsen, "Can Faith Validate Godtalk?" pp. 173–84; "Religious Perplexity and Faith," pp. 1–17). So God, believers correctly say, is a mystery or mysterious. But the mystery cannot be so deep that all we have are verbal formulas, nondeviant collections of words, expressing we know not what. But that, I think, is all that we have for key religious utterances. This, of course, runs against the sensitivities of religious people. But all the same it seems to me to be so.

My criterion (putative criterion) for factual significance given in the third full paragraph on page 133 intended to help us sort out (provide a kind of litmus test for) sentences used to make claims about the world: what the world (the universe) is like (including things in the universe) and what realities transcendent to the universe are like, if such there is or even can be, and, on the other hand, which sentences are unintelligible or incoherent verbal formulas. (Certainly "Bush sleeps slower than Kerry" as distinct from "Bush talks slower than Kerry" is one of them. I want to say that "God created the heavens and the earth" is like "Bush sleeps slower than Kerry," only less obviously so. It is only that in our tribe we have gotten used to hearing the former but not the latter. But no more sense can be made of the latter than the former.)

So "God created the heavens and the Earth" belongs on the incoherent or unintelligible side. My criterion for factual significance may be too narrow to capture all factual significance. Certainly it is if we count as true sentences expressing facts those true mathematical, moral, and aesthetic sentences expressing mathematical, moral, and aesthetic facts. And that at least seems perfectly proper as we have seen. And we should say these types of sentences are true if we stick with the way "fact" and "true" are ordinarily used as I intend to do. No more than Wittgenstein do I want to "sublime" language. Yet when we are intending to pick out claims that (if you will, to *sound* for the moment scientistic) give us information about the world (including things in it) and about the "supernatural world" as well (if sense can be made of that) such that we can have a criterion, a litmus paper for, those sentences which do and those sentences which don't so function, then in that context my criterion for factual significance has a point. Here there may be sentences in the indicative mode which, while looking like *informative* sentences, are utterly indeterminate when we utilize such a criterion. Perhaps no criterion will suffice and we will just have to use our nose. But I argue carefully on pages 94 to 99 for such a criterion so employed and what I say is not obviously wrong so employed (or so I think), and it very well might be essentially right.

III

I have in the text drawn attention to considerations such as the following in arguing that nonanthropomorphic conceptions of God are incoherent: God is said to be a person (thus an individual) but is also said to be infinite, but "an infinite individual" is a contradiction in terms; God is said to be transcendent to the world yet to act in the world—another contradiction; God is said to be a person and to be a spirit without a body—another contradiction, for a "bodiless person" is a contradiction in terms. Some have thought this is too quick a way with dissenters. These considerations indeed can't be decisive or clinching arguments for nothing can be. To see how this is so, note, for one example, how this is set out by Theodore M. Drange:

(1) If God exists, then he is nonphysical.
(2) If God exists, then he is a person (or a personal being).
(3) A person (or personal being) needs to be physical.
(4) Hence, it is impossible for God to exist (from 1–3). (Drange, "Incompatible-Properties Arguments," p. 193)

This is a *valid* argument (assuming we can make some sense of "God"). But is it a *sound* one? Are all the premises true? I accept and defend premise 3, as do many people, but such an astute fellow atheist as J. L. Mackie does not. The dispute between us turns on the issue of whether the very idea of a "bodiless person" is consistent and coherent. Mackie thinks it is and I do not. So, as Drange well realizes, the above argument with respect to its soundness is controversial.

It in turn rests on what should be said about personal identity. Again we get controversy. And so on and so on. We never get over any important matter something which is beyond controversy. We never, over such at least putatively substantive matters, get certainty though some arguments may have far greater plausibility than others. The same considerations, though perhaps less obviously, obtain for my other two arguments.

In a useful collection of essays titled *The Impossibility of God* (2003, edited by Michael Martin and Rick Monnier), all the essays try to show that the very concept of God in the Judeo-Christian-Islamic traditions (and most significantly in what J. L. Mackie calls ordinary theism and Alvin Plantinga calls standard theism) is contradictory or in some other way incoherent and that God so conceived does not and indeed cannot exist. Hence the title *The Impossibility of God*. The various authors identify, as the editors put it, the concept of God and specific elements within that concept that they consider to be contradictory in some way (p. 14). As Martin and Monnier are well aware, there are a variety of concepts of God. (I would prefer to say a variety of conceptualizations of what is taken to be the concept of God.) But what is actually done—and I think usefully—is to zero in on standard or ordinary theism. There we have a relatively determinate conception of God. With such a conception they try to show, by a variety of arguments, why such a God is an impossibility. (Remember that Paul Tillich and quite a few other theologians, and perhaps even such an astute religious thinker as Simone Weil, would have welcomed this.)

Martin and Monnier categorize these arguments as: (1) definitional disproofs of the existence of God; (2) deductive evil disproofs of the existence of God; (3) doctrinal disproofs of the existence of God; (4) multiple attributes disproofs of the existence of God; and (5) single attributive disproofs of the existence of God. They all involve deductive arguments attempting not only to be valid arguments but sound as well against the existence of God. Argument (1) tries to show (the mirror image of Anselm's ontological proof of God's existence) that if we have an adequate understanding of what God is—the definition of "God"—we can know that God cannot exist; (2) is a logical argument from evil for God's nonexistence, claiming a contradiction between the attributes of God and the existence of evil; (3) argues that there is a contradiction between the attributes of God and particular religious doctrines, stories, or teachings about God; (4) argues that there is a contradiction between two or more of God's attributes; and (5) argues that there is a self-contradiction within a single attribute of God. I do not, in *Atheism and Philosophy*, use such a typology or stress deduction, but I do argue that the very concept of God (where nonanthropomorphic) is contradictory or otherwise incoherent so *The Impossibility of God*, where correctly reasoned, is a welcome supplement.

The papers in *The Impossibility of God* are invariably carefully argued, some, of course, more convincingly so than others. And they are all deductive proofs for the nonexistence of God. All come at least close to being valid arguments. Are they sound arguments? If we mean by "sound arguments" valid arguments that can *plausibly* be said to be arguments whose premises are true, then they are sound arguments. If by "sound arguments" we mean valid arguments with premises that are *unassailably known to be true*, then none of them are sound arguments. (I will in a moment illustrate this with respect to arguments of types 1 and 2.) The second sense of "sound argument" shows the inherent limitations to giving a disproof of God's existence (or for that matter, a proof). What I do think is that what these arguments taken together show is that not one of them gives an *unassailable* argument for the nonexistence of God. There are various ways their premises can be challenged; and while none of them is absolutely conclusive, when taken together they give sufficiently plausible arguments to make belief in the existence of God problematic to say the least. As C. S. Peirce recognized (and some of the medievals as well), to rely on a single chain of deductive argument is a mistake. There will always be something challengeable in it. But for the point or points in question to be established, to have a number of carefully constructed plausible arguments is far more reasonable than relying on a single chain of argument no matter how carefully constructed. We should not put all our eggs in one basket.

When we reflect on these diverse forceful arguments taken as a whole it is hard not to believe that the case for the nonexistence of God is very strong. But we should also recognize that a Kierkegaard could respond: strong but not decisively carrying the day. But in turn we should take to heart the remark of the editors of *The Impossibility of God* that "[a]rguments for the impossibility of God are not about certainty but rather about [to be pleonastic] rational justification" (p. 14). Fallibilism, we should have learned by now, is inescapable, at least over matters of substance.

I want to illustrate this first with (1), the definitional disproofs argument, and then with (2), the arguments from evil. Conventional wisdom has it that there can neither be ontological proofs nor ontological disproofs of the existence of God. And I think that here conventional wisdom is right. Neither Norman

Malcolm with his careful attempt at an ontological proof nor J. N. Findlay with his careful attempt of an ontological disproof of the existence of God has been successful (Malcolm, *Knowledge and Certainty*, pp. 141–62; Findlay, "Can God's Existence Be Disproved" and "God's Nonexistence," pp. 19–30). Even they have come to realize that their deductive arguments are not without blemish (Malcolm, p. 162; Findlay, "God's Nonexistence," pp. 27–30). And no one has succeeded where these sophisticated and carefully formed arguments have failed. Malcolm, conceiving of God, plausibly following Anselm, as that which nothing greater than can be conceived, claims correctly, that such a being would be a necessary being (have necessary existence), that is, be an eternal being, but, he stresses, an eternal being could not just happen to be in existence, come into existence, or cease to exist. And while an eternal being couldn't cease to exist or come into existence, it could be the case that there are no eternal beings. Eternally (if you will) there may be no eternal beings. So we have not established that God must exist.

Findlay defines God as the adequate object of religious attitudes. This, as the editors paraphrase him, "leads irresistibly, by the sheer logic of this definition, to the conclusion that God's existence is necessary. However, in the light of the hypothetical predications, necessary existence is a contradiction in terms, and therefore God does not and cannot exist" (Martin and Monnier, *The Impossibility of God*, p. 18). But this assumes that the necessary existence we are talking about is *logically* necessary existence, and then it correctly claims that "logically necessary existence" is self-contradictory. There can be no such necessary existence. But, while God's necessary existence cannot be logically necessary existence, God's necessary existence is not the self-contradictory notion of logically necessary existence but *aseity* (complete independence). God's existence is necessary in the sense that God is not dependent on anyone or anything for his existence. God, as a matter of fact, exists completely independently of everything else and in that way his existence is necessary. So there is another way to construe "necessary existence" such that Findlay has not disproved God's existence. He has not shown there can be no necessary beings but only that there can be no *logically* necessary beings. Moreover, the most adequate object of a religious attitude cannot be something which is self-contradictory. Again we have not gained anything decisive.

Similar things can be said (though less clearly) about (2), the argument from evil to the nonexistence of God. God, by definition, is omnipotent, omniscient, and perfectly good, and yet evil plainly exists. As wholly good, God wants to eliminate evil completely and being omnipotent has unlimited power to do so; as omniscient he knows everything including what is good. Yet there manifestly is evil, so God does not and cannot exist as long as there is some evil in the world.

There are many quite ineffective and question-begging arguments against this and Mackie deftly disposes of them. However, Mackie quite rightly takes seriously what has been called the free will defense. This argument rests on a premise which Mackie accepts (as I do) that even an omnipotent God or any omnipotent being cannot do what is logically impossible. He cannot make, for example, a round square or make two plus two equal five. But such limitations are not limitations on his omnipotence because they ask him to do what is logically impossible and that is nonsense. However, God, as omnipotent, can do anything that it is logically possible to do. The free will argument crucially relies on these considerations for, it is claimed, God cannot—logically cannot—completely eliminate evil while still creating human beings who are free. That, so goes the argument, is like trying to make a round square. God cannot make a human being genuinely free (not just compatibilist free) and for it to be not possible for such free human beings not to choose evil or at least sometimes to choose evil. God couldn't create them genuinely free and yet create them so they couldn't do that. God wants to create genuinely free persons. But then God cannot make a state of affairs that exemplifies p and not p.

Mackie responds that God, if there is a god, if he can create humans who *sometimes* freely choose good (as he can), why could he then not create all human beings as beings who always choose good and thus, by God's doing this, there will be no evil (or at least no evil caused by human beings), and this being so is inconsistent with the existence of God *and* the existence of evil. But since there is plainly evil (including evil caused by human beings) there can be no God.

The argument now gets very arcane. Alvin Plantinga, who is the most prominent proponent of the free will defense, continues to argue for contra-causal freedom against compatibilist accounts, for a miniscule amount of evil as all that is necessary for the free will defense. But in doing so he assumes fallen angels (to account for animal suffering), individual essences, possible worlds in which in some of the beings (being contra-causally free) sometimes will do what is evil and that this must obtain (God or no God) in at least some possible world. But God is not responsible for evil if he could not—logically could not—avoid creating a world including the whole spectrum of possibile worlds in which there were genuinely free persons and no evil.

Much of this comes to Plantinga's resisting Mackie's claim that it is not logically impossible that God should create human beings such that they will always freely choose what is good. Mackie argues plausibly, I think, that even in its strongest versions the free will defense fails (Mackie, "The Problem of Evil," pp. 91–95). Still compatibilism can be challenged (and is challenged). It is still not completely clear that God can create free human beings whom he cannot control or that he can create a genuinely free being whom he can control. If he wants people, as he does for their own greatest good, to be genuinely free then he cannot completely control them. And remember that there is agreement between Mackie and Plantinga that it is not incompatible with God's omnipotence that he cannot do what is logically impossible. And at least in some possible world (so Plantinga argues) some people will choose evil or at least some things which are evil.

However, there are Mackie-type replies to this and so on and so on. We again get nothing *utterly* decisive here and even if we did in this domain (over evil and God) we should heed Mackie's warning:

> We cannot, indeed, take the problem of evil as a conclusive disproof of traditional theism, because, as we have seen, there

is some flexibility in its doctrines, and in particular in the additional premises needed to make the problem explicit. There *may* be some way of adjusting these which avoids an internal contradiction without giving up anything essential to theism. But none has yet been clearly presented, and there is a strong presumption that theism cannot be made coherent without a serious change in at least one of its central doctrines. (Mackie, "The Problem of Evil," p. 95)

But the object lesson here is again that we do not get certainty, self-evidence, or unassailability that at last brings inquiry or perplexity to an end; that gives us the absolutely *last* word concerning God, or anything else which is at least putatively substantive. But that notwithstanding, we can see that some arguments are more plausible (as I think obtains in this case for Mackie in his dispute with Plantinga), sometimes even much more plausible than others. Among other things some will have fewer arcane premises and obscure concepts or conceptions (e.g., fallen angels). Note how far Plantinga is driven in the direction of arcaneness to defend his claims. There Mackie's argument against the free will defense and more generally his argument against the compatibility of God and evil is more plausible. But it still is not decisive. But it is not a matter of "You pays your money and you takes your chances." Again, if we are reasonable, we will acquiesce in fallibilism, but *not* in the belief that anything goes.

The three arguments I mentioned earlier in this preface and have deployed in the text of this book and in my *Naturalism and Religion* are all of the multiple attributes disproofs type except that they are not strictly disproofs for they do not appeal to deductive arguments but rather appeal to what I take to be inconsistencies and incoherencies in the very uses of words (e.g., "infinite person," "bodiless person," "person who is *transcendent* to the world and is an *agent in* the world"). Generally I think so proceeding is more direct, neater, and less pedantic than the setting out of formal proofs, though sometimes, as with the problem of evil, a deductive proof is useful. However, I think most of the work in this conceptual domain is done by carefully attending to the uses of our terms both in *first-order* language-games and in theological-philosophical or sometimes just plain people's generalizations about the *first-order* use of religious discourse—*second-order* discourse if you will. But both techniques are useful and again none of these types of arguments (or any others that are substantive) is going to yield anything that is through and through decisive.

I want in line with the arguments I have just been making in this section to cite a telling passage from J. N. Findlay:

> [T]here can be nothing really "clinching" in philosophy: "proofs" and "disproofs" hold only for those who adopt certain premises, who are willing to follow certain rules of argument, and who use their terms in certain definite ways. And every proof or disproof can be readily evaded if one questions the truth of its premises or the validity of its type of inference, or if one finds new senses in which the terms may be used. And it is quite proper, and one's logical duty, to evade an argument in this manner, if it leads to preposterous consequences. (Findlay, "God's Non-Existence," p. 27)

Surely this is right and a further reason for the acceptance of the fallibilism I have been urging and for not putting too much trust in deductive arguments. This is further exacerbated by the often problematicity of what is and what isn't "preposterous" or of what is "mind-boggling." Mackie's sense of preposterousness or mine will sometimes (perhaps even frequently) not be the same as Plantinga's or Hartshorne's and what boggles their minds may not boggle ours.

In *The Impossibility of God* there is a confusion of proof and justification and a melding of them together (p. 14). *But proof is not justification.* Justification, as John Rawls well puts it, is argument, not typically deductive, though it may have deductive elements, "addressed to those who disagree with us, or to ourselves when we are of two minds" (Rawls, *A Theory of Justice,* p. 508). He goes on to add that it "presumes a clash of views between persons or within one person and seeks to convince others, or ourselves, of the reasonableness of the . . . [beliefs] upon which our claims and judgments" relative to our beliefs concerning religion (as well as other things) are founded (p. 508). Being designed to be reconciled by reason, that is careful reflection, impartial characterization, deliberation, and scrupulous argument,

> justification proceeds from what all parties to the discussion hold in common. Ideally, to justify [a conception of God or to give reasons for rejecting such a conception] to someone is to give him a proof of its principles from premises that the parties to the discussion accept, these principles having in turn consequences that match our considered judgments. Thus mere proof is not justification. A proof simply displays logical relations between propositions. But proofs become justifications once the starting points are mutually recognized, or the conclusions so comprehensive and compelling as to persuade us of the soundness of the conception expressed by the premises. (Rawls, *A Theory of Justice*, p. 508)

In trying to so establish things we do not proceed by attempting to find self-evident or unassailable principles "from which a sufficient body of standards and precepts can be derived to account for our considered judgments" (Rawls, *A Theory of Justice*, p. 506). To think we can do this presumes our starting points are self-evident truths, perhaps even necessary truths, and that by a single chain of valid deductive reasoning we can attain an unassailable conclusion. We should not use such a Cartesian method but proceed in a more Peircean way as was described earlier, which broadly speaking is also in a Rawlsian way. We should not give "first principles or conditions therein, or definition either" special pride of place "that permit a peculiar place in justifying" either religious principles or atheism or indeed anything else, formal systems apart. In seeking to justify an atheistic view of the world, as I do, these elements, though important, have no special place but "justification rests upon our entire conception and how it fits in with and organizes our considered judgments in reflective equilibrium. . . . Justification is a matter of the mutual support of many considerations, of everything fitting into one coherent view" (Rawls, *A Theory of Justice*, p. 507).

I have deliberately adapted Rawls's account meant for the justification of a theory of justice to the issue of justifying a religious point of view or an atheistic point of view as the case may be and to show that one point of view here is more adequate than another. I hope and believe I do not, in making that adaptation, distort Rawls's own view. But I do put it to purposes other than he intended. But at any rate it is how I think we should proceed in trying to justify either an atheistic point of view or a religious one. It is a coherence view (though relying on the *initial* plausibility of our considered judgments). It relies on many diverse elements (including deductive elements), but it is quite different from a purely deductive model, such as we see deployed in *The Impossibility of God*.

It is plausible to object that however well such a coherence method will work in moral theory and in normative political theory, it will not work in considering the choice between religious belief and atheism. The chasms in the latter case are just too deep. In the Rawlsian method we speak of starting points mutually recognized, of proceeding from what parties to the discussion hold in common, of relevant considered judgments mutually shared, but in the debate between atheism and theism, the argument goes, there are not things mutually shared. We are too far apart to make fruitful discussion possible.

I believe that is false though it is understandable if we look at some discussions of atheism versus theism that many think otherwise. So why do I say it is false? Because we find along with deep disagreement much that is held in common (and relevantly so) by both theists and atheists, and this can and does yield some starting points which are mutually recognized. There are some considered judgments or convictions held in common between many atheists and many theists (e.g., respect for all persons, for sound arguments, for avoiding internecine warfare, for avoiding religious hatred, for respect for evidence, for integrity, for tolerance, and so on and so on). There are also more determinate grounds that are held in common between them. That can be seen from my illustrations above of so-called definitional disproofs of the existence of God and the so-called problem of evil disproofs of the existence of God.

Atheists and theists who are philosophically literate and know something about at least one of the religions they are discussing, namely Judaism, Christianity, or Islam, will very often hold in common the following beliefs:

(1) That God (if there is one) is that which nothing greater than can be conceived.

(2) That this would be the adequate object of such theistic religious attitudes.

(3) That this in turn is the being (if such a being exists) most worthy of worship.

(4) That there can be no logically necessary beings.

(5) An eternal being could not come into existence or cease to exist.

(6) That God (if there is one) is an eternal being.

(7) We cannot sensibly ask whether a being which is eternal actually exists. If it is an eternal being it must exist. Still there may be no eternal beings.

(8) The God of our theistic religions, if he exists, is omnipotent, omniscient, and perfectly good.

(9) There is evil in the world.

(10) There is considerable agreement (though not complete, e.g., William of Ockham) that an omnipotent God cannot do what is logically impossible and that that is no limitation to his omnipotence. But there is also agreement that God (if there is one) can do anything that is logically possible to do (if he can act at all).

(11) That existence is not a predicate, but necessary existence is.

There will be widespread agreement here between philosophically literate (where "philosophically literate" need not be controversially characterized) atheists, agnostics, and theists alike.[3] These will be beliefs, and important beliefs, held in common despite on other matters a deep disagreement. They can be used as starting points mutually held in common when they begin to deliberate together in the Rawlsian manner described above. There may be, these common starting points, these toeholds, notwithstanding, too many deep disagreements for them to be able to so resolve their disagreements. They may, as it is said, at the end of the day (if there is an end of the day, i.e., a final last position resulting from deliberation and of taking matters to heart, having kept in mind the burdens of judgment) where they just must, if they are reasonable, just have to agree to disagree. But they may not be in that pickle. Instead, if they keep cool and if they carefully and with integrity carry through this Rawlsian method, they may find a way to agreement over at least some important matters. Their considered judgments in general and wide reflective equilibrium (though we would also have to say always for a determinate time) may yield either atheism, agnosticism, or theism (usually theism of a determinate sort). We will not know until we have tried and tried hard. But even then we will not know anything decisive and for all time.

In *Atheism and Philosophy* and more extensively and more explicitly in *Naturalism Without Foundations* and in *Naturalism and Religion*, I use that Rawlsian method to make a strong case for atheism. But then, of course, I may be wrong. But the same obtains for any agnostic or theist. But this is our inescapable situation and we should just learn to live with it and not go on the illusory quest for certainty.

IV

Some people have said (my close friend Hendrik Hart, as well as Peter Winch and D. Z. Phillips) that I am too rationalistic and intellectualistic about religion and that this blinds me so that I do not see some things that are utterly crucial about it. I don't think so but then again I may not be able to see the beam in my own eye.

Let us look into that. Not about me, of course, or certainly not essentially about me, and, when about me, me merely taken as a token of a type. Put more generally, I think it is frequently the case with philosophers (theists and Hegelian or Whiteheadian believers, on the one hand, and agnostics and atheists on the other) that they are indeed often too intellectualistic and too rationalistic concerning religion. Swinburne and Plantinga on the theist side and Flew and most of the authors writing in *The Impossibility of God* on the other side, seem to me too rationalistic and too intellectualistic. They all seem to me to need a good soaking in Pascal, Nietzsche, Kierkegaard, Barth, and Wittgenstein. Perhaps such intellectualism is an occupational disease of the philosophy of religion. But one can err on the other side too as Kierkegaard does. Be that as it may, I want to pursue a little of what is involved here for I think it is important and something that we secularists and humanists frequently are not sufficiently attentive to.

Norman Malcolm, a card-carrying member of what I have called (perhaps tendentiously) Wittgensteinian Fideism, remarks that we (or at least many of us) just uncritically assume that in order for religious belief to be intellectually respectable it ought to have an intellectual justification (Malcolm, "The Groundlessness of Belief"; Nielsen in this volume, pp. 221–24). We should see instead religion as a form of life; it integrally involves language embedded in action. It, no more than any other form of life, Malcolm has it, stands in need of justification. Perhaps it could have none. In any event, it does not need one. We are just enculturated into our forms of life. For many, some of them are religious, and we could, speaking generally of forms of life, neither think nor act without them. It is one of the primary pathologies of philosophy, Malcolm continues, to believe we must justify our forms of life. Just that is a pervasive mistake among philosophers for forms of life are neither well-grounded nor ill-grounded but are ungrounded and unavoidably so. They are just there, like our lives. There is no question, Malcolm claims echoing Wittgenstein, of reasonable/unreasonable here.

We have, Malcolm claims, an irrational fear of groundless beliefs. Yet we all live in a sea of groundless beliefs. And any particular belief must precede doubt and rely on groundless beliefs. Most of them are perfectly benign; and some, such as the need for air to live and rest to be able to work, are simply inescapable while, of course, not being logical truths or otherwise conceptual truths. Moreover, not everything we believe we believe for a reason, but Malcolm misses the Peircean and Deweyian point that wherever the itch of *real* doubt comes for a given belief, or cluster of beliefs, no matter what it is or what they are, if we have some specific reason for doubting it (them) and not mere Cartesian methodological doubt(s) (what Peirce called paper doubts) we can do so and we can reason about them. We do not need to just respond to such live doubts with our hearts—with our gut feelings—though this may cause (trigger) the doubt still we can and should use our big brains in such problematic situations to examine the situation, giving weight to our feelings, but not just blindly to follow them. Intelligence, as Dewey likes to say, always has a role. This is not to think of ourselves as just thinking machines, shrinking our abilities to feel, but as creatures with both the capacity to reason and to feel and, attending to both, to deliberate—using both cognitive and affective faculties—about what to do, how to live, and what to believe. There, given what religious beliefs are, and given a world of conflicting *claimed* revelations, we, if we wish to be reasonable, should not just let our feelings carry the day.

"Well, why then be reasonable?" we can imagine Dostoevsky's underground man asking. Because, as John Rawls argues, that is an essential part of what it is to be human and for us to be able to live together with reciprocity. This is not rationalism or intellectualism run wild, but just being humanly reflective and making reflective endorsements. The emotional side of us by our so proceeding need not be atrophied.

But doesn't the heart have its reasons that reason does not know? I think this familiar remark of Pascal's rings something like a sympathetic chord with most of us. The thing is to figure out just what it means and comes to and whether someone who is critical of religion, someone who is a secularist all the way down, cannot acknowledge that and take it to heart.

I am loath to speak of an "emotional way of knowing." That sounds too obscurantist and sometimes is sinister. (Remember Mussolini on "thinking with your blood.") Yet we sometimes come to a place that looks sinister, someone makes a proposal that looks fishy, sometimes by just a kind of gut feeling one feels that someone is faking or is untrustworthy. Sometimes at a party one looks across the room at one's spouse and senses one's spouse is bored, wants to leave, or laugh ironically. One sometimes feels depressed, alienated, afraid, or feels like a lost dependent child. And sometimes such things give us a clue to something important in one's life and the lives of others. If one is religious one may feel somehow a place is holy or that something is sacred or even a hard-bitten old atheist like me may sometimes feel the urge to pray that his friend dying in agony need not suffer so or that there be more decency in our world where decency is in short supply.

Sometimes these feelings are not reliable indicators of anything going on in the world but are just expressive of our own emotions—emotions which may be leading us down the garden path. But sometimes they are reliable indicators of things in the world. We, particularly if we are perceptive, can sometimes trust our feelings: they answer sometimes to something real. But it is also the case—or so it seems to me—in all the above cases that *both* feeling and thinking, probably in an unscrambled and perhaps often unscramblable way, are intertwined. We have nothing that is just delivered by the feelings without cognitive tips and cognitive content.

To probe whether this is intellectualist dogma on my part or just being sensible about what is involved, I want to work with a detailed example given by Cohn Lyas, something of a Wittgenstein philosopher, in his *Peter Winch*. The example and his commentary on it reveal something of his own work and of the work of that paradigmatic Wittgensteinian philosopher Peter Winch on religion (pp. 142–44). People, Winch argues (as does Wittgenstein), have primitive reactions to pain in crying and holding the injured part. This comes to sometimes be replaced by such expressions as "Ouch" or "It hurts so" or "I'm in terrible pain." These are expressive utterances replacing crying but are expressive of our pain and not descriptive of it. Analogously "other aspects of one's life of feeling get expressed in which the primitive reactions upon which religion alone can be based can be articulated" (p. 143). Religious expressions get their sense "from spontaneous reactions to experience" (p. 143). To show the force of this it is valuable and perhaps necessary to work with a detailed example. Lyas obliges with what I think is a very good one. I can see no other way of bringing out the force of what he and Winch are saying here than by quoting it in full, noting also Lyas's perceptive commentary and then differently commenting on it myself.

Keep firmly in mind that we are trying to find out whether our emotions can lead us to God or whether, for all their sometimes genuineness, we play tricks with ourselves here. The example Lyas sets out is taken from Virginia Woolf's novel *To the Lighthouse*. Mrs. Ramsey is a main character in the novel and the wife of an eminent philosopher. She is modeled on Virginia Woolf's mother who was the wife of a then (late nineteenth century) eminent philosopher, Lesile Stephen, Virginia Woolf's father. (See the discussion of his views in this volume, pp. 58–61.) It is significant to note that Virginia Woolf herself reacted against what she took to be the overintellectualism of her deeply agnostic father. Be that as it may, in the passage I shall quote, Lyas seeks to illustrate Winch's expressive conception of religion and religious discourse. A conception with which Lyas himself plainly has sympathy. In the novel Mrs. Ramsey sits knitting and as the evening comes on, the light of the beams of the lighthouse sweeps across her. She becomes meditative and somehow feels liberated. Now the passage:

> Beneath it is all dark, it is all spreading, it is unfathomably deep; but now and again we rise to the surface and that is what you see us by. Her horizon seemed to her limitless. There were all the places she had not seen; the Indian plains; she felt herself pushing aside the thick leather curtain of a church in Rome. This core of darkness could go anywhere, for no one saw it. They could not stop it, she thought, exulting. There was freedom, there was peace, there was, most welcome of all, a summoning together, a resting on a platform of stability. Not as oneself did one ever find rest, in her experience (she accomplished here something dexterous with her needles), but as a

wedge of darkness. Losing personality one lost the fret, the
hurry, the stir; and there rose to her lips always some exclama-
tion of triumph over life when things come together in this
peace, this rest, this eternity; and pausing there she looked out
to meet that stroke of the lighthouse, the long steady stroke,
the last of the three, which was her stroke, for watching them
in this mood always at this hour one could not help attaching
oneself to one thing especially of the things one saw; and this
thing, the long steady stroke was her stroke. Often she found
herself sitting and looking, sitting and looking, with her work
in her hands until she became the thing she looked at—that
light for example. And it would lift up on it some little phrase
or other which had been lying in her mind like that—"Children don't forget, children don't forget"—which she would
repeat and begin adding to it, It will end, It will end, she said.
It will come, it will come, when suddenly she added, We are in
the hands of the Lord.

But instantly she was annoyed with herself for saying that.
Who had said it? Not she; she had been trapped into saying
something that she did not mean. . . .

What brought her to say that: "We are in the hands of the
Lord?" she wondered. The insincerity slipping in among the
truths roused her, annoyed her. She returned to her knitting
again. How could any Lord have made this world? she asked.
With her mind she always seized the fact that there is no
reason, order, justice: but suffering, death, the poor. No happiness lasted, she knew that. (pp. 69–71)

Now for Lyas's commentary on this which is intended both
to express his own views and to elucidate Winch's. Mrs. Ramsay,
though living in an agnostic ambience and an agnostic herself,
lives beyond that ambience in a largely Christian culture and has
the weight of that pervasive culture as something given to her. It
is natural, Lyas comments, that in the context we see Mrs. Ramsey
to be in, that she should both utter "We are in the hands of the
Lord" and for her to react to her own saying of that as she does.
Lyas comments, "Those words were the *only* ones that seemed to
her at that moment to say what she wanted to say and they got
that meaning from *that* experience in *those* circumstances" (Lyas,

Peter Winch, p. 145). Winch's suggestion is that "religious utterances arise in this way, as primitive reactions that articulate an
inner life of feeling, no less than the pain language articulates the
inner life of sensation" (Winch, "Review," pp. 222–23). But, Lyas
adds correctly, that Mrs. Ramsey "immediately rejects her mode
of thought. But the novelist is careful to add 'with her mind she
seized the fact that there is no reason, order, justice'" (Lyas, *Peter
Winch*, p. 145). Lyas takes it that the crucial lesson to be learned
from this is "that someone might try to intellectualize something
that was not delivered by the route of the intellect. . . . But it
would be equally possible to say that, in thinking that way about
the experience, one falsified it" (p. 145).

How (if at all) does so thinking about it falsify it? Mrs.
Ramsey acknowledges the naturalness in the circumstances of
her saying it, but she is annoyed with herself for saying it and
realizes how senseless (cognitively senseless but not emotionally
senseless) it is for her to say it. How does this falsify the *experience*: a spontaneous primitive reaction in that situation for
someone acculturated as she was. How (if at all) does her so
thinking about her experience falsify it? As Lyas recognizes, a
Chinese brought up in the pervasively atheistic culture since the
Chinese Revolution, but having a similar experience in a similar
situation and with little understanding of Christianity, except to
have been taught something of how "God" is used in a Christian
culture, might be baffled by Mrs. Ramsey's remark. By contrast,
I, crusted old atheist that I am, though raised and living in a
Judeo-Christian culture, would understand Mrs. Ramsey's
remark and, unlike the Chinese, see the naturalness of it in those
circumstances. I might so respond in such a circumstance myself.
So I might spontaneously utter, so placed, "We are in the hands
of the Lord" while a second's reflection would lead me to my
firm belief that there can be no Lord—no God—that we can be
in the hands of. How, I ask again, can that understanding negate
or falsify the *experience* that gave rise to the utterance of "We are
in the hands of the Lord"?

Consider this analogy. I am sitting in my garden reading. An
adolescent walks by and just nonchalantly, though not aiming at

me or even seeing me, tosses an empty beer can over the wall into my garden. My primitive reaction is to utter to myself "That pig!" but a moment's reflection leads me to think to myself that there by the grace of a different social conditioning, genetic inheritance, and age go I. But that does not falsify my primitive reaction expressed in "That pig!" that articulates my spontaneous feelings. Why should it be different for Mrs. Ramsey, aside, of course, from the quality of the experience? Moreover, how does this show—in any way show—that in so reflecting we have falsified the experience or that our emotions take us to a realization that God, my Savior, exists or even can exist? If we say that belief in God or an understanding of "God" just comes to having such primitive reactions or any kind of reactions and "God" is just an expression of them then we are back with something like the reductionist accounts of Braithwaite and Hare which are not only reductionist but are a *reductio ad absurdum* because there we have an interpretation of God-talk which in no way corresponds to our actual God-talk—e.g., "God created the world out of nothing" would have to mean something like "People express certain sentiments out of the contingencies and stresses of their lives." But then on that or any similar understanding of "God created the world out of nothing," people would have to have existed for it to make sense that God created the world out of nothing; but if God created the world out of nothing there were no people around to witness that act of creation or to express their feelings concerning it. We cannot take belief in God or belief that God exists to be talk of either describing our experience or to be expressions of our experience. God is not just a human experience or a projection of that experience. Such a conceptualizing of that experience or so understanding God could only come from someone who was an atheist. Metaphysical religiosity remains part of the orientation of the believer. That aside, I am sure that Winch and somewhat sure that Lyas would not intend to say that—would not intend to construe "God" in that reductionist way. But that is what their accounts seem at least to come to. Have I been uncharitable and, if so, how?

I feel the power of the Virginia Woolf passage. It seems to me to get some things emotionally just right. But I do not see, nor do

I think, Woolf intends to be saying or implying, that our emotions lead us to God but that such emotions, such attunements, to at least some people, are important to the living of a human life and that, with Leslie Stephen no doubt in mind, we shouldn't be overly rationalistic. What, if anything can, can lead us to God or even to an understanding of what it is to be led to God? If anything can lead us to God it would be our emotions and thoughts working in tandem. (They hardly can help doing that anyway, they are so inseparably entwined. But I leave that aside here.) Perhaps, I think very probably, no one could understand, except perhaps in the most rudimentary and crudest sense, God-talk if they did not have a certain kind of emotional life. If they did not, for example, respond in an attuned way to plain chant (though I am not saying there is any one thing that it is essential for them to respond to). But having that emotional life is not even remotely sufficient to be able to have a belief in God or even to grasp what it is to believe in God. We have to have certain conceptualizations and certain other beliefs as well. Belief in God is not just a matter of reason, but it is not just a matter of the emotions either. The heart has no reasons that reason cannot know, though that does not entail or give to understand that we do not have many groundless beliefs. We live, as Wittgenstein realized, in a sea of them. But we are none the worse off for all of that.

NOTES

1. The qualifier "almost always" is made to accommodate certain rare but terrible situations. Suppose I survive a plane crash in the midst of a desert. It may be crucial for my survival that I think I can walk out while on the best evidence it is very unlikely though still not impossible. It is better that I believe, in that situation, that improbability than I believe what is best justified on the evidence to believe.

2. Unless these language-games are so radically changed that they are hardly religious language-games anymore and do not meet Jewish, Christian, or Islamic *expectations* of what these religions will hold out for them. D. Z. Phillips seems to me paradigmatic of someone who so radically changes religious language-games.

3. I hope I do not beg any important questions by speaking of being "philosophically literate." What I think—though I speak only of Western societies—is that people who are (a) well educated philosophically and (b) have a good participant's understanding or a participant-like understanding of Jewish, Christian, or Islamic language-games and practices would assent to propositions 1 through 11 with the *possible* exception of 6 and 11.

BIBLIOGRAPHY

Bentley, Arthur, and John Dewey. *Knowing and the Known*. Boston: Beacon Press, 1949.

Braithwaite, R. B. "An Empiricist's View of the Nature of Religious Belief." In *The Logic of God*, edited by L. Diamond Malcolm and Thomas Litzenburg Jr., pp. 127–47. Indianapolis: Bobbs–Merrill, 1975.

Brandon, Robert, ed. *Rorty and His Critics*. Oxford, UK: Blackwell, 2000.

Brown, Stuart C., ed. *Reason and Religion*. Ithaca, NY: Cornell University Press, 1977.

Carnap, Rudolf. "Truth and Confirmation." In *Readings in Philosophical Analysis*, edited by Herbert Feigl and Wilfrid Sellars, pp. 119–27. New York: Appleton-Century Crofts, 1949.

Drange, Theodore M. "Incompatible-Properties Arguments: A Survey." In Martin and Monnier, *The Impossibility of God*, pp. 185–97.

Findlay, J. N. "Can God's Existence Be Disproved?" In Martin and Monnier, *The Impossibility of God*, pp.19–26.

———. "God's Non-Existence: A Reply to Mr. Rainer and Mr. Hughes." In Martin and Monnier, *The Impossibility of God*, pp. 27–30.

Hägerström, Axel. *Philosophy and Religion*. Translated by Robert T. Sandin. London: Allen and Unwin, 1964.

Hare, R. M. "The Simple Believer." In *Religion and Morality*, edited by Gene Outka and John P. Reeder Jr., pp. 393–427. Garden City, NY: Anchor Books, 1973.

Lyas, Colin. *Peter Winch*. Teddington, UK: Acumen, 1999.

Mackie, J. L. "The Problem of Evil." In Martin and Monnier, *The Impossibility of God*, pp. 73–96.

Malcolm, Norman. "The Groundlessness of Belief." In Brown, *Reason and Religion*, pp. 143–57.

———. *Knowledge and Certainty*. Englewood Cliffs, NJ: Prentice-Hall, 1963.

Martin, Michael, and Ricki Monnier, eds. *The Impossibility of God.* Amherst, NY: Prometheus Books, 2003.

Nielsen, Kai. "Can Faith Validate God-talk?" *Theology Today* 20 (1963): 173–84.

———. *God, Scepticism and Modernity.* Ottawa, Ontario: University of Ottawa Press, 1989.

———. *Naturalism and Religion.* Amherst, NY: Prometheus Books, 2001.

———. *Naturalism without Foundations.* Amherst, NY: Prometheus Books, 1996.

———. *On Transformation Philosophy: A Metaphysical Inquiry.* Boulder, CO: Westview Press, 1995.

———. "Religious Perplexity and Faith." *Grande Review* 8, no. 1 (Fall 1965): 1–17.

———, and D. Z. Phillips, eds. *Wittgensteinian Fideism?* London: SLM Press, 2006.

Rawls, John. *A Theory of Justice.* Cambridge, MA: Harvard University Press, 1999.

Rorty, Richard. *Philosophy and the Mirror of Nature.* Princeton, NJ: Princeton University Press, 1979.

———. *Philosophy and Social Hope.* Harmondsworth, UK: Penguin Books, 1999.

———. "Response to Habermas." In Brandon, *Rorty and His Critics*, pp. 56–64.

———. "Universality and Truth." In Brandon, *Rorty and His Critics*, pp. 1–30.

Sober, Elliott. "Testability." *Proceedings and Addresses of the American Philosophical Association* 73, no. 3 (1999): 47–76.

Winch, Peter. "Review of Norman Malcolm." *Philosophical Investigations* 15 (1992): 222–23.

———. *Trying to Make Sense.* Oxford, UK: Blackwell, 1987.

Woolf, Virginia. *To the Lighthouse.* 1927. Reprint, Harmondsworth, UK: Penguin Books, 1992.

1

Introduction

How Is Atheism to Be Characterized?

Many, perhaps most, educated twentieth-century believers and non-believers alike are perplexed about the concept of God and other central religious notions of the Jewish-Christian-Islamic faiths. Key concepts of such religions—God, heaven, hell, sin, the Last Judgment, a human being's chief end, being resurrected, and coming to be a new man with a new body—are all to one degree or another problematic. Indeed, their very intelligibility or rational acceptability are not beyond reasonable doubt. These concepts form a system. Indeed, a religious faith or a religion should be seen as a system of salvation and we should recognize that we cannot properly understand these concepts in isolation or apart from understanding the rationale of the form of life of which they are an integral part. But in the various cultures of the West, if our socialization has been even remotely normal, we know how to play Jewish or Christian language-games and in varying degrees, we even have some understanding of those forms of life. Yet what I said initially still remains true: many of us—believers and nonbelievers alike—remain perplexed by the fundamental concepts of the dominant religion in our culture. We know how to use these terms perfectly well and we have a reasonable understanding of why they have remained in circulation, for we acknowledge many of the aspirations that religion answers to. Yet we remain thoroughly perplexed over whether these terms in their religious employments answer to anything real or even to anything we can coherently conceive.

    I shall in this collection of essays probe why this is so, and in the course of this probing I shall define, explicate, and defend atheism as a form of skepticism concerning religion. Perhaps "atheism" is a crude word, gesturing too overtly at something that many people, touched deeply by modern sensibilities about science and philosophy and more broadly by contemporary intellectual culture, instinctively feel, but will not affirm so flatly or so unequivocally as I do. Their reasons vary; some of them are aesthetic, including a wish (surely well grounded) not to be caught up in yet another "orthodoxy" or some "smelly little ideology." While sharing their desire to stay utterly clear of a kind of "church outside any church," I shall seek, without dogmatism and hopefully in tune with sophisticated developments in philosophy, to defend a form of atheism. (Part of the task will be to make clear what atheism comes to.)

In the first two essays collected here, "The Making of an Atheist" and "Does God Exist?: Reflections on Disbelief," I try in an elementary way to show something of my road to this atheism and something of its rationale. In the middle essays, starting with "Agnosticism" and ending with "The Burden of Proof and *The Presumption of Atheism*," I both explicate and probe the core of my defense of atheism and show, as well, in the first of these essays, something of its historical roots.

"The Primacy of Philosophical Theology" turns to an examination of a claim, central to powerful strands of Protestant theology, which would set forth an appeal to revelation and faith as a block to skeptical critiques of religion. I argue that problems of relativity and arguments about the coherence of God-talk serve to undermine such apologetic moves. Karl Barth or no Karl Barth, we cannot in this way escape the critique of religion. (Barth, who is arguably the most important Protestant theologian of the twentieth century, thought, much like Luther, that the rationalistic arguments of philosophy and natural theology could only lead to unbelief. Our acceptance of the claim of Christianity must rest solely on revelation.)

In "Religious Ethics Versus Humanistic Ethics," I return to themes pursued in my *Ethics Without God* and elsewhere.[1] I criticize both Divine Command and Natural Law conceptions of ethics and attempt to show the bankruptcy of the popular apologetic move that if God is dead nothing matters.

Finally, in "Religion and Rationality" and "The Embeddedness of Atheism," I return to underlying philosophical topics—topics that cut to the heart of the matter—discussed in "In Defense of Atheism" and in my previous books: *Contemporary Critiques of Religion, Skepticism* and *An Introduction to the Philosophy of Religion*. I try in these last two essays to probe what the elusive appeal to religion comes to in the broader context of exploring the underlying philosophical questions about the rationality of religious belief.

II

In the remainder of this introduction, I shall seek perspicuously to characterize atheism and to contrast it with agnosticism and with religious belief-systems. What it is to be an atheist is not as unproblematic as it is frequently thought to be. I shall move from common but less adequate characterizations to what I take to be the proper delineation of what it is to be an atheist. With that characterization before us, I shall in the first instance try to show some of the attractions of this position and then close this introductory essay by criticizing a brisk way of dismissing my whole project.

A central common core of Judaism, Christianity, and Islam is the affirmation of the realitiy of one and only one God. Adherents to these religions believe that there is a God who created the universe out of nothing and who is taken to have absolute sovereignty over all His creation, including, of course, human beings—beings who are not only utterly dependent on this creative power but who are also sinful and who, according to the faithful, can only make adequate sense of their lives by accepting without question God's ordinances for them. The varieties of atheism are quite numerous but all atheists are united in rejecting such a set of beliefs, which are central to the religious systems of Western cultures.

However, atheism casts a wider net and rejects all belief in "spiritual beings," and to the extent that belief in spiritual beings is definitive of what it is for a belief-system to be religious, atheism rejects religion. Thus, it is not only a rejection of the central conceptions of Judeo-Christianity; it is, as well, a rejection of the religious beliefs of such African religions as those of the Dinka and the Nuer, the anthropomorphic gods of classical Greece and Rome, and the transcendental conceptions of Hinduism and Buddhism.[2] Sometimes atheism is viewed simplistically as a denial of "God" or of "the gods" and, if religion is to be defined in terms of the belief in "spiritual beings," then atheism is the rejection of all religious belief.

However, if any tolerably adequate understanding of atheism is to be achieved, it is necessary to give a careful reading to "rejection of religious belief" and to realize how frightfully inadequate it is to characterize atheism as the denial of God (or the gods) or of all spiritual beings.

To say that atheism is the denial of God (or the gods) and that it is the opposite of theism, a system of belief which affirms the reality of God and seeks to demonstrate His existence, is inadequate in several ways. First, not all theologians who regard themselves as defenders of the Christian faith or of Judaism or Islam regard themselves as defenders of theism. The influential twentieth-century Protestant theologian Paul Tillich, for example, regards the God of theism as an idol and refuses to construe God as a being, even a supreme being, among beings or as an infinite being above finite beings.[3] God, for him, is being-itself, the ground of being and meaning. The particulars of Tillich's view are in certain ways idiosyncratic as well as obscure and problematic; but they have had a considerable impact on our cultural life, and his rejection of theism while retaining a belief in God is not eccentric in contemporary theology, though it may very well be an affront to the plain believer.

Secondly, and more importantly, it is not the case that all theists seek to demonstrate or even in any way rationally to establish the existence of God. Many theists regard such a demonstration as impossible, and fideistic believers (e.g., Georg Hamann and Søren Kirkegaard) believe such a demonstration to be undesirable even if it were possible, for, in their view, it would undermine faith. If we could prove, i.e., come to know for certain, that God exists, then we would not be in a position to accept Him on faith as our Sovereign Lord with all the risks that faith entails. There are theologians who have argued that for genuine faith to be possible God must necessarily be a hidden God, the mysterious ultimate reality, whose existence and authority we must accept simply on faith. This fideistic view has not, of course, gone without challenge from inside these major faiths. But it is of sufficient importance to raise serious questions about the adequacy of the above theism.

It should also be noted that not all denials of God come to the same thing. Sometimes believers deny God while not being at all in a state of doubt that God exists. Many willfully reject what they take to be His authority by not acting in accordance with what they take to be His will, while others simply live their lives as if God did not exist. In this important way, they deny Him in practice while in a sense remaining believers. But neither of the above deniers are atheists (unless we wish, misleadingly, to call them "practical atheists"). They are not even agnostics. They would never question the existence of God, even though they deny Him in other ways.

To be atheists we need to deny the *existence* of God. It is frequently, but I shall argue mistakenly, thought that this entails that we need to believe that it is false that God exists or, alternatively, that we must believe that God's existence is a speculative hypothesis of an extremely low order of probability.[4] Such a characterization, I shall argue, is defective in a number of ways. For one it is too narrow. There are atheists (including this atheist) who believe that the very concept of God, at least in developed and less anthropomorphic forms of Judeo-Christianity, is so incoherent that certain central religious claims, such as "God is my creator to whom everything is owed," are not genuine truth-claims. That is to say, as claims they are neither true nor false. Yet, believers do indeed take such religious propositions to be true, and *some* atheists, unlike this atheist, believe they are false; and there are agnostics who cannot make up their minds whether the propositions (putative propositions) are true *or* false. (The latter consider religious claims to be one or the other but believe that we cannot determine which.) It will be the underlying burden of my argument to show that all three stances are mistaken, for such putative truth-claims are not sufficiently intelligible to be genuine truth-claims that are either true or false. In reality there is nothing here to be believed or disbelieved, though, for the believer, there remains a powerful and humanly comforting illusion that there is.

While the above considerations about atheism and intelligibility will, if well-taken, show that the second characterization of atheism is too narrow, it would also be accurate to say that, in a way, the characterization is too broad. There are fideistic believers who quite unequivocally believe it to be the case that, when looked at objectively, propositions about God's existence have a very low probability weight. They do not believe in God because it is probable that He exists—they think it is more probable that He doesn't—but because such a belief is thought by them to be necessary to make sense of human life. The short of it is that such a characterization of atheism would not distinguish a fideistic believer (e.g., Blaise Pascal or Søren Kierkegaard) or an agnostic (e.g., T. H. Huxley or Leslie Stephen) from an atheist such as Baron Holbach or Thomas Paine. They all believe that propositions of the form "There is a God" and "God protects humankind," however emotionally important they may be, are, when viewed objectively, nothing more than speculative hypotheses of an extremely low order of probability. But this, since it does not distinguish believers from nonbelievers, and does not distinguish agnostics from atheists, cannot be an adequate characterization of atheism.

It may be retorted that if *a prioriism* and dogmatic atheism are to be avoided we must regard the existence of God as a hypothesis. There are no ontological (purely *a priori*) proofs or *disproofs* of God's existence. Without such a proof or disproof it is not reasonable (or at least ill-advised) to rule in advance that to say "God exists" makes no sense. It has often been argued—and not unreasonably—that all the atheist can reasonably claim is that there is no evidence that there is a God and that without such evidence he is justified in asserting that there is no God. Some opponents of this view have insisted that it is simply dogmatic for an atheist to assert that no possible evidence could ever provide grounds for a belief in God. Instead, it is argued, atheists should justify their unbelief by supporting (if they can) the assertion that no evidence currently warrants a belief in God. If atheism is justified, the advocate will have shown that in fact there is no evidence that God exists. But, the argument goes, it should not be part of his task to try to show that there couldn't be *any* evidence for the existence of God. If the atheist could somehow survive the death of his pressent body (assuming for the nonce that such talk makes sense) and came, much to his surprise, to stand in the presence of God, his answer should be "Oh! Lord you didn't give me enough evidence!" His belief that there is no God would have turned out to have been mistaken all along and now he realizes that he had believed something to be false that in fact was true. Given what he had come to experience in this transformed state, he now sees that he was mistaken in his judgment that there is no God. Still, he was not unjustified, in the light of the evidence available to him during his "earthly life," in believing that God did not exist. That judgment, given what he knew at the time, is not rendered unreasonable in the light of evidence that only could become available to him later. The reasonableness of our judgments should be assessed in the light of the evidence available to us at a given time. Not having any such post-mortem experiences of the presence of God (assuming for the occasion that he could have them), as things stand, and in the face of the evidence he actually has, and is likely to be able to get, he should say that it is false that God exists. When we legitimately assert that a proposition is false we need not be certain that it is false. "Knowing with certainty" is not a pleonasm. The claim is that this tentative posture is the reasonable position for the atheist to take.

An atheist who argues in this manner may also make a distinctive burden-of-proof argument. Given that God (if there is one) is by definition a very *recherché* reality, a reality that must be transcendent to the world, the burden of proof is not on the atheist to give grounds for believing that there is no reality of that order. Rather, the burden of proof is on the believer to give us evidence for God's existence, i.e., something to show that there is such a reality. Given what God must be, if there is a God, the believer needs to present the evidence for such a very strange reality. He needs to show that there is more in the world than is disclosed by our common experience. The scientific method, broadly conceived as a resolutely empirical method, and the scientific method alone, such an atheist asserts, affords a reliable method for establishing what is in fact the case. The believer will in turn assert that in addition to the varieties of empirical facts there are also "spiritual facts" or "transcendent facts," i.e., the fact that there is a supernatural, self-existent eternal power. To this the atheist can, and should, retort that such "facts" have not been shown to us. The believer has done nothing to deliver the goods here. No such facts have been presented. Atheists of the "we-don't-have-enough-evidence" variety will argue, against what they take to be dogmatic *a prioristic* atheists, that the atheist should be a fallibilist and remain open-minded about what the future may bring. After all, they argue, there may be such "transcendent facts," such *recherché* metaphysical realities.

It is not that such a fallibilistic atheist is really an agnostic who believes that he is not justified in either asserting that God exists or denying that He exists, and that to be maximally reasonable over this issue, what he must do is suspend belief. On the contrary, such an atheist believes he has very good grounds indeed, as things stand, for denying the existence of God. But what he will not deny is that things could be otherwise and, if they were, that he would not be justified in asserting that it is false that there is a God. Using reliable empirical techniques—proven methods for establishing matters of fact—he has found nothing in the universe that would make a belief in God's existence justifiable or even, everything considered, the most rational of the available options. He therefore draws the atheistic conclusion (also keeping in mind his burden-of-proof argument) that God does not exist. But his denial of God's existence is not set forth dogmatically in a high *a priori* fashion. The atheist remains a thorough and consistent fallibilist.

III

Such a form of atheism (the atheism of those pragmatists who are also naturalistic humanists) is not adequate. This can be seen if we take careful note of the concept of God in our forms of life. Unlike Zeus or Wotan, in developed forms of Judaism, Christianity, and Islam, God is not, like Zeus or Wotan, construed in a relatively plain anthropomorphic way.[5] Nothing that could count as "God" in such religions could possibly be observed, literally encountered, or detected in the universe. God, on such a conception, is transcendent to the world; He is conceived of as "pure spirit," an infinite individual who created the universe out of nothing and who is distinct from it, though, for Christians, God, in the form of Christ, is said to have walked the earth. Thus, somehow, for Christians—and only for Christians—God is said to be both transcendent and immanent. He is "pure spirit" *and* a person with a material embodiment. God is said to be an eternal transcendent reality but he is also said to be immanent. This appears at least to be incoherent, but, incoherent or not, Christians whose beliefs are at all close to established orthodoxy will not abandon their claim that God is transcendent to the world. Such a "transcendent reality"—a reality understood to be an ultimate mystery— can not be identified in the same way that objects or processes in the universe are identified. There can be no pointing at God, no ostensive teaching of "God," to show what "God" means. The word "God" can only be taught intra-linguistically. Someone who does not understand what the word "God" means can be taught by using descriptions such as "the maker of the universe," "the eternal, utterly independent being upon whom all other beings depend," "the first cause," "the sole ulti-mate reality," "a self-caused being," and the like. For someone who does not understand such descriptions (putative descriptions), there can be no understanding of the concept of God. Yet there is a very good reason for saying that we do not understand such "descriptions": they do not give us an empirical foundation for *what* we are talking about when we speak of God. The key terms employed in these "descriptions" are themselves no more capable of ostensive definition (i.e., capable of having their referents pointed out) than is "God." Unlike the referent for the term "Zeus," what is allegedly referred to by the term "God" is not construed anthropomorphically. (That does not mean that anyone has actually pointed to Zeus or observed Zeus but it does mean that we know roughly what it would be like to do so. We know, that is, roughly what would constitute pointing to Zeus.)

In coming to understand what is meant by "God," in such re-ligious discourses, we must come to understand that God, whatever else He is, is a being that could not possibly be observed in any way. He could not be anything that is empirically detectable (again a pleo-nasm). Moreover, God is said by believers to be an intractable, ulti-mate mystery. A nonmysterious God would not be the God of Judaism, Christianity, and Islam.

The relevance of the preceding to our second characterization of atheism is that, if "God" is taken to be a transcendent mystery, we should then come to see that it is a mistake to claim that His existence can rightly be treated as a hypothesis and that it is also a mistake to claim that we, by the use of the experimental method or some deter-minate empirical method, can come to confirm or disconfirm God's existence as we could if He were an empirical reality. Such a proposed way of coming to know, or failing to come to know, God makes no sense for anyone who understands what kind of reality God is sup-posed to be. Anything whose existence could be so verified would not be the God of developed Judeo-Christianity. God could not be a reality whose presence is even faintly adumbrated in experience, for anything that could count as the God of Judeo-Christianity must be transcen-dent to the world. Anything that could actually be encountered or experienced could not be an eternal transcendent reality. This is indeed a conceptual argument, but it is an argument that has been made, and should be made, as indeed any argument should be made, in a thor-oughly fallibilistic spirit. It is a putatively *a priori* claim, but whether it is a valid claim, whether it is genuinely *a priori* (analytically true or in some weaker way conceptually true) as its defenders claim, is in turn a thoroughly fallible belief. There need be, and indeed should be, nothing dogmatic about such a defense of atheism.

So at the very heart of a religion such as Christianity there is a cosmological belief—a thoroughly metaphysical belief—in a reality that is alleged to transcend the "empirical world." It is the metaphysical belief that there is an eternal, ever-present creative source and sustainer of the universe. The problem is how we could come to know or reasonably believe that such a strange reality exists or come to understand what such talk is about.

It is not that God is like a theoretical entity, such as a proton or neutrino in physics. Such theoretical entities, where they are construed as realities rather than as heuristically useful conceptual fictions, are thought to be part of the actual furniture of the universe. They are not said to be transcendent to the universe. Rather, they are invisible entities logically on a par with specks of dust and grains of sand only much much smaller. Theoretical entities are not a different kind of reality; it is only the case that they, as a matter of fact, cannot be seen. Indeed, we have no understanding of what it would be like to see a proton or a neutrino—in *that way* they are like God—and no provision is made in physical theory for seeing them. Still, there is no *logical* ban on our seeing them as there is on seeing God. We cannot correctly say that it is *logically* impossible that they could be seen.

Though invisible, theoretical entities are among the things in the universe and thus they can be postulated as causes of the things we do see. Since this is so, it becomes at least logically possible indirectly to verify by empirical methods the existence of such realities. It is also the case that there is no *logical* ban on establishing what is necessary to ascertain a causal connection, namely a constant conjunction of two discrete empirical realities. However, for the nonanthropomorphic conceptions of God of developed forms of Judeo-Christianity, no such constant conjunction can be established or even intelligibly asserted between God and the universe; thus the existence of God is not even indirectly confirmable or disconfirmable. God is not a discrete empirical thing or being and the universe is not some gigantic thing or process over and above the various particular things and processes in the universe of which it makes sense to say it has or had a cause. A particular thing in the universe could cause another particular thing. It is one discrete thing making another discrete thing happen. It is between things of this type that we can establish a constant conjunction. But neither "God" nor "the universe" are words standing for realities of which we have any idea at all what it would be like for them to stand in constant conjunction. Indeed, such talk has no intelligible home here. We have no basis for saying one is the cause of the other. But then there is no way, directly or indirectly, that we could empirically establish even the probability that there is a God since we have already disposed of the claim that God could be directly observed.

IV

There is the gnostic reply that God's existence can be established or made probable in some nonempirical way. There are, that is (or so the claim goes), truths about the nature of the cosmos that are neither capable of nor standing in need of verification. There is, gnostics claim against empiricists, knowledge of the world that transcends experience and comprehends the sorry scheme of things entire.

Since the thorough probings of such epistemological foundations by David Hume and Immanuel Kant, skepticism about how, and indeed even that, such knowledge is possible has become very strong indeed.[6] With respect to knowledge of God in particular both Hume and Kant provide powerful critiques of the various traditional attempts to prove in any way His existence. (Kant set forth such an analysis of prevailing doctrine even though he remained a steadfast Christian.) While some of the *details* of their arguments have been rejected and refinements rooted in their argumentative procedures have been developed, there remains a very considerable consensus among contemporary philosophers and theologians that arguments like those developed by Hume and Kant show that no proof (*a priori* or empirical) of God's existence is possible.[7] And, alternatively, to speak of "intuitive knowledge" (an intuitive grasp of being, or of an intuition of the reality of the divine being) as gnostics do is to appeal to something that lacks sufficient clarity to be of any value in establishing or even understanding anything.

There is another turn that should be considered in this initial laying out of the problems with which I shall wrestle. Prior to the rise of anthropology and the scientific study of religion, an appeal to revelation and authority as a substitute for knowledge or warranted belief might have been thought to possess considerable force. But with a knowledge of other religions and their associated appeals to "Revealed Truth," such arguments are without probative force. Claimed (alleged) revelations are numerous, diverse, and not infrequently conflicting; we cannot claim by simply appealing to a given putative revelation, at least not without going in a very small and vicious circle, that it is the "true revelation" or the "genuine revelation" and that other so-called revelations are actually mistaken or, where nonconflicting, they are mere approximations of the truth. Similar things need to be said for religious authority. Moreover, it is at best problematic whether faith could sanction our speaking of testing the genuineness of revelation or of the acceptability of religious authority. Indeed, if something is a "genuine revelation," we cannot use our reason to assess it. But our predicament is that, as a matter of anthropological fact, we have this diverse and sometimes conflicting field of alleged revelations with no way of deciding or even having a reasonable hunch which, if any, of the candidate revelations is the genuine article. But even if we allow for the necessity of some tests for the genuineness of revelation, we still have a claim that clearly will not do, for such a procedure would make an appeal to revelation or authority supererogatory. Where such tests are allowed, it is not revelation or authority that can warrant the most fundamental religious truths on which the rest depend. It is something else, namely, that which establishes the genuineness of the revelation or authority. It is that which guarantees these religious truths (if such there be) including the proposition that God exists. But then the question surfaces again as to what that fundamental guarantee is or could be. Perhaps such a belief is nothing more than a cultural myth? There is, as we have seen, neither empirical knowledge nor *a priori* knowledge of God, and talk of "intuitive knowledge" is without logical force.[8]

If the above considerations are near to the mark, it is unclear what it would mean to say, as some agnostics and even some atheists have, that they are "skeptical God-seekers" who simply have not found, after a careful examination, enough evidence to make belief in God warranted or even reasonable. That is so because it is very unclear what it would be like to have or, for that matter, to fail to have evidence for the existence of God. It isn't that the "God-seeker" has to be able to give the evidence, for if that were so no search would be necessary; but he, or at least somebody, must at least be able to conceive what *would count* as evidence if he had it so that he, and we, would have some idea of what to look for. We need at least to have some idea of what evidence would look like here. But it appears that it is just this that we do not have.[9]

The response might be given that it is enough for the God-seeker not to accept any *logical* ban on the possibility of there being evidence. He need not understand what it would be like to have evidence in this domain. I would, in turn, retort that when we consider what kind of transcendent reality God is said to be, it appears at least, as I remarked earlier, that there is an implicit *logical* ban on the presence of empirical evidence (a pleonasm) for His existence.

Someone seeking to resist this conclusion might try to give empirical anchorage to talk of God by utilizing the following fanciful hypothetical case. It is important not to forget, however, that things even remotely like what I shall now describe do not happen. The fanciful case is this: Suppose thousands of us were standing out under the starry skies and we all saw a set of stars rearrange themselves to spell out "God." We would be utterly astonished and indeed rightly think we had gone mad. Even if we could somehow assure ourselves that this was not some form of mass hallucination, though how we could do this is not evident, such an experience would still not constitute evidence for the existence of God, for we still would be without a clue as to what could be *meant* by speaking of an infinite individual transcendent to the world. Such an observation (i.e., the stars rearranging themselves), no matter how well confirmed, would not ostensively fix the reference range of "God." Talk of such an infinite individual would still remain incomprehensible and it would also have the same appearance of being incoherent. We do not know what we are talking about in speaking of such a transcendent reality. All we would know is that something very strange indeed had happened—something we would not know what to make of.[10]

The doubt arises (or at least it should arise) as to whether believers or indeed anyone else, in terms acceptable to believers, can give an intelligible account of the concept of God or of what belief in God comes to once the concept is thoroughly de-anthropomorphized. It is completely unclear how we could give such a term any empirical foundation. We do not know what it would be like to specify the denotation (the referent) of a nonanthropomorphic God.

V

Reflection on the above cluster of claims should lead us to a more adequate statement of what atheism is and indeed as well to what an agnostic or religious response to atheism should be. Instead of saying that an atheist is someone who believes that it is false or probably false that there is a God, a more adequate characterization of atheism consists in the more complex claim that an atheist is someone who rejects belief in God for at least one of the following reasons (the specific reason will likely depend on how God is being conceived): (1) if an anthropomorphic God is proposed, the atheist rejects belief in God because it is false or probably false that there is such a God; (2) if it be a nonanthropomorphic God (i.e., the God of Luther and Calvin, Aquinas and Maimonides), he rejects belief in God because the concept of such a God is either meaningless, unintelligible, contradictory, incomprehensible, or incoherent; (3) the atheist rejects belief in God (here we speak of the God portrayed by some modern or contemporary theologians or philosophers) because the concept of God in question is such that it merely masks an atheistic substance, e.g., "God" is just another name for love or simply a symbolic term for moral ideals.[11]

Such a ramified conception of atheism, as well as its more reflective opposition, is much more complex than the simpler conceptions of atheism we initially considered. From what has been said about the concept of God in developed forms of Judeo-Christianity, it should be evident that the more crucial form of atheist rejection is not the one asserting that it is false that there is a God but instead the form of atheism that rejects belief in God based on the contention that the concept of God does not make sense: it is in some important sense incoherent or unintelligible. (Note: I do not say that it is unintelligible or meaningless full stop. It is very important to keep this in mind, particularly when reading the essay entitled "In Defense of Atheism.")

Such a broader conception of atheism, of course, includes everyone who is an atheist in the narrower sense, i.e., the sense in which atheism is identified with the claim that "God exists" is false; but the converse plainly does not obtain. Moreover, this broad conception of atheism does not have to say that religious claims are in all aspects meaningless. The more typical, less paradoxical, and less tendentious claim is that utterances such as "There is an infinite, eternal creator of the universe" are incoherent and the conception of God reflected therein is in a crucial respect unintelligible and, because of that, in an important sense inconceivable and incredible: incapable of being a rational object of belief for a philosophically and scientifically sophisticated person touched by modernity.[12] This is a central belief of many contemporary atheists. And it is just such an atheism that I shall defend in this volume. I shall argue that there (a) are good *empirical* grounds for believing that there are no Zeus-like spiritual beings and (b) that there are also sound grounds for believing that the non-anthropomorphic or at least radically less anthropomorphic conceptions of God are incoherent or unintelligible. (Remember that both of these conceptions admit of degree.) If these two claims can be justified, the atheist, to understate it, has very strong grounds for rejecting belief in God.

Atheism, as we have seen, is a critique and a denial of the central metaphysical belief-systems of salvation involving a belief in God or spiritual beings; however, a sophisticated atheist will not simply contend that all such cosmological claims are false but will take it that some are so problematic that, while purporting to be factual, they actually do not succeed in making coherent factual claims. In an important respect they do not make sense, and while believers are under the illusion that something intelligible is there in which to

believe, in reality this is not the case. These seemingly grand cosmological claims are in reality best understood as myths or ideological
claims reflecting a humanly understandable confusion on the part of
the people who make them.[13]

It is not a well-taken rejoinder to atheistic critiques to say, as some
contemporary Protestant and Jewish theologians have, that belief in
God is the worst form of atheism and idolatry, for the language of
Christian and Jewish belief, including such sentences as "God exists"
and "God created the world," is not to be taken literally but rather as
symbol or metaphor. Christianity, as Reinhold Niebuhr (a theologian
who defends such views) once put it, is "true myth." On such an
account, the claims of religion are not to be understood as metaphysical claims trying to convey some extraordinary facts but as metaphorical and analogical claims that are not understandable in any
other terms. But this claim is incoherent: if something is a metaphor,
it must at least in principle be possible to say what it is a metaphor
of.[14] Thus metaphors cannot be understandable *only* in metaphorical
terms. All metaphors and symbolic expressions must be capable of
paraphrase, though, what is something else again, a user of such
expressions may not be able on demand to supply that paraphrase.
Moreover, and more simply and less controversially, if the language
of religion becomes little more than the language of myth and religious
beliefs are viewed simply as powerful and often humanly compelling
myths, then we have conceptions that actually possess an atheistic
substance.[15] The believer is making no cosmological claim; he is making no claim that the atheist should feel obliged to deny. It is just that
the believer's talk, including his unelucidated talk of "true myths," is
language that has a more powerful emotive force for many people. But
if the believer follows these theologians or Christian philosophers
down this path, he will have abandoned his effort to make truth
claims that are different from those made by the atheist.

VI

Many skeptics would prefer to think of themselves as agnostics rather
than atheists because it seems less dogmatic. In my essay on "Agnosticism," I shall examine in some detail what is involved here; but
initially, and in a preliminary way, I want now to show something of
what is at stake.

Agnosticism has a parallel development to that of atheism. An
agnostic, like an atheist, asserts that we can neither know nor have
sound reasons for believing that God exists; but, unlike the atheist,
the agnostic does not think we are justified in saying that God does

not exist or, stronger still, that God cannot exist. Similarly, while some contemporary atheists will say that the concept of God in developed theism does not make sense and thus Jewish, Christian, and Islamic beliefs must be rejected, many contemporary agnostics will believe that, though the concept of God is radically problematic, we are not in a position to be able rationally to decide whether, on the one hand, the terms and concepts of such religions are so problematic that such religious beliefs do not make sense or whether, on the other, they still have just enough coherence to make a belief in an ultimate mystery a live option for a reflective and informed human being, even though the talk of such belief is indeed radically paradoxical and in many ways incomprehensible.

Such an agnostic recognizes that our puzzles about God cut deeper than perplexities concerning whether it is possible to attain adequate evidence for God's existence. Rather, he sees clearly the need to exhibit an adequate nonanthropomorphic, extra-linguistic referent for "God." (This need not commit him to the belief that there is any theory-independent acquisition of data.) Believers think that even though God is a mystery such a referent has been secured, though what it is still remains obscure. Atheists, by contrast, believe, as we have seen, that it has not been secured, and indeed some of them believe that it cannot be secured. To speak of mystery here, they maintain, is just an evasive way of talking about what we do not understand. Instead of being candid about their total incomprehension, believers use the evasive language of mystery. Contemporary agnostics (those agnostics who parallel the atheists characterized above) remain in doubt about whether our talk of God in this halting fashion just barely secures such reference or whether it fails after all and "God" refers to nothing religiously acceptable.

Intense religious commitment, as the history of fideism makes evident, has sometimes combined with deep skepticism concerning man's capacity to know God. It is agreed by almost all parties to the dispute between belief and unbelief that religious claims are paradoxical, and if there is a God, He is indeed a very mysterious reality. Furthermore, criteria for what is or is not meaningless and what is or is not intelligible are deeply contested; at least there seem to be no generally accepted criteria here.

Keeping these diverse considerations in mind, in the arguments between belief, agnosticism, and atheism, it is crucial to ask whether we have any good reason at all to believe that there is a personal creative reality that exists beyond the bounds of space and time and that transcends the world. Do we even have a sufficient understanding of such talk so that the reality to which it refers can be the object of religious commitment? We cannot have faith in or accept on faith that which we do not at all understand. We must at least in some way understand what it is we are to have faith in if we are actually to have faith in it. If someone asks me to trust *Irglig,* I cannot do so no matter how strongly I want to take that something-I-know-not-what simply on trust.[16]

What appears at least to be the case is that it is just a brute fact that there is that indefinitely immense collection of finite and contingent masses or conglomerations of things and processes we use the phrase "the universe" to refer to. There is no logical or rational necessity that there are any of these things or anything at all. It just manifestly is so. That we can in certain moods come to feel wonder, awe, and puzzlement that there is a world at all does not license the claim that there is a noncontingent reality on which the world (the sorry collection of such things entire) depends. It is not even clear that such a sense of contingency gives us an understanding of what a "noncontingent thing" could be. Some atheists (including this atheist) think that the reference range of "God" is so indeterminate and the concept so problematic that it is impossible for someone to be fully aware of this fact and, if the person is being nonevasive, to believe in God. Believers, by contrast, think that neither the reference range of "God" is so indeterminate nor the concept of God so problematic as to make belief in God irrational or incoherent.[17] We do know, they claim, that talk of God is problematic, but we do not know, and we cannot know, whether it is so problematic as to be without a religiously appropriate sense. After all, God is supposed to be an ultimate mystery. Agnostics, in turn, say that there is no reasonable decision procedure here that would enable us to resolve the issue. We do not know and cannot ascertain whether "God" secures a religiously adequate referent. In reflecting on this issue, we should strive to ascertain whether (1) a "contingent thing" is a pleonasm, (2) an "infinite individual" is without sense and (3) whether when we go beyond anthropomorphism (or try to go beyond it), we have a sufficient understanding of *what* is referred to by "God" to make faith a coherent possibility. I shall argue that "a contingent thing" is pleonastic, that "infinite individual" is without sense, and that the last question should be answered in the negative. The agnostic, by contrast, is not led to faith, but he does believe that such questions cannot be answered.

In "Religious Ethics Versus Humanistic Ethics," I argue that it will not do to take a Pascalian or Dostoyevskian turn and claim that, intellectual absurdity or not, religious belief is, humanly speaking, necessary, for without belief in God, morality does not make sense and life is meaningless.[18] That claim is false; for even if there is no God and no purpose *to* life there are purposes *in* life.[19] There are things we care about and want to do that can remain perfectly intact even in a Godless world. God or no God, immortality or no immortality, it is vile to torture people just for the fun of it; and friendship, solidarity, love, and the attainment of self-respect are human goods even in an utterly Godless world. There are intellectual puzzles about how we know these things are good but that is doubly true for the distinctive claims of a religious ethic. With them, we have the standard perplexities concerning how we can know some things to be good and other things to be bad, as well as the additional perplexities concerning how we can come to understand, let alone assess, the truth of the distinctively religious claims embedded in these systems of belief. But that latter perplexity is one that the atheist can put to the side. However, with the moral beliefs just mentioned, the point is that these things are acknowledged to be desirable by believer and nonbeliever alike. How we can know they are desirable provides a philosophical puzzle for both believer and skeptic. But whether these things are desirable or not has nothing to do with whether God exists. When we reflect carefully on the fact that certain purposes remain intact even in a Godless world, we will, as a corollary, come to see that life can have a point even in a world without God.

VII

The kind of religious response I shall primarily be concerned with and will attempt to criticize, with what I hope is sensitivity and understanding, is a tortured religiosity that is well aware of the problematic nature of religious concepts and the questionable coherence of religious beliefs, yet still seeks to make sense of these beliefs and continues the attempt to bring to the fore their vital human import in the teeth of their paradoxical nature and their apparent incoherence. Such Jews, Moslems, and Christians seem to me to have taken to heart the problems posed by modernity.

There is, however, a growing movement in popular religion, with some representation in intellectual circles as well, that seeks to turn its back on these problems with what seems to be an obtuseness that is both peculiar and disheartening. Religious discourse does not seem to them paradoxical, and religious concepts, including the concept of God, do not seem to them problematic. "We know well enough what we are talking about when we talk about or to God," so they tell us. Christian revelation, they aver, is perfectly intact and the moral vision of that religion, viewed along orthodox lines, provides a firm and evident foundation for the moral life. There is no reason to follow a Kierkegaard, to say nothing of a Nietzsche, regarding any of these things. We can be quite confident of the coherence of God-talk and of the integrity of the Christian faith. The central philosophical task, such traditional Christian philosophers believe, is to provide a sound proof for the existence of God. Of course, they also aver, even without proof, we still have the certainty of revelation; but with proof as well, we have a philosophical basis for a foundationalist account in philosophical theology that would rationalize belief.

This view is the counterpart of both the simpler view of atheism, which regards the key theistic beliefs as simply false, and of a simple agnosticism, which believes that we understand the beliefs well enough but just do not have enough evidence to make a responsible judgment about their truth. Such an agnostic believes that theistic beliefs are plainly either true or false, but whether they are true *or* false is something he believes cannot be established. By contrast, as the previous sections of this chapter have brought to the fore, my atheism and its parallels in religious belief and agnosticism, is principally taken up, in reflecting on religious belief, with the logically prior questions of the coherence of God-talk. Our concern is with whether we have anything sufficiently unproblematic in the religious discourse of developed Judeo-Christianity such that something could really count there as religious truth. Such a view is very distant from Neo-Conservative Christianity.

Alvin Plantinga, a representative (indeed a well-known philosophical representative) of this fundamentalist Christian faith, has tried in short order to set aside those philosophical perplexities as unreal pseudo-problems.[20] In bringing this introductory chapter to a close, I want to note his line of argumentation—a line that is common enough in some circles—and succinctly to set out my response.

What is common ground between us is that we both take "God" to be some sort of referring expression. My skeptical questions, in light of this, can be put in the following terms. Where "God" is not employed purely anthropomorphically to refer to a kind of cosmic mickey-mouse, to whom or to what does "God" refer? Is it a proper name, an abbreviated definite description, a special kind of descriptive predictable, or what? How could we be acquainted with, or otherwise come to know, what "God" stands for or characterizes? How do we—or do we—identify or individuate God? What are we talking about when we speak of God? What or who is this God we pray to, love, make sense of our lives in terms of, and the like?

We know, since we know how to use God-talk, that in talking about God, we are talking about a being of infinite love, mercy, power, and understanding. But such talk does not relieve our puzzlement. What literally are we talking about when we speak of this being? Of what kind of reality, if indeed it is of any kind of reality at all, do we speak when we use such awesome words? Do we really understand what we are talking about here? There is a challenge here to faith that has bothered many a believer and nonbeliever alike. It is a challenge that can perhaps be met, but it is puzzling and, to some, a disturbing challenge all the same.[21]

Plantinga remarks to the question "Who or what is God?" that the "question is the sort to which a definite description provides the appropriate answer."[22] The appropriate definite descriptions, Plantinga confidently remarks, are "the creator of the Universe," "the omnipotent, omniscient, and wholly good person," "the Father of Our Lord and Savior Jesus Christ." There is no more problem with "Who or what is God?," he incautiously proclaims, than there is with the definite descriptions supplied by way of an answer to the question "Who is Sylvia?," namely, such things as "the first person to climb the North Ridge of Mount Blanc" or "the local news announcer."

It is very difficult not to believe that Plantinga is being thoroughly disingenuous here. He knows full well that there are puzzles about the very understanding of the alleged definite descriptions answering to "God" in a way that there is no puzzle about the definite descriptions specifying for us who Sylvia is. He insinuates that it is as silly to be perplexed about who is God as it is, after some straightforward definite descriptions have been given, to be perplexed about who is Sylvia. But he *must* know that there are perplexities about "creator of the universe," "omnipotent, omniscient, and wholly good person," or "Our Savior Jesus Christ" that are just as considerable as our perplexities about "God." As Ronald Hepburn pointed out years ago, Jesus Christ in Christian theology is taken to be the Son of God, and if we are puzzled about what we are talking about in speaking of God, we are going to be no less puzzled about what we are talking about in speaking of "the Son of God." And the phrases "the creator of the universe" or "the omnipotent, omniscient, and wholly good person" are, as the history of their discussion makes evident, thoroughly puzzling phrases. Many theologians (sincere and believing Christians), troubled by what, if any, appropriate sense could be given to them, have, as we have remarked, sought analogical or symbolic readings of these phrases. Plantinga writes with what at least appears to be an arrogant unconcern for years and years of our intellectual history. When he remarks that these definite descriptions are entirely appropriate "since God is a person—a living being who believes and knows, speaks and acts, approves and disapproves," he is either being evasively disingenuous or almost unbelievably naive. For people who do not construe God as a kind of cosmic Mickey Mouse, it has been a key task to demythologize such talk so that it can be seen to be something that a nonsuperstitious person might possibly accept. There can be no taking it as unproblematical in the way Plantinga attempts to.[24]

This is an extreme case of what I call "being bloody minded about God." It is a blind and stubborn refusal to face up to problems where there are indeed problems or where at least there certainly appear to be problems for religious belief and understanding. Perhaps, just perhaps, some subtle Wittgensteinian technique could show us that there are, after all, no problems here, or perhaps we can find a way to meet these problems, but the kind of footstamping that Plantinga engages in is not even a beginning. It is a kind of misplaced Mooreanism, buttressed by some jargon taken from modal logic, where no such appeal to common sense is possible. What we need to recognize is that the concept of God is very problematic indeed. What is crucially at issue is to ascertain, if we can, whether sufficient sense can be made of religious conceptions to make faith a live option for a reflective and concerned human being possessing a reasonable scientific and philosophical understanding of the world he lives in, or whether some form of atheism or agnosticism is the most nonevasive option for such a person. It is with some of the many facets of this issue that I shall wrestle in the pages to follow.

NOTES

1. Kai Nielsen, *Ethics Without God* (Prometheus Books: Buffalo, New York, 1973); Kai Nielsen, "Linguistic Philosophy and 'the Meaning of Life,' " in E. D. Klemke (ed.) *The Meaning of Life* (New York: Oxford University Press, 1981, pp. 177-204; Kai Nielsen, "An Examination of the Thomistic Theory of Natural Law," *Natural Law Forum*, 4 (1959); and Kai Nielsen, "The Myth of Natural Law," in Sidney Hook (ed.) *Law and Philosophy* (New York University Press: New York, 1964).

2. For a clear statement of what anthropomorphism is see John Skorupski, *Symbol and Theory* (London: Cambridge University Press, 1976), p. 65.

3. Paul Tillich's massive *Systematic Theology* is very hard going indeed. The writing is cumbersome and obscure beyond any rational excuse. However, in his more popular writings, what he wants to say, at least on a superficial level, attains some measure of clarity. His *The Courage To Be,* (New Haven: Yale University Press, 1952) in most places has this quality, but most clearly and most revealingly of all a scattered group of his popular essays captures, I believe, what made Tillich important to a number of people touched deeply by modernity who were not philosophers or theologians. He spoke to people who had a need to believe but could not swallow the old supernaturalistic framework. Braithwaite and Hare also tried to answer to such needs but their gruel was too thin for people with such religious aspirations. But Tillich and his popularizing disciple Bishop Robinson filled the bill. See the following short essays, all by Tillich: "Religion," *Perspectives* 15 (Spring, 1956): 43-48; "The God above God," *The Listener* (August 3, 1961); "The Lost Dimension in Religion" in *Adventures of the Mind*, Richard Thruelson and John Kebler

(eds.), (New York: Vintage Books, 1960); "The Idea of God as Affected by Modern Knowledge" in *In Search of God and Immortality*, (Boston: Beacon Press, 1961), no editor; "The Relationship Today Between Science and Religion" in *The Student Seeks An Answer* (Waterville, Maine: Colby College Press, 1960), pp. 297-306. For important critiques of Tillich see the essays on Tillich in Sidney Hook (ed.), *Religious Experience and Truth* (New York: New York University Press, 1961); Paul Edwards, "Professor Tillich's Confusions," *Mind* 74 (1965); and Alistair M. MacLeod, *Tillich* (London: George Allen & Unwin Ltd., 1973). For more sympathetic elucidations and examinations of Tillich (examinations that attend to some of the above criticisms of Tillich), see Malcolm L. Diamond, *Contemporary Philosophy and Religious Thought* (New York: McGraw-Hill Book Company, 1974), pp. 301-389; and William L. Rowe, *Religious Symbols and God* (Chicago: The University of Chicago Press, 1968).

4. In the sorting out of this issue the exchange between Sidney Hook and myself is, I believe, instructive. See Kai Nielsen, "Religion and Naturalistic Humanism: Some Remarks on Hook's Critique of Religion" in Paul Kurtz (ed.) *Sidney Hook and the Contemporary World* (New York: John Day Company, 1968), pp. 257-279; Kai Nielsen, "Secularism and Theology: Remarks on a Form of Naturalistic Humanism," *The Southern Journal of Philosophy* XIII (Spring, 1975): 109-126; Sidney Hook, "For An Open-Minded Naturalism," *The Southern Journal of Philosophy* XIII (Spring, 1975): 127-136; and his *The Quest For Being* (New York: St. Martin's Press, 1960), particularly pp. 115-135, 145-195.

5. John Skorupski gives us a good sense of such an anthropomorphism in the following passage: "A very common feature of traditional religious cosmologies is the belief that there are procedures which, if followed, will give a man the ability to see the spirits around him. Or people often believe that there are certain places such as streams or glades in which gods may be encountered—not simply in the sense that their presence is felt but in the sense that one might get a glimpse of them." John Skorupski, op.cit., p. 65.

6. This can survive a very thorough rejection of the methodological and epistemological programmes of both Hume and Kant and the traditions they have spawned in contemporary philosophy. This is shown clearly in the work of Richard Rorty, whose *Philosophy and the Mirror of Nature* (Princeton, New Jersey: Princeton University Press, 1979) is one such rejection—indeed a very persuasive rejection. Yet, for all his historicism, Rorty remarks, without any ambivalence at all, "that the preservation of the values of the Enlightenment is our best hope," pp. 335-6. And, for all his distance from positivism, Rorty also declares "the positivists were absolutely right in thinking it imperative to extirpate metaphysics, when 'metaphysics' means the attempt to give knowledge of what science cannot know," p. 384.

7. There has, of course, been some dissent, principally from neo-scholastic philosophers and, as well, from two modal-logic-with-God philosophers, Charles Hartshorne and Alvin Plantinga. But these are backward looking, rear-guard operations of little cultural or intellectual significance.

8. There is often an attempt at such a point to make an appeal to faith. In addition to "The Primacy of Philosophical Theology," reprinted here, I

have tried critically to examine such moves in my "Can Faith Validate God-talk?" *Theology Today* XX (July, 1963); "Faith and Authority," *The Southern Journal of Philosophy* 3 (Winter, 1965); and "Religious Perplexity and Faith," *Crane Review* VIII (Fall, 1965).

9. This is one of the central things at issue in my exchange with Sidney Hook. See the references in footnote 4.

10. I have tried to defend this in my "On the Rationality of Radical Theological Neo-Naturalism," *Religious Studies* (1978): 193-204; in my "Radical Theological Non-Naturalism," *Sophia* XVIII (July, 1978): 1-6; and in my essays reprinted in *The Logic of God: Theology and Verification,* Malcolm L. Diamond and Thomas V. Litzenburg (Indianapolis, IN: The Bobbs-Merrill Company, 1975).

11. Richard B. Braithwaite, "An Empiricist's View of the Nature of Religious Belief" in *The Logic of God,* pp. 127-149 and R. M. Hare, "The Simple Believer" in *Religion and Morality,* Gene Outka and John Reeder, Jr. (Garden City, NY: Anchor Books, 1973), pp. 393-427.

12. See my penultimate essay in this volume, my "Principles of Rationality," *Philosophical Papers* III (October, 1974): 55-89 and my "Christian Empiricism," *The Journal of Religion* 61 (April, 1981): 146-167. The latter contains a critique of Braithwaite's and Hare's "Christian empiricism."

13. This claim is most extensively developed in my "On Speaking of God," *Theoria* XXVII (1962): 110-137. This essay is reprinted, together with a number of my other essays, in *Analytical Philosophy of Religion in Canada,* Mostafa Foghfowry (ed.), (Ottawa, ON: The University of Ottawa Press, 1982).

14. See here William P. Alston, "Tillich's Conception of a Religious Symbol" in *Religious Experience and Truth,* pp. 12-26 and chapter 7 of Paul Henle (ed.), *Language, Thought and Culture* (Ann Arbor, MI: The University of Michigan Press, 1958).

15. Sidney Hook, "The Atheism of Paul Tillich," in *Religious Experience and Truth,* pp. 59-63 and his *The Quest For Being,* pp. 145-171.

16. For the argument for this, see my "Can Faith Validate God-talk?" *Theology Today* XX (July, 1963).

17. Kai Nielsen, "On Fixing the Reference Range of 'God,'" in *The Logic of God,* pp. 330-340.

18. See Kurt Baier's essay and my essay in E. D. Klemke's (ed.) *The Meaning of Life,* pp. 81-117 and 177-204 and my *Ethics Without God,* pp. 48-64.

19. See Baier's essay cited above.

20. The citations in the text come from Plantinga's response to my "Religion and Groundless Believing," Frederick Crosson (ed.) *The Autonomy of Religious Belief* (Notre Dame, IN: The University of Notre Dame Press, 1981). The exchange took place at the conference on "Religion and Forms of Life" at the University of Notre Dame in 1979. See, as well, Plantinga's "Analytic Philosophy and Christianity," *Christianity Today* (October 25, 1963): 75-78 and his "Verificationism" in *The Logic of God,* pp. 446-455, and my response to it in my *Contemporary Critiques of Religion* (New York: Herder and Herder, 1971), pp. 55-71.

21. The challenge is powerfully put from the side of religious belief by Michael Durrant, *The Logical Status of 'God'* (New York: Macmillan, 1973)

and his *Theology and Intelligibility* (Boston: Routledge and Kegan Paul, 1973).

22. In his response to my "Religion and Groundless Believing."

23. Ronald Hepburn, *Christianity and Paradox* (London: Watts, 1958), chapter 5. But also see, to tease the matter out a little more, John Hick's response in his "A Philosopher Criticizes Theology," *The Modern Quarterly* 31 (1962): 103-110.

24. Plantinga, op. cit.

2

The Making of an Atheist

I will be autobiographical though not simply and solely autobiographical. But perhaps an account of my evolution from an amorphous Protestantism, through Catholicism, through several varieties of agnosticism and atheism will do something more than exhibit some of the psychodynamics of belief and unbelief. However, like any other autobiographical account, it is exposed to Goethe's revealing irony about *Dichtung und Wahrheit* (poetry and truth).

My mother came from rural North America and my father from a Danish proletarian background remarkably like that powerfully described by the Danish novelist Martin Anderson-Nexo in *Under the Open Sky*. Around the turn of the century, my grandfather on my father's side, after years as an alcoholic, converted from Lutheranism to a fiercely held Seventh-Day Adventism. In this venture he carried with him—at least nominally—his large and impoverished family. The effect on my father, as far as I can ascertain, was for the most part to induce a rather indulgent skepticism, coupled with the belief that somehow some kind of religion is important for social stability and, for many though not for all, for psychological stability. My mother, by contrast, had a vague Protestant background, though as she grew older—she was in her forties when I was born—and her health deteriorated, she turned more and more to religion and for the last ten years of her life to Christian Science.

As an only and somewhat pampered child of middle-aged parents, and particularly as a rather lonely adolescent voraciously reading and with the standard adolescent obsessions about sex, I had my

From *The Humanist* (January/February, 1974): 14-15, 18-19. Reprinted by permission of the publisher.

struggles between belief and unbelief. During the latter part of that period I went to a Catholic high school, not at all because it was Catholic but simply to play on their basketball team. However, some of the priests who taught me were reflective and interesting men, and this, together with the rather different way of life at the school, generated in me a curiosity about religion in general and Catholicism in particular. This concern about religion was enhanced and pushed in a somewhat different direction by the reading of as much of Dostoevsky and Tolstoy as I could come by during isolated yet cherished summer vacations.

During the war years, as a thoroughly ill-adjusted cadet-midshipman in the American Merchant Marine, I read, or (as in the case of Dante) tried to read, classical Catholic authors and, probably without much understanding, Schopenhauer and Nietzsche. While traveling around the Pacific in this hardly more than a late adolescent state on rather supererogatory wartime services, I reflected on religion and finally resolved to become a Catholic. I converted shortly after the end of the war and entered a Catholic university.

There I studied philosophy in some tolerably systematic fashion for the first time. From the more inadequate professors I got philosophy out of scholastic manuals and, from a bright and learned young professor from St. Michael's College at the University of Toronto, I got Plato, Aristotle, and Aquinas. It was, however, this very study which solidified and gave a rationale to the doubts with which I had lived for as long as I can remember thinking about belief. I came to see, after repeated reading and much discussion with my Catholic mentors, that one could not prove—in any reasonable sense of the word—that God existed. I came, in sum, to see that the claims of natural theology to a natural knowledge of God could not be sustained.

As I now know, there are further and more complicated moves within natural theology itself concerning such putative proofs, but it still seems to me, as it seemed to me then, that this matter of the proofs—that is, arguments purporting to establish the existence of God—is essential. Given the intelligibility and moral coherence of secular accounts of the world, given the very great diversity of religious beliefs (not all of which are even theistic), given the existence of informed, rational, and morally committed skeptics, and given the very peculiarity and obscurity of the concept of God, we are not justified in believing in God if no good evidence can be given for believing that God exists.

I had not yet come to appreciate the force of the Protestant counters to this; but, genetically and causally speaking, these considerations about the proofs were crucial for me. I should add that these considerations still seem crucial to me, though I now see that they need bolstering by all sorts of subsidiary arguments to be even re-motely decisive. That is to say, while they most certainly are not all of the matter, they are at the heart of the matter in any reasonable choice between belief and unbelief. (If we are so irrational about such a putative choice that there is in reality no choice in the matter one way or another, then we are in a different ballgame altogether, and the account we need to give will be a causal one.)

The diversity of my religious background was such that I could never take appeals to putative revelations as having much force. Al-leged revelations are myriad and often conflicting. In this, as far as I can now make out, I only generalized and rationalized my father's thorough skepticism concerning his parents' tenaciously held con-viction that their church, their isolated little sect, had the saving truth, while the surrounding Lutheran majority were sinfully deluded. Given the vast diversity of belief and commitment that actually obtains, if there are no sound arguments for believing in God, then it is irrational to believe.

After two years, I left the Catholic university and went to a secular one, with—among other things—the intent of seeing what they could teach me about philosophy. Slowly "a new world" opened up for me, though I continued to argue it out with "my old world." My own perceptions and reactions at that time, modified of course by my very different cultural situation, were strongly influenced by some of San-tayana's writings on morality and religion, and he in turn generated in me an interest in Spinoza.

At that time I had not yet felt or come to understand the reactionary and repressive side of Catholicism. Those of my former Catholic mentors who had influenced me were tolerant men, and they were either apolitical or were political beings concerned with social justice and, indeed, considering the Neanderthal ideological frame-work of the middle-American society in which I grew up, reasonably progressive. Only later did I come to understand the social evils of the Catholic Church and to see how very much these teachers of mine were in a minority among their fellow Catholics. (The Heinrich Bölls and Graham Greenes of Catholicism are rare. The reactionary and bigoted parish priests of southern Italy and Ireland are not exactly the norm either, but such attitudes are very pervasive within the Catholic Church.) But given this atypical experience and my own political immaturity, my struggles were not initially with a moral cri-tique of Catholicism but with whether its avowed claims were true. It became increasingly evident to me that they were not and that belief in God was the fairytale that Santayana said it was, though for some time I remained, like Santayana, wistful about that fairytale.

As a graduate student, I studied anthropology as well as philosophy, and, primarily through my acquaintance with the Freudian anthropologist Weston Labarre, I came gradually to view religion very differently. At approximately the same time, the related but still disparate influence of John Dewey and Karl Marx provided me with: 1) a humanistic and naturalistic framework in accordance with which to view the world, and 2) the beginnings of a social critique of religion.

Two years later, during a period of personal turmoil, I came to have some understanding of one side of the Protestant tradition, first, and rather peripherally, through Reinhold Niebuhr, and then, in depth and grippingly, through Søren Kierkegaard, who in spite of his conceptual confusions still strikes me as one of the most profound figures of the nineteenth century. I came to see, in studying him, how an intense faith could go hand-in-hand with a thorough agnosticism. In Kierkegaard, I saw what religion could mean to a man, on one hand assailed by doubts and aware of the intellectual affront and scandal of belief and, on the other, trying to come to grips with the entanglements of life and the despair that our condition can engender. (Kierkegaard would claim that our condition *must* engender such despair if we are aware.) After the rationalism and the illusory conviction of the certainty of scholasticism, this response to religion, coupled with his understanding of the complexities of moral psychology, exerted a lasting influence on my view of religion. But the counter-influence of Freud, the pragmatists, and Marx was too deep. One need not take an utterly stark leap of faith to make sense of one's ensnarled life, or to make sense generally of the life of the human animal, even if one pressed to the depths as Kierkegaard did. Indeed, one not only need not, but one could not, if one had a clear view of one's condition.

In the later years of my graduate work in philosophy, the influence of analytical philosophy, first logical empiricism and then later linguistic philosophy, gradually gained ground with me. Perhaps because of the prior influence of Peirce and Dewey, the tendency to think of it as something remote from the problems of men or concerned solely with "esoteric issues" never took hold of me. All my published work has been written in this mode, though the effects of the nonanalytic philosophers have remained, and such diverse figures as Kierkegaard, Nietzsche, Feuerbach, and Marx—increasingly Marx—continue to seem far more important to me than they do to most philosophers taken by "the linguistic turn."

Initially my chief interest in such an analytic manner of philosophizing was to apply techniques principally derivative from the later Wittgenstein to moral and social philosophy. When, mainly through the requirements of teaching, I came to consider religion again, the situation seemed to me (as it still seems to me) roughly as follows:

natural theology was clearly broken-backed. With slight modifications, the arguments of Hume and Kant undermine the classical attempts to give us grounds for believing in God, and no alternative avenues to justify belief are sustainable. Scholastic and quasi-scholastic philosophers who persist in such argumentation are reduced to an obscure kind of talk about "being," whose very intelligibility is thoroughly problematic. Religious philosophers and theologians out of a more Protestant tradition, who are antimetaphysical or simply nonmetaphysical in orientation, pose another more subtle and, *prima facie*, more interesting problem about giving a coherent account of religious belief. Such believers often argue or at least imply that they do not *deny* anything nonbelievers deny or doubt. They, too, do not believe in the God in which the skeptic does not believe. Hume, they agree and indeed often stress, has shown us that anthropomorphic gods could not reasonably be believed in. God could not be a mere existent or even a supernatural existent, a being among beings, a First Cause or some Prime Mover. Hume and Kant have clearly shown that we have no sound grounds for believing that such a God exists. Moreover, some of them also recognize that with Thomistic talk about Pure Actuality or Tillich's talk about Being-itself or anything of that order, it becomes utterly unclear what, if anything intelligible, is being affirmed that a skeptic could not affirm as well. With such Thomistic or Tillichian talk, there is a complicated jargon but no intelligible additional claims of substance. Yet these Protestant thinkers still give us to understand that they themselves believe in something mysterious and profound and crucial to the human condition of which the nonbeliever has no understanding or no real understanding. They seem, however, to be quite incapable of explaining or even describing what this "more" is, though they are confident that they are not just saying the same thing as the skeptic in a more obscure and heightened vocabulary. Given such a state of affairs, I came to wonder, as did many others, if, after all, there really is a more than *verbal* difference and a difference in attitude between the sophisticated believer and the skeptic or whether such a believer actually succeeds in believing anything intelligible or coherent at all that is distinct from the purely secular beliefs of the skeptic.

As I wrestled with the ins and outs of this, the conviction gradually firmed up that nonanthropomorphic conceptions of God are so problematic, so, at least apparently, incoherent, that they are of doubtful intelligibility and that it is this characteristic that accounts for the persistent failures of natural theology. Once we leave a Zeus-like conception of God, a god we know does not exist, we become entangled in a conception of God that simply does not make sense. By this, I do not mean that "God" is meaningless; "God" has nondeviant uses in our language, and believers and nonbelievers alike know how to engage in God-talk. What I mean in saying that such God-talk does not make sense is that believers are committed to such claims as "God loves all his creation," and "There is a divine reality which transcends all finite realities." And yet, while such uses of language are putative truth-claims, we have no idea at all what would or, even in principle could, establish or disestablish such claims so that we could have some idea whether the persons attempting to assert or deny a claim were probably or even possibly saying something that is true. At least we appear not to know how to do more than *verbally* distinguish their alleged assertions and denials. Like "The underground will be here in five minutes," "No it will not, the subway will be here in five minutes," "There is a divine reality which transcends all finite realities," and "There is no such reality," are equally compatible with anything and everything of a directly or indirectly experiential sort that we can even conceive as coming to pass. But to say that p and not-p are truth-claims, when we do *not* understand what it would be like to state their truth-conditions so that we could distinguish between p being true or even possibly being true and not-p being true or even possibly being true, is to say something of very dubious intelligibility.

There are similar problems about the identification of the referent of "God." "God" is supposed to be a referring expression or at least in some way meaningful; but just *what* does "God" refer to and how do we identify the supposed referent of "God" where God is not Zeus-like? Again we seem to be lost here. But if we cannot, even in a stammering manner, say *what* it is we are talking about when we speak of God, our conceptions of God are incoherent.

Related to the above problem is the problem about the attenuation of predications concerning "God." Believers say "God loves us," but "loves" when applied to God undergoes such a radical sea-change that it seems not to mean at all what it means when it is said that "Gandhi loves even the least among us." No matter how much evil obtains in the world, believers still go on saying, "God loves us." What would have to transpire for it to be correct or even possibly justified to say, "God does not love us"? Believers seem to be quite unprepared to say, or often enough even to recognize, the need for trying to make some specifications here. But then has not "love" been emptied of all its meaning? This attenuation of predicates is so thorough for "love," and other predicates as well, that we have still further grounds for wondering whether talk of God even makes sense.

In short, I have come not to believe in God, not only because I am convinced that there is no evidence or good grounds for believing that God exists, but also because I believe that the very concept or (if you will) notion of God (where nonanthropomorphic) is so problematic that there is nothing statable which could even be the grounds for such a belief. There is, to put it crudely, nothing to believe, but it is a mistake to go on to say, "But then there is nothing to disbelieve either," for the Jew or Christian is attempting to make a positive claim and this claim is being rejected as incoherent in its nonanthropomorphic forms. (Only a few philosophers take such anthropomorphic conceptions seriously; theologians, interestingly enough, are as dismissive of these conceptions as I am.) That, at least, is my central reason, though not my only reason, for not having any religious allegiance at all.

The criteria for "intelligibility" and "coherence" utilized above can be and have been challenged. Among other things, it has been alleged that there is a confusion in such talk between "unintelligibility" and "irrationality." Some Wittgensteinian philosophers, whom I have characterized as Wittgensteinian fideists, have even argued that the very criteria of intelligibility and rationality are so dependent on particular forms of life, particular culture patterns, and historically distinct ways of doing things that no such general challenge of intelligibility can properly be made of a whole domain of discourse or form of life such as religion. There are myriads of different forms of life, all culturally and historically contingent and each with its distinctive or at least partially distinctive criteria of intelligibility, rationality, and truth. No such general challenge, as I have made, can properly be made of a belief in God.

I have attempted in various places to meet such a fideist challenge, but, even if I have been completely unsuccessful and we are caught in such a relativism and historicism, it would seem that that too would make it impossible reasonably to believe in God or at least to believe in the God of Judaism or Christianity. Such religions purport, as doctrines of salvation, to provide us with the Truth and the Way; but, if criteria of truth, rationality, and intelligibility are all that culturally and/or mode-of-discourse relative, talk of "The Truth" and "The Way" surely is without sense or at least without any reasonable purport.

There have been some who have thought, quite apart from these Wittgensteinian considerations, that, though God-talk is of a very problematical intelligibility, religious belief—scandal to the intellect or not—remains a human necessity, for without it morality will be groundless and life will make no sense. But this is plainly an error. The torturing of innocent children, the wanton slaying of human beings, the utter neglect of the needs of a human being or the treatment of him as a *mere* means to further some end are evils whether or not God exists. Moreover, the mere fact that an omnipotent, all-knowing being wills something does not make it good. Whether or not something is good or bad is independent of whether it was willed, commanded, or ordained. Human beings are intelligent beings with interests, purposes, and needs. Moralities exist to answer to these interests and needs and to adjudicate in a just way between conflicting interests and desires. In sum, we can, and some of us do, ground morality in an utterly secular way, and there is no reason to believe that a religious morality can provide us with a "higher" alternative morality. What we should recognize is that there is good reason to believe that any morality, religious or secular, that did not turn to considerations of justly adjudicating conflicting interests and to the satisfaction of human needs would be a sadly deficient morality. Similarly, Pascal and Dostoevsky to the contrary notwithstanding, life need not be meaningless for a human being in an utterly Godless world. His life need not be pointless, for he can reflectively form intentions and act on those intentions and purposes and find satisfaction in so doing.

In fine, there are no good intellectual grounds for believing in God and very good ones, perhaps even utterly decisive ones, for not believing in God; and there is no moral or human need, let alone necessity, for a nonevasive and informed person in the twentieth century to have religious commitments of any kind.

3

Does God Exist?
Reflections on Disbelief

Introduction

Religious people in our culture say things like this: "All mighty God we have sinned against you," "The Lord will comfort us," "We will be happy with God in heaven," "To God our lives lie open," "God is our All Mighty and Eternal Father whose realm extends beyond the bounds of space and time," "God will protect us, enlighten us, and liberate us from fear and crippling anxiety," and "God's Kingdom is coming to bring on a new world."

We hear such things repeatedly and wonder whether we have any good reason to believe that they are true or even probably true or whether they can be reasonably believed by properly informed people. Moreover, some of us wonder whether such utterances are sufficiently intelligible to make their acceptance a coherent object of faith. Can we reasonably believe that such claims—and indeed the central claims of Judaism and Christianity as well—make statements which are either true or false?

I believe that we should answer all those questions in the *negative*. Religious belief—or at least belief in God—should be impossible for someone living in our century, who thinks carefully about these matters and who has a tolerable scientific education and good philosophical training. It is not so hard to convolute oneself into religious belief if one has philosophical expertise but little knowledge of the world and it is easy enough to be a believer if one is a scientist and philosophically naive. However, if we have a scientific education and philosophical sophistication, along with a willingness to reflect on such matters, these things, taken together, should undermine religious belief. I want

From *Free Inquiry* 1 (Spring, 1981): 21-26. Reprinted by permission of the publisher.

to go some of the way toward showing that this is so and why it is so. I shall principally argue on two fronts. First, familiarly—and only in a sketchy manner—I shall argue in Part I against the various attempts to prove that God exists, that revelation is reliable, that morality requires religious belief, and that God can be known directly in religious experience. The first part of my argument will be to show that none of these apologetic appeals work. I do not claim originality here, but I do claim that what I argue is a good approximation of the truth. In Part II, the skeptical perplexities turn principally on questions concerning how we might establish the truth or probable truth of the claims of Judaism or Christianity and whether we could reasonably accept them as articles of faith. I shall turn in Part III to the vexed question of whether such religious beliefs could even count as genuine truth-claims. When we examine closely the truth of religion, our concern should gradually turn to questions about the meaning or intelligibility of the key claims of religion. In *some sense,* God-talk is plainly meaningful. Believers and nonbelievers alike know how to use religious vocabulary nondeviantly, but, to put it at first crudely, we can, if we reflect, come to wonder if such talk makes sense. This strikes us immediately when we study primitive religions. Our familiarity with Christian or Jewish discourse may dull our perceptions here. Yet if we try for a moment to look at our own religious talk with the eyes of an anthropologist coming from an alien culture, we should at least begin to feel the strangeness of talk of God in which God is said to be an "omnipresent, almighty Father whose realm extends beyond the bounds of space and time." What is this *realm* beyond space and time? Try to think very literally about this. What are we really doing here? What does "God" or "heaven" denote or stand for? What are you really referring to when you speak of God? What are you worshipping when you worship God? I shall, after I have examined attempts to prove the viability of religious belief, turn to these questions and attempt to show that the very concept of God is of such a low order of intelligibility that belief in him is unjustified. Belief in God is an ideological belief that distorts our understanding of reality. This is not just an innocent distortion. For often, where we have such beliefs or are affected by such beliefs, they distort our lives. They are not, I shall argue, humanly desirable saving myths. In Part IV I shall turn to these considerations by briefly considering what interests religion answers to, and what, under certian societal conditions, socially necessary illusions religion secures.

I

In the Middle Ages, it was generally thought that we could quite definitely prove the existence of God. There were a few skeptics, of course, but they were intellectual outcasts, very much in the minority. With the unfolding of the industrial revolution and the deepening effect of the Enlightenment, this intellectual attitude shifted. Hume and Kant came along—Hume an agnostic and Kant a fideistic Christian—and together they provided powerful philosophical arguments designed to show that we could not prove that God exists. Culturally speaking, though the battle took centuries to unwind, Hume and Kant won. Or, whatever the etiology, the *Zeitgeist* shifted in their favor. It is now a philosophical and, in many quarters, even a cultural commonplace to say that we cannot prove that God exists. Reason and observation cannot show the unprejudiced mind, willing to follow the argument and evidence wherever it will go, that there is a God. What Hume and Kant struggled to establish, many of us take as almost a cultural dogma, so that in one sense we have not earned our right to disbelief. Moreover, this disbelief in the proofs is common ground between skeptics and many believers. They, of course, differ over religious commitment, but not over such a common cultural orientation. It is indeed true that from time to time, some philosopher—sometimes even some relatively distinguished philosopher—comes to believe that, after all, one or another of these proofs, usually in some increasingly esoteric version, works, but very few people are convinced.[1] If he is clever enough or has enough weight in his profession, what happens is that his refurbished version of one of the proofs turns out to be a source of intellectual exercise which for a time helps fill the pages of professional philosophical journals and gives people (often people without the slightest interest in religion) who delight in solving puzzles a chance to strut their stuff: to whet their philosophical knives and show their philosophical wares. But, just as the *Zeitgeist* cut against the skeptic in the Middle Ages, so the *Zeitgeist* in our time, Billy Graham notwithstanding, favors skepticism about proofs. Even the appeal to religious experience isn't what it once was.

However, the *Zeitgeist* may not speak the truth and, even if God is on the side of the big battalions, truth isn't a camp follower, so I will turn now to a rapid fire examination of the traditional proofs.[2]

The first arguments I shall consider are arguments that philosophers call arguments of the *ontological* type. They perhaps fascinate philosophers more than any of the other type proofs and would, if correct, be strict demonstrations of the reality of God, making the denial of God's existence into a self-contradiction. The person articulating such an argument claims, as Anselm did in the Middle Ages and Descartes in the seventeenth century, that to conceive of God clearly is to realize that he *must* exist. "God is that than which no greater can be conceived but then God must exist or he would not be the greatest conceivable being."

But to say that God exists is not to amplify our concept of God, it is not to further characterize God, but to say that there is one or that the concept of God has exemplification. Our concept of the greatest conceivable being is not altered by whether or not that concept is exemplified in reality. Its exemplification or lack thereof does not make the *concept* greater. Our concept of God—our concept of the greatest conceivable being—is not altered by whether there is or isn't such a being. So such an ontological argument fails.

Ontological type arguments are not helped by alternatively arguing that God by definition is an eternal being and that an eternal being could not come to exist, just happen to exist, or cease to exist, but exists necessarily. Thus God *must* exist if God is conceivable at all, for a necessary or eternal being cannot cease or even just contingently exist. He must exist necessarily. Thus, if we can conceive of God at all then God must exist. Against this it should be noted that while an eternal being could not come to exist or just cease to exist, it still could *eternally* be the case that there are no eternal beings. Thus to conceive of an eternal being is not to establish that there actually is one. What our conceptualization tells us is that if there is one he or it exists timelessly.

A second type of argument that has also been popular was articulated by Thomas Aquinas in the thirteenth century and repeated in various formulations ever since. Such arguments, often called "*cosmological* arguments," might, rather pretentiously, be referred to as arguments from the matter-of-fact nature of the world. If certain empirical facts actually obtain, so the argument goes, then either a) God must exist or b) (and more weakly) the postulation of God is the best explanation of those undeniable facts. The plain facts that Aquinas had in mind are that there are contingent beings or beings who owe their existence to some other beings. He argued there could not be an infinite series of such beings with no noncontingent being who brought them into existence and sustains their existence. For, if there were no such noncontingent being, even now there would be nothing, for something cannot come from nothing. And since such a series must finally come to an end, nothing could have gotten started in the first place or be ultimately sustained or explained, if there were not at least one self-existent, necessary being who owes its existence to no other reality. All other realities are said to depend upon it.

However, this cosmological argument will not do, for it confuses an *infinite* series with a very long *finite* series. Nothing will have to have gotten started or needed a first sustainer in the first place, if the series is genuinely infinite, for an infinite series, no matter of what type, can have no first member. And, while there will be no *ultimate* explanation of why there is anything at all, there is no good reason to believe that we can, let alone must, have explanations *of that type*. That is to say, there are no good grounds for believing that there are, let alone that there must be, such ultimate explanations. In that special sense it need not be the case that there is a reason for everything.

There is a distinctive form of cosmological argument usually tagged "the argument from design." It was very popular in the eighteenth century and remained popular even in Darwin's time. It is probably, in nonphilosophical circles, still the most favored of the attempts to prove—in this case inductively establish—the existence of God. The argument contends that the universe shows an orderliness and design that can be adequately accounted for only by an infinite and perfect designer of the universe, and that being we call God. But the order we observe, which is surely order *in* the universe and not *of* the universe, is such that it hardly evidences the marks of a perfect designer. Rather, if a designer at all, it bears the marks of an apprentice designer or a decrepit designer whose powers and insight were failing. More fundamentally, this familiar Humean point aside, the observed order in the world (universe) does not show or even lend any probability to the claim that the world (universe) is ordered let alone that the world (universe) is designed. Indeed no clear sense has been given to the phrase "The universe is designed." An observed pattern of things, no matter how intricate, does not show that there was or is an orderer or designer.

Since the destructive attacks of Hume and Kant, it has become rather common, *particularly* in certain Protestant circles, to claim that we do not need the proofs, even if we could have them, for we have a much surer way of knowing God, namely through direct religious experience. At least some people, so the claim goes, have an immediate, direct awareness of the reality of God which is so compelling that the person who has the experience cannot deny this reality. But such a claim—at least construed in some tolerably literal way—cannot be right. Perhaps Zeus (if there is a Zeus) could be so encountered, but the God of our developed Judeo-Christian-Islamic religions cannot be so encountered or encountered at all. God is a Pure Spirit, a being "out of time," transcendent to the world. If we just think what those conceptions literally connote, there can be no encountering—meeting—such a being. Any being which could be met with—seen, observed, in any way sensed—would not be the God of the developed Judeo-Christian-Islamic strand. God is supposedly a mysterious infinite being "beyond the world," "beyond space and time." He could not be observed, as Kierkegaard quipped, like a great green parrot. But then what is it to be aware of God, to stand in the presence of God, to experience God?

To experience God, some have said in reply, is to experience (or perhaps experience to the full) one's finitude, to have feelings of dependency, awe, wonder, dread or to feel a oneness and a love and a sense of security, no matter what happens. But these are plainly human experiences, psychological experiences, which can have purely secular readings or interpretations. They can be, as they were by Feuerbach, Freud, and Marx, understood as a distinctive and often a psychologically and socially compelling kind of human reaction to certain conditions of human living. They can readily be fit into a purely secular or scientific world perspective. Why should we multiply conceptions beyond need and say these understandable human experiences are also experiences of God or that they are best explained as experiences of God or as attesting to the reality of God or as showing that somehow we stand in the presence of God? We are not justified in postulating such odd entities unless there is reason to think that the phenomena cannot be adequately explained by reference to less *recherché* realities, which are plainly realities of our familiar spatio-temporal framework. Plainly, such experiences can be explained in natural or secular terms, so there is no warrant for postulating God to account for them.

It is sometimes said, trying to make the argument turn in another direction, that religious experiences are *self-authenticating* experiences and thus we can know, if we actually have them, that they must be experiences of God. But the only experiences which can plausibly be considered self-authenticating—that is, can be plausibly considered experiences which guarantee the reality of what is said to be experienced—are experiences of psychological realities, such as the fact that I am in pain, am tired or that I now intend to have a drink before I go to bed. But no nonpsychological experiences carry this indubitability. I may be perfectly confident that I am seeing an exit sign at the end of the hall and still be mistaken or I may be quite confident that what I hear is the surf breaking and still be mistaken. We may be justifiably confident that we feel anxiety, but we cannot be so confident that we have experienced God. There is no religious experience which guarantees that our experience is an experience of God. This can be asserted without for a moment doubting that some people have religious experiences. The psychological reality of such experience is one thing, that these experiences are actually experiences of God is another.[3]

The cluster of arguments above has a definite skeptical thrust. If these arguments are in the main right, and we recognize them to be right but we are still trying to cling to religious beliefs, we seem at least to be thrown back on a straight appeal to faith. To have religion at all, we must have religion without foundations: Christianity or Judaism without rational grounds. If it is responded that we have foundations rooted solely in religious authority, we should in turn ask: Why should we accept the authority of a given scripture, faith or religious tradition? Why Jesus rather than Buddha or Mohammed? We need to recognize that there are many faiths, many religious traditions, many alleged revelations. If we look on the matter as social anthropologists would—that is if we are genuinely empirical about religions—we need to count them in the thousands. Why then opt for any particular one? Why claim or believe that a certain religion is the Truth and the Way? And if there is no decent answer to these questions, why go in for any religious faith at all? If there is no proof for the existence of God, no independent way of establishing or making credible his existence, isn't a claim that Christianity is the Truth and the Way both incredibly arrogant, ethnocentric, and arbitrary? Moreover, we must recognize that these different faiths, different religions do not, in various ways, symbolize the same Transcendent reality. They are sometimes radically different. Some do not have anything like a God at all and they by no means say the same thing. Furthermore, there are no nonethnocentric criteria for determining "the higher" and "the lower" religions. And that we have a higher material and scientific culture does not show our superiority in other aspects of culture. It may well be that man cannot judge of the authenticity of a revelation. How is man to judge God's revealed word? But when there is a host of putative revelations all claiming to be genuine, a reasonable person is not justified in claiming that one of these putative revelations is *the* true revelation: the genuine word of God which is to provide us with the Truth and the Way.[4]

Finally, an anguished Christian or Jew, looking for some way of anchoring his claim to religious truth, might *a là* Pascal, claim, absurdity or not, that we need religion to make sense of our tangled lives and to give our morality some foundation. If God is dead, he echoes a Dostoevskian character, nothing matters. But that is false. For God or no God, killing of innocent children, allowing people to starve when it can be prevented, lying simply to further one's convenience or treating other human beings as means to further one's ends are plainly vile. Whatever philosophical account we give of the wrongness of these things, we know that, if anything is wrong, these things are wrong and that, even in a Godless world, they would still be wrong, and that God's commanding us to do them could not make them right or morally justified. Without God there may be no purpose to life, but life can still be purposeful, be worth living, even if there is no overarching purpose to life. Even if there is no purpose *of* life or purpose *to* life there can be purposes *in* life, e.g., to cure the sick, to achieve racial equality and social justice, to achieve happiness and a fuller and more varied life for oneself and for those to whom one relates, to achieve love and close human bonds and solidarity. These are the purposes we human beings can have and they can remain intact in a Godless world.[5]

II

If the arguments above have been close to their mark, claims to religious truth are groundless and indeed Holmesless Watsons. There is no reason to think we have any justified religious truth claims at all or that we need to make a religious leap in the dark to give moral endeavor a point or to make sense out of our tangled lives. But troubles for the believer do not end here and indeed what may be the deepest and most characteristic contemporary malaise has not yet even been mentioned. The trouble is traceable to problems about the very meaning of religious utterances and to our religiously dominant nonanthropomorphic conceptions of God. The worry is that God-talk may not come to anything sufficiently coherent to be capable of even making false claims.[6] Reflect back on the religious utterances we mentioned at the outset. A Christian believer says "Almighty God we have sinned against you" or "God's kingdom is coming to bring on a new world and a new man" or "God is our almighty and eternal Father whose realm extends beyond the bounds of space and time." How are we to understand what is being said here or indeed do we understand what is being said? The words are familiar enough, but do they make sense? In the above arguments about truth in religion we have assumed that we have at least a *minimally coherent* set of concepts embedded in our God-talk, but that we just do not know if the claims of religion are true. But it is this very assumption which is now coming under fire. Certain central concepts, including the concept of God, are so problematic that it is questionable whether we can know or reasonably believe or even justifiably take on trust that these concepts can be put to work to make religious claims which are either true or false.

The believer talks of God and claims to pray and confess to God. *Who* or *what* is he praying and confessing to? (If you do these things, ask it as a question for yourselves.) Once we leave an anthromorphic and idolatrous conception of God, where God—as a kind of cosmic Mickey Mouse—is a being among beings, it is unclear to what or to whom we are referring when we use that term. What does "God" denote or stand for? "God," unlike "Hans" or "Erika" or "Mexico," cannot be ostensively defined or taught. As we have seen, it doesn't even make sense to speak of seeing or encountering God. We can't literally be aware of God or stand in the presence of God. The term "God" can only be introduced intra-linguistically through definite descriptions. It is understandable that we might try to help a person puzzled about what we are talking about in speaking of God. We might try to elucidate how "God" is used in such religious utterances as we have quoted, by introducing the term intra-linguistically via definitive descriptions. We can say, to use some typical examples,

(1) "God is the only infinite individual."
(2) "God is the maker of the universe."
(3) "God is the only ultimate reality upon whom all other realities depend."
(4) "God is the only person transcendent to the world."
(5) "God is the foundation of the world."
(6) "God is the sole self-existent reality upon whom all other realities depend."

We should note, however, that the alleged definite descriptions we introduced to make it possible to answer our question *who* or *what* is God are at least as puzzling as "God." We should ask if we actually understand what they mean. What is it for something to "transcend the world" or to be "an ultimate reality" or "a foundation of the world" or an "infinite individual" or even "the maker of the universe"? These phrases have a cluster of varied and complicated resonances and they are believed to be key elements in Christian cosmologies, but do they have a sufficiently unproblematic meaning for us to understand what we are asserting or denying when we use them? Do we have any idea of what we are talking about or even any understanding of what is being referred to when we use them?

I think it is questionable that we do. To probe and to begin to test that claim, consider someone who says "God is the maker of the universe." Suppose A asserts it (tries to assert it) and B denies it (tries to deny it). That is, A avows it and B refuses to make that avowal. What support could either provide to establish or even to give a somewhat greater probability to his or her view? What *experienceable* states of affairs count *for* one view and *against* the other such that on balance we are justified in claiming greater probability for one view over the other?

It seems that nothing does. But if every actual or possible happening is equally compatible with either claim, then one must wonder what each is asserting. How could one sentence succeed in asserting something different than the other sentence is used to assert? What is one claiming that the other is denying? If that question cannot be answered—and it appears that it cannot—then the alleged assertions really fail genuinely to assert anything. Since such claims purport to assert "grand cosmological facts," the claims are thus unmasked as incoherent conceptions. They don't and can't do what they purport to do. Moreover, it isn't the situation where we just have two theories equally compatible with the available evidence. What we have is one set of putative claims—the religious ones—claiming to assert something thoroughly different, through and through mysterious, and of a quite different order. Yet there are no differences of an experientially specifiable sort between the two accounts. Experientially the believer cannot show what *more* he is asserting, can't elucidate, except in equally perplexing terms, what he means to be saying that the non-believer is not, so that the suspicion is very difficult to resist that there is, after all, no nonverbal difference between them.

Some Christians of a rather empiricist bent would accept much of the general thrust, if not the details, of the above arguments.[7] They would agree that the above "definite descriptions" are in reality *Ersatz* descriptions which are as problematic as the concept whose sense or at least whose reference they are trying to secure. However, they would argue that there is another definite description readily available to Christians which is far less problematic and is one of the most basic things we can say about God. Indeed it is a something that gives the term an empirical anchorage and enables us to describe or characterize God uniquely such that we can answer the question "Who is God?" The definite description in question is this: "God is the being who raised Jesus from the dead." Here we have talk that relates to the spatio-temporal framework we are in and with which we are familiar. It is a description that gives us a sense of who we are talking about when we talk of or to God. Unlike the alleged definite descriptions I trotted out, this one is linked with the spatio-temporal framework in which we live. Moreover, the claim is falsifiable and verifiable (confirmable and disconfirmable). If in some future situation, after the dissolution of our present bodies, we find out that God did not raise Jesus from the dead, we will have disconfirmed our claim. That is to say, if we discover in that world that Jesus is alive and well and all things are subordinate to him, then we will have confirming evidence that God raised Jesus form the dead. If, however, we do not discover this, we will have disconfirming evidence.

We thus have shown, this Christian defense contends, how key strands of God-talk are verifiable and we have given some determinate sense to "God" by showing who it is we are talking about when speaking of God. But, we are not out of the dark woods yet, for "Jesus is alive and all things are subordinate to him" is equally compatible with "God raised Jesus from the dead" and "It is not the case that God raised Jesus from the dead." But then we have not succeeded by that device in distinguishing what counts for one assertion and against the other. But if we cannot do that, we cannot distinguish between what one is asserting and the other denying, so that we cannot—except in a verbal way—distinguish these claims. Moreover, we have trouble with "God raised Jesus from the dead," for while we understand but do not believe that "Peter raised Jesus from the dead," it is not clear what it *means* to speak of *God*, i.e., "a pure spirit," doing such things and it is not clear what (*if* anything) more is asserted by "God raised Jesus from the dead" than by "Jesus rose form the dead." How can "a pure spirit," "a being beyond space" and "out of time" coherently be said to *do* any of these things? How can a being "out of time" and "beyond space" act "in time" to raise up anything and do all that without a body? It looks like language and indeed sense have gone on a holiday. If nothing more is asserted by the employment of "God raised Jesus from the dead" than is asserted by "Jesus rose from the dead," then we do not have anything that atheists could not consistently assert. If something more is intended, then what this additional (more) is must be explained, but this has not been done and it is not evident that it can be done. But in lieu of an answer here this definite description is little, if any, improvement over the *Ersatz* definite descriptions I have given. We are still at a loss to say *who* God is and we cannot *point* either.

If the central thrusts of these arguments is correct, then Christianity is wedded to conceptions so problematic that Christian faith is rendered incoherent. (But then, given its guidance and salvation functions, it will be exposed as an ideology. This seems to be the position we are in.) We do not understand what "God" is supposed to refer to and the constituent terms in the supposedly elucidating descriptions are equally puzzling about their referent. And the sentences in which these terms are employed are such that we have no idea whether their truth or falsity is ascertainable. We do not know how to distinguish, except purely verbally, between their assertions and their denials.

III

Let us suppose (in order to continue the argument) that Christianity has been so exposed. Let us now ask what interests it answers to and what socially necessary illusions it secures. How does it serve to block our understanding of the foundations of society and deflect unreasonably our actions as human agents?

Christianity in particular, and religion in general, arises as a response to human suffering, degradation, and exploitation in societies. Faced with this, it develops eschatological hopes for a new time and a new man grounded in a radical transformation of man and social relations such that, when we have shuffled off these mortal coils, we will in Heaven at last have a society based not on man's inhumanity to man but on love, in which a genuine classlessness, and in that sense equality, will have been obtained, where there will no longer be any master and slave, and there will be a genuine human flourishing. This, demythologized, is the utopian ideal which Theodor Adorno says should guide our critique of ideology. But in its religious form the hope for a classless and truly human society, through an ideological conjuring trick, has been *projected* into some peculiar never-never land called Heaven. What we have here is a disguised ideologically distorted expression of genuinely human emancipatory interests and enduring human hopes. But, given the repressive and authoritarian nature of our societies, this hope is placed off in "a spiritual world" after "bodily death." Man, in such an ideology, is seen as a sinful, largely selfish and aggressive creature who must be tamed into giving unto Caesar what is Caesar's and unto God what is God's and who must obey duly constituted authority. The ideology tells us we must learn not to aspire to, let alone seize, what is not "ours" but instead accept our God-given place in society, do our share, and accept God's will unquestionably. We must come to know our station and its duties; we must accept our lot. It is within this framework that we have our various entitlements and our just deserts. We are enjoined to accept a social order whose foundations are built on miracle, mystery, and authority and indeed on an authority which can rightly claim neither a rational nor a morally justified authority. The foundations of society are actually obscured from us and our condition in this world—which need not be so fixed—is made to seem fixed, as a consequence of our fallen nature. Everything, or almost everything, is, as the crude image goes, "Pie in the sky by and by."

While there have been, and continue to be, as a tiny minority in the Christian Church, such truly admirable charismatic figures as Dietrich Bonhoeffer, Martin Luther King, Daniel Berrigan and Beyers Naude, generally and massively, the Christian Church stands, and has for a long time stood, on the side of reaction and repression. (We should remember Luther and the German peasants and not forget the horrible fate of his perhaps equally great contemporary Thomas Muntzer, who did stand with the German peasants.) Suffering, degraded, and exploited human beings have been repeatedly taught to accept their fate as part of God's providential order and have projected to a "Spiritual World" and a "New Time" what could be distinctively human hopes, aspirations, and earthly expectations. Religion has deflected them from going after what they might have collectively struggled to achieve in this world, by instilling in them an attitude of resignation concerning this world and replacing their worldly hopes with eschatological ones concerning another far better but purely "spiritual world" which was to be their reward for the patient acceptance of the evils in this world. One was to accept one's worldly masters here and look to this "new spiritual world" where such exploitation and degradation would finally cease. It is there and only there that they shall overcome.

We should clearly recognize, in this heavenly swindle, the ideological function of such age-old religious apologetics. It was a brilliant inspiration, for it both leaves scope for utopian hopes and effectively pacifies the masses, deflecting them from the struggle to achieve their actual liberation. As Feuerbach saw, the ideals and moral qualities that should properly be made the objects of purely human ideals are projected onto God. As our concept of God is enriched our concept of man is impoverished. Here we have for a people caught in such repressive societies, a socially necessary but still an ideologically distorted false consciousness. Religion cons them into accepting a dehumanizing *status quo*. It sings of man's liberation while helping to forge his chains.

In asking what is to be done, we should answer that we must break the spell of this false consciousness and make the demystified, ideologically unravelled, and utterly secularized positive side of Christian utopian hopes the object of our realistic endeavors. With the ideal of a classless unauthoritarian society before us, a genuine human flourishing for all can be obtained and the maxim of egalitarian justice for a materially enriched society can not only be inscribed on our banners but conditioned in our hearts.[8]

NOTES

1. Norman Malcolm's resurrection of the ontological argument is the most striking example. But Charles Hartshorne, Alvin Plantinga, and Richard Taylor have gone off on their own special tangents.

2. I examine these proofs in some detail in my *Reason and Practice*.

3. C. B. Martin has powerfully argued these matters in his *Religious Belief*. I have also elaborated these notions in my *Skepticism*.

4. For further arguments about an appeal to faith and revelation see my "Can Faith Validate God-talk?", *Theology Today* (July, 1963), "Religious Perplexity and Faith," *Crane Review* (Fall, 1965), and my "The Primacy of Philosophical Theology," *Theology Today* (July, 1970).

5. See here my *Ethics Without God* and my "Linguistic Philosophy and 'The Meaning of Life,'" *Cross-Currents* 14 (Summer, 1964).

6. The claims made here have been developed in my *Contemporary Cri-*

tiques of Religion and my *Skepticism.* They are most succinctly made in my "In Defense of Atheism" in *Perspectives in Education, Religion and the Arts,* Howard Kiefer and Milton Munitz (eds.), chapter 5 of the present volume.

7. James Moulder pressed something like this against me, though I would not like to saddle him with my particular formulation.

8. Some of the conceptual underpinning for this last section occurs in my "On Speaking of God," *Theoria* 28 (1962), Part Two, "Religious Perplexity and Faith," *Crane Review* (Fall, 1965), "God as a Human Projection," *The Lockhaven Review* 1 (1967), and "Religiosity and Powerlessness," *The Humanist* (May/June, 1977). I have tried to say what that maxim of egalitarian justice is in my *Equality and Liberty: A Defense of Radical Egalitarianism* (Totowa, NJ: Rowman and Allanheld, 1985).

4

Agnosticism

I

Agnosticism is a philosophical and theological concept which has been understood in various ways by different philosophers and theologians. T. H. Huxley coined the term in 1869, and its first home was in the disputes about science and religion, naturalism and supernaturalism, that reached a climax during the nineteenth century. To be an agnostic is to hold that nothing can be known or at least that it is very unlikely that anything will be known or soundly believed concerning whether God or any transcendent reality or state exists.

It is very natural for certain people conditioned in certain ways to believe that there must be some power "behind," "beyond," or "underlying" the universe which is responsible for its order and all the incredible features that are observed and studied by the sciences even though these same people will readily grant that we do not know that there is such a power or have good grounds for believing that there is such a power. While the admission of ignorance concerning things divine is usually made by someone outside the circle of faith, it can and indeed has been made by fideistic Jews and Christians as well.

Some writers, e.g., Robert Flint and James Ward, so construed "agnosticism" that (1) it was identified with "philosophical skepticism" and (2) it allowed for there being "theistic agnostics" and "Christian agnostics." However, the more typical employment of "agnosticism" is such that it would not be correct to count as agnostics either fideistic believers or Jews and Christians who claim that we can only gain knowledge of God through some mystical awareness or "ineffable knowledge." It surely was this standard but more circumscribed sense of "agnosticism" that William James had in mind when he made his famous remark in his essay "The Will to Believe" that agnosticism was the worst thing that "ever came out of the philosopher's workshop." Without implying or suggesting any support at all for James's value judgment, we shall construe agnosticism in this rather more typical manner. Given this construal (1) "theistic agnosticism" is a contradiction and thus one cannot be a Jew or a Christian and be an agnostic and (2) also agnosticism is *neutral* vis-à-vis the claim that there can be no philosophical knowledge or even scientific or common-sense knowledge. We shall then take agnosticism to be the more limited claim that we either do not or cannot know that God or any other transcendent reality or state exists and thus we should suspend judgment concerning the assertion that God exists. That is to say, the agnostic neither affirms or denies it. This, as should be evident from the above characterization, can take further specification and indeed later such specifications will be supplied. But such a construal captures in its characterization both what was essentially at issue in the great agnostic debates in the nineteenth century and the issue as it has come down to us.

II

T. H. Huxley was by training a biologist, but he had strong philosophical interests and as a champion of Darwinism he became a major intellectual figure in the nineteenth century. In his "Science and Christian tradition" (in *Collected Essays*), Huxley remarks that agnosticism is a method, a stance taken toward putative religious truth-claims, the core of which is to refuse to assent to religious doctrines for which there is no adequate evidence, but to retain an open-mindedness about the possibility of sometime attaining adequate evidence. We ought never to assert that we know a proposition to be true or indeed even to assent to that proposition unless we have adequate evidence to support it.

After his youthful reading of the Scottish metaphysician William Hamilton's *Philosophy of the Unconditioned* (1829), Huxley repeatedly returned to questions about the limits of our possible knowledge and came, as did Leslie Stephen, to the empiricist conclusion that we cannot know anything about God or any alleged states or realities "beyond phenomena." Whether there is a God, a world of demons, an immortal soul, whether indeed "the spiritual world" is other than human fantasy or projection, were all taken by Huxley to be *factual questions* open to careful and systematic empirical investigation. In short, however humanly important such questions were, they were also "matters of the intellect" and in such contexts the central maxim of the method of agnosticism is to "follow your reason as far as it will take you, without regard to any other consideration. And negatively: In matters of the intellect do not pretend that conclusions are certain which are not demonstrated or demonstrable" (Huxley, pp. 245-46). Operating in accordance with such a method does not justify "the denial of the existence of any Supernature; but simply the denial of the validity of the evidence adduced in favor of this, or that, extant form of Super-naturalism" (p. 126). Huxley found that he could no more endorse materialism, idealism, atheism, or pantheism than he could theism; all claimed too much about essentially contested matters. Huxley felt that people espousing such world views were too ready to claim a solution to the "problem of existence," while he remained painfully aware that he had not succeeded in coming by such a solution and in addition retained "a pretty strong conviction that the problem was insoluble" (pp. 237-38).

This conviction is at the heart of his agnosticism. Huxley was convinced that Kant and Hamilton had established that reason fails us—and indeed *must* fail us—when we try to establish that the world is finite in space or time or indefinite in space or time, rational or irrational, an ordered whole or simply manifesting certain ordered features but not something properly to be called an ordered whole. Answers to such questions reveal something about our attitudes but can never provide us with propositions we can justifiably claim to be true or even know to be false. Agnosticism is a confession of honesty here. It is "the only position for people who object to say that they know what they are quite aware they do not know" (p. 210).

Such skepticism concerning the truth-claims of religion and metaphysics, including, of course, metaphysical religiosity, should not be taken as a denial that there can be reliable knowledge. Rather Huxley argued, as John Dewey did far more systematically later, that we can and do gain experimental and experiential knowledge of nature, including human nature, and that this, by contrast with so-called "supernatural knowledge," becomes increasingly more extensive and reliable. And while remaining an agnostic, Huxley saw in science—basically the scientific way of fixing belief—a fundamental and well grounded challenge to the authority of the theory of the "spiritual world."

Whatever may have been the case in the seventeenth century, there was in Huxley's time a state of war between science and religion. Huxley took science to be a challenge to claims of biblical infallibility and revelation. The whole supernatural world view built on the authority of the Bible and revelation must come under scientific scrutiny and when this is done it becomes gradually apparent that the use of the scientific method and appeals to scientific canons of criticism give us a far more reliable method of settling belief than do the scriptures and revelation.

To commit ourselves to the Bible as an infallible authority is to commit ourselves to a world view in which we must believe that devils were cast out of a man and went into a herd of swine, that the deluge was universal, that the world was made in six days, and the like. Yet such claims are plainly and massively contravened by our actual empirical knowledge such that they are quite beyond the boundaries of responsible belief. About such matters, Huxley argues, we ought not to be at all agnostic. Moreover, we cannot take them simply as myths, important for the biblical and Christian understanding of the world, if we are to take seriously biblical infallibility and the authority of revelation. For the Judeo-Christian world view to establish its validity, it must provide us with adequate grounds for believing that there are demons. But there is no good evidence for such alleged realities and to believe in them is the grossest form of superstition (Huxley, p. 215).

Even if we fall back on a severe Christology, we are still in difficulties, for it is evident enough that Jesus believed in demons and if we are to adopt a radical Christology and take Jesus as our infallible guide to the divine, we are going to have to accept such superstitious beliefs. Such beliefs affront not only our intellect—our credibility concerning what it is reasonable to believe—they also affront our moral sense as well (p. 226). Yet once we give up the Gospel claim that there are "demons who can be transferred from a man to a pig," the other stories of "demonic possession fall under suspicion." Once we start on this slide, once we challenge the ultimate authority of the Bible, and follow experimental and scientific procedures, the ground for the whole Judeo-Christian world view is undermined.

Huxley obviously thinks its credibility and probability is of a very low order; an order which would make Christian or Jewish belief quite impossible for a reasonable and tolerably well informed man. Those who claim to know that there are such unseen and indeed utterly unseeable realities, are very likely people who have taken "cunning phrases for answers," where real answers are "not merely actually impossible, but theoretically inconceivable." Yet as an agnostic one must always—even for such problematical transcendental claims—remain open to conviction where evidence can be brought to establish the truth of such transcendent religious claims.

Leslie Stephen in his neglected *An Agnostic's Apology* (1893) remarks that he uses "agnostic" in a sense close to that of T. H. Huxley. To be agnostic, according to Stephen, is to reject what he calls "Dogmatic Atheism," i.e., "the doctrine that there is no God. . ."; it is, instead, (1) to affirm "what no one denies," namely, "that there are limits to the sphere of human intelligence" and (2) also to affirm the controversial empiricist thesis "that those limits are such as to exclude at least what Lewes called 'Metaempirical knowledge' " (p. 1). ("Metaempirical knowledge" is meant to designate all forms of knowledge of a transcendent, numinal, nonempirical sort.)

Stephen makes apparent the empiricist commitments of his conception of agnosticism in characterizing gnosticism, the view agnosticism is deliberately set against. To be a gnostic is to believe that "we can attain truths not capable of verification and not needing verification by actual experiment or observation" (ibid., pp. 1-2). In gaining such a knowledge gnostics in opposition to both Hume and Kant claim that by the use of our reason we can attain a knowledge that transcends "the narrow limits of experience" (p. 1). But the agnostic, firmly in the empiricist tradition, denies that there can be any knowledge of the world, including anything about its origin and destiny, which transcends experience and comprehends "the sorry scheme of things entire." Such putative knowledge, Stephen maintains, is illusory and not something "essential to the highest interests of mankind," providing us, as speculative metaphysicians believe, with the solution to "the dark riddle of the universe." (p. 2).

In a manner that anticipates the challenge to the claims of religion and metaphysics made by the logical empiricists, Stephen says that in addition to the problem of whether they can establish the truth or probable truth of "Religious truth-claims" there is the further consideration—actually a logically prior question—of whether such putative claims "have any meaning" (p. 3).

It should be noted that Stephen does not begin *An Agnostic's Apology* by discussing semantical difficulties in putative religious truth-claims but starts with problems connected with what W. K. Clifford was later to call "the ethics of belief." We indeed would all want—if we could do it honestly—to accept the claim that "evil is transitory . . . good eternal" and that the "world is really an embodiment of love and wisdom, however dark it may appear to us" (p. 2). But the rub is that many of us cannot believe that and in a question of such inestimable human value, we have "the most sacred obligations to recognize the facts" and make our judgments in accordance with the facts. But the facts do not give us grounds for confidence in the viability of Judeo-Christian beliefs. Rather we are strongly inclined when we inspect these beliefs to believe they are wish fulfillments. And while it may indeed be true that for the moment dreams may be pleasanter than realities, it is also true that if we are bent on attaining a more permanent measure of happiness, it "must be won by adapting our lives to the realities," for we know from experience that illusory

consolations "are the bitterest of mockeries" (ibid.). The religious plat-
itudes "Pain is not evil," "Death is not a separation," and "Sickness is
but a blessing in disguise" have tortured sufferers far more than "the
gloomiest speculations of avowed pessimists" (ibid.).

However, the problem of *meaning* cuts to a deeper conceptual
level than do such arguments about the ethics of belief. Where Judeo-
Christianity does not have a fideistic basis, it is committed to what
Stephen calls gnosticism. But does not such a doctrine fail "to recognize the limits of possible knowledge" and in trying to transcend these
limits does it not in effect commit the gnostic to pseudo-propositions
which are devoid of literal meaning? Logical empiricists later answered
this question in the affirmative and while it is not crystal clear that
Stephen's answer is quite that definite, it would appear that this is
what he wants to maintain. And if that is what Stephen is maintaining,
there can, of course, on his account, be no knowledge of the divine.

Stephen raises this key question concerning the intelligibility of
such gnostic God-talk, but he does little with it. Instead he focuses on
some key questions concerning attempts by theologians to undermine
agnosticism. He first points out that an appeal to revelation is no
answer to the agnostic's denial that we have knowledge of transcendent realities or states, for in claiming to rely exclusively on revelation
these theologians acknowledge that "natural man can know nothing
of the Divine nature." But this, Stephen replies, is not only to grant
but in effect to assert the agnostic's fundamental principle (p. 5). He
points out that H. L. Mansel in effect and in substance affirms agnosticism and that Cardinal Newman with his appeal to the testimony
of conscience does not provide a reliable argument on which to base a
belief in God nor does he undermine the agnostic's position, for "the
voice of conscience has been very differently interpreted." Some of
these interpretations, secular though they may be, have all the appearances of being at least as valid as Newman's, for all that Newman
or anyone else has shown. Moreover, on any reasonable reading of a
principle of parsimony, they are far simpler than Newman's interpretation. Thus Newman's arguments in reality prove, as do Mansel's,
that a man ought to be an agnostic concerning such ultimate questions where reason remains his guide and where he does not make
an appeal to the *authority* of the Church. They, of course, would have
us accept the authority of the Church, but how can we reasonably do
so when there are so many Churches, so many conflicting authorities,
and so many putative revelations? Where reason can only lead us to
agnosticism concerning religious matters, we can have no ground for
accepting one Church, one religious authority, or one putative revelation rather than another. We simply have no way of knowing which
course is the better course. Agnosticism, Stephen concludes, is the

only reasonable and viable alternative.

Like Huxley, and like Hume before him, Stephen is skeptical of the *a priori* arguments of metaphysics and natural theology. "There is not a single proof of natural theology," he asserts, "of which the negative has not been maintained as vigorously as the affirmative" (p. 9). In such a context, where there is no substantial agreement, but just endless and irresolvable philosophical controversy, it is the duty of a reasonable man to profess ignorance (p. 9). In trying to escape the bounds of sense—in trying to gain some metaempirical knowledge—philosophers continue to contradict flatly the first principles of their predecessors and no vantage point is attained where we can objectively assess these endemic metaphysical conflicts that divide philosophers. To escape utter skepticism, we must be agnostics and argue that such metaphysical and theological controversies lead to "transcending the limits of reason" (p. 10). But the only widely accepted characterization of these limits "comes in substance to an exclusion of ontology" and an adherence to empirically based truth-claims as the only legitimate truth-claims.

It will not help, Stephen argues, to maintain that the Numinous, i.e., the divine, is essentially mysterious and that religious understanding—a seeing through a glass darkly—is a knowledge of something which is irreducibly and inescapably mysterious. In such talk in such contexts, there is linguistic legerdemain: we call our doubts mysteries and what is now being appealed to as "the mystery of faith" is but the theological phrase for agnosticism (p. 22).

Stephen argues that one could believe knowledge of the standard types was quite possible and indeed actual and remain skeptical about metaphysics. It is just such a position that many (perhaps most) contemporary philosophers would take. In taking this position himself, Stephen came to believe that metaphysical claims are "nothing but the bare husks of meaningless words." To gain genuine knowledge, we must firmly put aside such meaningless metaphysical claims and recognize the more limited extent of our knowledge claims. A firm recognition here will enable us to avoid utter skepticism because we come to see that within the limits of the experiential "we have been able to discover certain reliable truths" and with them "we shall find sufficient guidance for the needs of life" (p. 26). So while we remain religious skeptics and skeptical of the claims of transcendental metaphysics, we are not generally skeptical about man's capacity to attain reliable knowledge. Yet it remains the case that nothing is known or can be known, of the alleged "ultimate reality"—the Infinite and Absolute—of traditional metaphysics and natural theology (p. 26). And thus nothing can be known of God.

III

Before moving on to a consideration of some twentieth-century formulations of agnosticism and to a critical examination of all forms of agnosticism, let us consider briefly a question that the above characterization of Huxley and Stephen certainly should give rise to. Given the correctness of the above criticisms of Judaism and Christianity, do we not have good grounds for rejecting these religions and is not this in effect an espousal of atheism rather than agnosticism?

We should answer differently for Huxley than we do for Stephen. Huxley's arguments, if correct, would give us good grounds for rejecting Christianity and Judaism; but they are not sufficient by themselves for jettisoning a belief in God, though they would require us to suspend judgment about the putative knowledge-claim that God exists and created the world. But it must be remembered that agnosticism is the general claim that we do not know and (more typically) cannot know or have good grounds for believing that there is a God. But to accept this is not to accept the claim that there is no God, unless we accept the premiss that what cannot even in principle be known cannot exist. This was not a premiss to which Huxley and Stephen were committed. Rather they accepted the standard agnostic view that since we cannot know or have good reasons for believing that God exists we should suspend judgment concerning his existence or nonexistence. Moreover, as we shall see, forms of Jewish and Christian fideism when linked with modern biblical scholarship could accept at least most of Huxley's arguments and still defend an acceptance of the Jewish or Christian faith.

Stephen's key arguments are more epistemologically oriented and are more definitely committed to an empiricist account of meaning and the limits of conceivability. As we shall see in examining the contentions of some contemporary critics of religion, it is more difficult to see what, given the correctness of Stephen's own account, it could *mean* to affirm, deny, or even doubt the existence of God. The very concept of God on such an account becomes problematical. And this makes what it would be to be an agnostic, an atheist, or a theist problematical.

The cultural context in which we speak of religion is very different in the twentieth century than it was in the nineteenth (cf. MacIntyre, Ricoeur). For most twentieth-century people with even a minimal amount of education, the authority of science has cut much deeper than it did in previous centuries. The cosmological claims in the biblical stories are no longer taken at face value by the overwhelming majority of educated people both religious and nonreligious. Theologians working from within the circle of faith have carried out an extensive program of demythologizing such biblical claims. Thus it is evident that in one quite obvious respect the nineteenth-century agnostics have clearly been victorious. There is no longer any serious attempt to defend the truth of the cosmological claims in the type of biblical stories that Huxley discusses.

However, what has not received such wide acceptance is the claim that the acceptance of such a demythologizing undermines Judaism and Christianity and drives an honest man in the direction of agnosticism or atheism. Many would claim that such demythologizing only purifies Judaism and Christianity of extraneous cultural material. The first thing to ask is whether or not a steady recognition of the fact that these biblical stories are false supports agnosticism as strongly as Huxley thinks it does.

Here the new historical perspective on the Bible is a crucial factor. The very concept of the authority of the Bible undergoes a sea change with the new look in historical scholarship. It is and has been widely acknowledged both now and in the nineteenth century that Judaism and Christianity are both integrally linked with certain historical claims. They are not sufficient to establish the truth of either of these religions, but they are necessary. Yet modern historical research—to put it minimally—places many of these historical claims in an equivocal light and makes it quite impossible to accept claims about the literal infallibility of the Bible. Conservative evangelicalists (fundamentalists) try to resist this tide and in reality still battle with Huxley. They reject the basic findings of modern biblical scholarship and in contrast to modernists treat the Bible not as a fallible and myth-laden account of God's self-revelation in history but as a fully inspired and infallible historical record. Conservative evangelicalists agree with modernists that revelation consists in God's self-disclosure to man, but they further believe that the Bible is an infallible testimony of God's self-unveiling. Modernists by contrast believe that we must discover what the crucial historical but yet divine events and realities are like by a painstaking historical investigation of the biblical material. This involves all the techniques of modern historical research. The various accounts in the Bible must be sifted by methodical inquiry and independently acquired knowledge of the culture and the times must be used whenever possible.

Conservative evangelicalism is still strong as a cultural phenomenon in North America, though it is steadily losing strength. However it is not a serious influence in the major seminaries and modernism has thoroughly won the day in the intellectually respectable centers of Jewish and Christian learning. Huxley's arguments do come into conflict with conservative evangelicalism and his arguments about the plain falsity, utter incoherence, and sometimes questionable morality of the miracle stories and stories of Jesus' actions would have to be met by such conservative evangelicalists. But the modernists would be on Huxley's side here. So, for a large and respectable element of the Jewish and Christian community, Huxley's arguments, which lead him to reject Christianity and accept agnosticism, are accepted but not taken as at all undermining the foundations of Judaism or Christianity.

Huxley's sort of endeavor, like the more systematic endeavors of David Strauss, simply helps Christians rid the world of the historically contingent cultural trappings of the biblical writers. Once this has been cut away, modernists argue, the true import of the biblical message can be seen as something of decisive relevance that transcends the vicissitudes of time.

However, this is not all that should be said vis-à-vis the conflict between science and religion and agnosticism. It is often said that the conflict between science and religion came to a head in the nineteenth century and now has been transcended. Science, it is averred, is now seen to be neutral concerning materialism or any other metaphysical thesis and theology—the enterprise of attempting to provide ever deeper, clearer, and more reasonable statements and explications of the truths of religion—is more sophisticated and less vulnerable to attacks by science or scientifically oriented thinkers. Still it may be the case that there remain some conflicts between science and religion which have not been overcome even with a sophisticated analysis of religion, where that analysis takes the religions of the world and Christianity and Judaism in particular to be making truth-claims.

Let us consider how such difficulties might arise. Most Christians, for example, would want to claim as something central to their religion that Christ rose from the dead and that there is a life after the death of our earthly bodies. These claims seem at least to run athwart our scientific understanding of the world so that it is difficult to know how we could both accept scientific method as the most reliable method of settling disputes about the facts and accept these central Christian claims. Moreover, given what science teaches us about the world, these things could not happen or have happened. Yet it is also true that the by now widely accepted new historical perspective on the Bible recognizes and indeed stresses mythical and poetical strands in the Bible stories. And surely it is in this nonliteral way that the stories about demons, Jonah in the whale's belly, and Noah and his ark are to be taken, but how far is this to be carried with the other biblical claims? Are we to extend it to such central Christian claims as "Christ rose from the Dead," "Man shall survive the death of his earthly body," "God is in Christ"? If we do, it becomes completely unclear as to what it could mean to speak of either the truth or falsity of the Christian religion. If we do not, then it would seem that some central Christian truth-claims do clash with scientific claims and orientations so that there is after all a conflict between science and religion.

Given such a dilemma, the agnostic or atheist could then go on to claim that either these key religious utterances do not function propositionally as truth-claims at all or there is indeed such a clash. But if there is such a clash, the scientific claims are clearly the claims to be preferred, for of all the rival ways of fixing belief, the scientific way of fixing belief is clearly the most reliable. Thus if there are good empirical, scientific reasons (as there are) for thinking that people who die are not resurrected, that when our earthly bodies die we die, and that there is no evidence at all, and indeed not even any clear meaning to the claim that there are "resurrection bodies" and a "resurrection world" utterly distinct from the cosmos, we have the strongest of reasons for not accepting the Christian claim that "Christ rose from the Dead." The scientific beliefs in conflict with that belief are ones that it would be foolish to jettison. But it is only by a sacrifice of our scientific way of conceiving of things that we could assent to such a central religious claim. Thus it is fair to say that our scientific understanding drives us in the direction of either atheism or agnosticism.

Some contemporary theologians have responded to such contentions by arguing that there are good conceptual reasons why there could not be, appearances to the contrary notwithstanding, such a conflict. "Christ" is not equivalent to "Jesus" but to "the son of God" and God is not a physical reality. Christianity centers on a belief in a deity who is beyond the world, who is creator of the world. But such a reality is in principle, since it is transcendent to the cosmos, not capable of being investigated scientifically but must be understood in some other way. God in his proper nonanthropomorphic forms is beyond the reach of evidence. Only crude anthropomorphic forms of Christian belief could be disproved by modern scientific investigations.

To believe that Christ rose from the dead is to be committed to a belief in miracles. But, it has been forcefully argued by Ninian Smart, this does not commit us to something which is antiscientific or that can be ruled out a priori (Smart) [1964], Ch. II; [1966], pp. 44-45). A miracle is an event of divine significance which is an exception to at least one law of nature. Scientific laws are not, it is important to remember, falsified by single exceptions but only by a class of experimentally repeatable events. Thus we can believe in the miracle of Christ's resurrection without clashing with anything sanctioned by science. It is a dogma, the critic of agnosticism could continue, to think that everything that can be known can be known by the method of science or by simple observation. A thoroughly scientific mind quite devoid of credulity could remain committed to Judaism or Christianity, believe in God, and accept such crucial miracle stories without abandoning a scientific attitude, i.e., he could accept all the findings of science and accept its authority as the most efficient method for ascertaining what is the case when ascertaining what is the case comes to predicting and retrodicting classes of experimentally repeatable events or processes.

Christians as well as agnostics can and do recognize the obscurity and mysteriousness of religious claims. The Christian should go on to say that a nonmysterious God, a God whose reality is evident, would not be the God of Judeo-Christianity—the God to be accepted on faith with fear and trembling. It is only for a God who moves in mysterious ways, that the characteristic Jewish and Christian attitudes of discipleship, adoration, and faith are appropriate. If the existence of God and what it was to act in accordance with His will were perfectly evident or clearly establishable by hard intellectual work, faith would lose its force and rationale. Faith involves risk, trust, and commitment. Judaism or Christianity is not something one simply must believe in if one will only think the matter through as clearly and honestly as possible.

What is evident is that the agnosticism of a Huxley and a Stephen at least—and a Bertrand Russell as well—rests on a philosophical view not dictated by science. James Ward saw this around the turn of the century and argued in his *Naturalism and Agnosticism* that agnosticism "is an inherently unstable position" unless it is supplemented by some general philosophical view such as materialism or idealism (p. 21). Yet it is just such overall views that Huxley and Stephen were anxious to avoid and along Humean lines viewed with a thoroughgoing skepticism.

In sum, the claim is that only if such an overall philosophical view is justified is it the case that there may be good grounds for being an agnostic rather than a Christian or a Jew. The overall position necessary for such a justification is either a postion of empiricism or materialism and if it is the former it must be a form of empiricism which in Jürgen Habermas's terms is also a scientism. By this we mean the claim that there are no facts which science cannot explore: that what cannot at least in principle be known by the method of science cannot be known. Where alternatively scientism is part of a reductive materialist metaphysics, there is a commitment to what has been called an "existence-monism," namely, the view that there is only one sort of level or order of existence and that is spatiotemporal existence. That is to say, such an existence-monist believes that to exist is to have a place in space-time. In support of this, he may point out that we can always ask about a thing that is supposed to exist *where* it exists. This, it is claimed, indicates how we in reality operate on materialist assumptions. And note that if that question is not apposite, "exists" and its equivalents are *not* being employed in their standard senses, but are being used in a secondary sense as in "Ghosts and gremlins exist merely in one's mind." Besides existence-monism there is the even more pervasive and distinctively empiricist position— a position shared by the logical empiricists, by Bertrand Russell, and by John Dewey—referred to as "methodological-monism": to wit "that all statements of fact are such that they can be investigated scientifically, i.e., that they can in principle be falsified by observation" (Smart [1966], p. 8).

However, critics of agnosticism have responded, as has Ninian Smart, by pointing out that these philosophical positions are vulnerable to a variety of fairly obvious and long-standing criticisms. Perhaps these criticisms can be and have been met, but these positions are highly controversial. If agnosticism is tied to them, do we not have as good grounds for being skeptical of agnosticism as the agnostics have for being skeptical of the claims of religion?

Some samplings of the grounds for being skeptical about the philosophical underpinnings for agnosticism are these. When I suddenly remember that I left my key in my car, it makes sense to speak of the space-time location of my car but, it is at least plausibly argued, not of the space-time location of my sudden thought. Moreover numbers exist but it hardly makes sense to ask *where* they exist. It is not the case that for all standard uses of "exist" that to exist is to have a place in space-time. Methodological-monism is also beset with difficulties. There are in science theoretically unobservable entities and "from quite early times, the central concepts of religion, such as God and nirvana already include the notion that what they stand for cannot literally be observed" (Smart [1962], p. 8). Moreover it is not evident that we could falsify statements such as "There are some graylings in Michigan" or "Every human being has some neurotic traits" or "Photons really exist, they are not simply scientific fictions." Yet we do recognize them (or so at least it would seem) as intelligible statements of fact. Such considerations led Ninian Smart to claim confidently in his *The Teacher and Christian Belief* (London, 1966) that "it remains merely a dogma to claim that all facts are facts about moons and flowers and humans and other denizens of the cosmos. There need be no general embargo upon belief in a transcendent reality, provided such belief is not merely based on uncontrolled speculation" (p. 51). Smart goes on to conclude that "the exclusion of transcendent facts rests on a mere decision" (p. 52). So it would appear, from what has been said above, that agnosticism has no solid rational foundation.

The dialectic of the argument over agnosticism is not nearly at an end and it shall be the burden of the argument here to establish that agnosticism still has much to be said for it. First of all, even granting, for the reasons outlined above, that neither the development of science nor an appeal to scientism or empiricism establishes agnosticism, there are other considerations which give it strong support. David Hume's *Dialogues Concerning Natural Religion* (1779) and Immanuel Kant's *Critique of Pure Reason* (1781) make it quite evident that none of the proofs for the existence of God work, i.e., they are not sound or reliable arguments. Furthermore it should be noted that their arguments do not for the most part depend for their force on empiricist assumptions and they most certainly do not depend on the development of science.

The most rigorous contemporary work in the philosophy of religion has not always supported the detailed arguments of Hume and Kant but it has for the most part supported their overall conclusions on this issue. Alvin Plantinga, for example, in his *God and Other Minds* (1967) rejects rather thoroughly the principles and assumptions of both existence-monism and methodological-monism and he subjects the particulars of Hume's and Kant's views to careful criticism, yet in the very course of giving a defense of what he takes to be the rationality of Christian belief, he argues that none of the attempts at a demonstration of the existence of God have succeeded. He is echoed in this claim by such important contemporary analytical theologians as John Hick and Diogenes Allen. This lack of validated knowledge of the divine or lack of such warranted belief strengthens the hand of the agnostics, though it is also compatible with fideism or a revelationist view such as Barth's, which holds that man on his own can know nothing of God but must rely utterly on God's self-disclosure.

IV

In the twentieth century a distinct element comes to the fore which counts in favor of agnosticism but also gives it a particular twist. This new turn leads to a reformulation of agnosticism. It states agnosticism in such a manner that it becomes evident how it is a relevant response to one of the major elements in contemporary philosophical perplexities over religion.

We have hitherto been talking as if God-talk is used in certain central contexts to make statements of whose truth-value we are in doubt. That is, there is no doubt that they have a truth-value but there is a doubt which truth-value they actually have. Theists think that at least some of the key Jewish or Christian claims are true, atheists think they are false, and traditional agnostics, as H. H. Price puts it in his *Belief* (London, 1969), suspend "judgement on the ground that we do not have sufficient evidence to decide the question and so far as he [the agnostic] can tell there is no likelihood that we ever shall have" (p. 445). But in the twentieth century with certain analytic philosophers the question has come to the fore about whether these key religious utterances have any truth-value at all.

A. J. Ayer defending the modern variety of empiricism called "logical empiricism" argued in his *Language, Truth and Logic* (London, 1935) that such key religious utterances are devoid of cognitive meaning. Such considerations lead Ayer to deny that he or anyone taking such a position could be either a theist, an atheist, or even an agnostic. In a well known passage Ayer comments that it is very important not to confuse his view with agnosticism or atheism, for, as he puts it:

> It is a characteristic of an agnostic to hold that the existence of a god is a possibility in which there is no good reason either to believe or disbelieve; and it is characteristic of an atheist to hold that it is at least probable that no god exists. And our view that all utterances about the nature of God are nonsensical, so far form being identical with, or even lending any support to, either of these familiar contentions, is actually incompatible with them. For if the assertion that there is a god is nonsensical, then the atheist's assertion that there is no god is equally nonsensical, since it is only a significant proposition that can be significantly contradicted. As for the agnostic, although he refrains from saying either that there is or that there is not a god, he does not deny that the question whether a transcendent god exists is a genuine question. He does not deny that the two sentences "There is a transcendent god" and "There is no transcendent god" express propositions one of which is actually true and the other false. All he says is that we have no means of telling which of them is true, and therefore ought not to commit ourselves to either. But we have seen that the sentences in question do not express propositions at all. And this means that agnosticism also is ruled out (p. 219).

Ayer goes on to remark that the theist's putative claims are neither valid nor invalid; they say nothing at all and thus the theist cannot rightly be "accused of saying anything false, or anything for which he has insufficient grounds" (ibid., p. 219). It is only when the Christian, so to speak, turns meta-theologian and claims that in asserting the existence of a Transcendent God he is expressing a genuine proposition "that we are entitled to disagree with him" (ibid.).

The central point Ayer is making is that such religious utterances do not assert anything and thus they can be neither doubted, believed, nor even asserted to be false. With such considerations pushed to the front, the key question becomes whether such religious utterances have any informative content at all.

There is something very strange here. Ayer, as we have seen, does not regard his position as atheistical or agnostic, for since such key religious utterances could not even be false, they could not be intelligibly denied and since they make no claim to be intelligibly questioned, they could not be sensibly doubted. But, as Susan Stebbing rightly observed, "the plain man would not find it easy to see the difference between Mr. Ayer's non-atheism and the fool's atheism" (Stebbing, p. 264). But before we say "so much the worse for the plain man," we should remember that to believe that such key religious utterances are unbelievable because nonsensical is even a more basic rejection of religious belief than simply asserting the falsity of the putative truth-claims of Christianity, but allowing for the *possibility* that they might be true.

Because of this altered conceptualization of the situation, Price and Edwards, have characterized both agnosticism and atheism in a broader and more adequate way which takes into account these problems about meaning, and I, as well, have done this in a more systematic and nuanced way in the introductory chapter. A contemporary agnostic who is alert to such questions about meaning would maintain that judgments concerning putatively assertive God-talk should be suspended for either of two reasons, depending on the exact nature of the God-talk in question: (1) the claims, though genuine truth-claims, are without sufficient evidence to warrant either their belief or categorical rejection, or (2) their meaning is so problematical that it is doubtful whether there is something there which is sufficiently intelligible or coherent to be believed. Where God is conceived somewhat anthropomorphically the first condition obtains and where God is conceived nonanthropomorphically the second condition obtains. The contemporary agnostic believes that "God" in the most typical religious employments is so indeterminate in meaning that he must simply suspend judgment about whether there is anything that it stands for which can intelligibly be believed. His position, as Price points out, is like the traditional agnostic's in being neutral between theism and atheism (p. 454). He believes that neither such positive judgment is justified, but unlike a contemporary atheist, on the one hand, he is not so confident of the unintelligiblity or incoherence of religious utterances that he feels that religious belief is irrational and is to be rejected, but, on the other hand, he does not believe one is justified in taking these problematic utterances as being obscurely revelatory of Divine Truth. Neither atheism nor any of the several forms of fideism is acceptable to him.

The contemporary agnostic sensitive to problems about the logical status of religious utterance simply stresses that the reasonable and on the whole justified course of action here is simply to suspend judgment. His doubts are primarily *doubts about the possibility of there being anything to doubt,* but, second-order as they are, they have an effect similar to the effect of classical agnosticism and they lead to a similar attitude toward religion. There is neither the classical atheistic denial that there is anything to the claims of religion nor is there the fideistic avowal that in spite of all their obscurity and *seeming* unintelligibility that there still is something there *worthy* of belief. Instead there is a genuine suspension of judgment.

The thing to ask is whether the doubts leading to a suspension of judgment are actually sufficient to *justify* such a suspension or, everything considered, (1) would a leap of faith be more justified or (2) would the overcoming of doubt in the direction of atheism be more reasonable? Or is it the case that there is no way of making a rational decision here or of reasonably deciding what one ought to do or believe?

It may indeed be true, as many a sophisticated theologian has argued, that religious commitment is perfectly compatible with a high degree of ignorance about God and the nature—whatever that may mean—of "ultimate reality." But, if this is the case and if our ignorance here is as invincible as much contemporary philosophical argumentation would have us believe, *natural theology* seems at least to be thoroughly undermined. In trying to establish whether the world is contingent or noncontingent, whether there is or can be something "beyond the world" upon which the world in some sense depends, or whether there is or could be an unlimited reality which is still in some sense personal, theological reasonings have been notoriously unsuccessful. About the best that has been done is to establish that it is not entirely evident that these questions are meaningless or utterly unanswerable.

Here a Barthian turn-away from natural theology is equally fruitless. To say that man can by his own endeavors know nothing of God but simply must await an unpredictable and rationally inexplicable self-disclosure of God—the core notion of God revealing himself to man —is of no help, for when we look at religions in an honest anthropological light, we will see, when all the world is our stage, that we have multitudes of conflicting alleged revelations with no means at all of deciding, without the aid of natural theology or philosophical analysis, which, if any, of these putative revelations are genuine revelations. It is true enough that if something is actually a divine revelation, it cannot be assessed by man, but must simply be accepted. But the agnostic reminds the revelationist that we have a multitude of conflicting candidate revelations with no means of reasonably deciding which one to accept. In such a context a reasonable man will remain agnostic concerning such matters. To simply accept the authoritative claims of a Church in such a circumstance is to fly in the face of reason.

The most crucial problem raised by the so-called truth-claims of

Judaism and Christianity is that of conceivability—to borrow a term that Herbert Spencer used in the nineteenth century and thereby suggesting that there are more lines of continuity between the old agnosticism and the new than this essay has indicated. The *incredibility*—to use Spencer's contrasting term—of these central religious claims is tied, at least in part, to their *inconceivability*. "God" is not supposed to refer to a being among beings; by definition God is no finite object or process in the world. But then how is the referring to be done? What are we really talking about when we speak of God? How do we or can we fix the reference range of "God"? God surely cannot be identified in the same manner we identify the sole realities compatible with existence-monism. There can be no picking God out as we would a discrete entity in space-time. Alternatively there are theologians who will say that when we come to recognize that it is just a brute fact that there is that indefinitely immense collection of finite and contingent masses or conglomerations of things, we use the phrase "the world" to refer to, and when we recognize it could have been the case—eternally the case—that there was no world at all, we can come quite naturally to feel puzzled about why there is a world at all.

Is there anything that would account for the existence of all finite reality and not itself be a reality that needed to be similarly explained? In speaking of God we are speaking of such a reality, if indeed there is such a reality. We are concerned with a reality not simply—as the world might be—infinite in space and time, but a reality such that it would not make sense to ask *why* it exists. Such a reality could not be a physical reality.

In sum, we have, if we reflect at all, a developing sense of the. contingency of the world. The word "God" in part means, in Jewish and Christian discourses, whatever it is that is noncontingent upon which all these contingent realities continuously depend. God is the completeness that would fill in the essential incompleteness of the world. We have feelings of dependency, creatureliness, finitude and in having those feelings, it is argued, we have some sense of that which is without limit. "God" refers to such alleged ultimate realities and to something richer as well. But surely this, the critic of agnosticism will reply, sufficiently fixes the reference range of "God," such that it would be a mistake to assert that "God" is a term supposedly used to refer to a referent but nothing coherently specifiable counts as a possible referent for "God," where "God" has a nonanthropomorphic employment.

Surely such a referent is not something which can be clearly conceived, but, as we have seen, a nonmysterious God would not be the God of Judeo-Christianity, But has language gone on a holiday? We certainly, given our religious conditioning, have a *feeling* that we understand what we are saying here. But do we? Perhaps, as Axel Hägerström thought, "contingent thing," "finite thing," and "finite reality" are pleonastic. For anything at all that exists, we seem to be able to ask, without being linguistically or conceptually deviant, why it exists. "The world" or "the cosmos" does not stand for an entity or a *class* of things, but is an umbrella term for all those things and their structural relations that religious people call "finite things" and many others just call "things." What are we talking about when we say there is something infinite and utterly different from these "finite realities" and that this "utterly other reality" is neither physical nor temporal, neither purely conceptual nor simply imaginary, but, while being unique and radically distinct from all these things, continuously sustains all these "finite things" and is a mysterious something upon which they are utterly dependent? Surely this is very odd talk and "sustains" and "dependent" have no unproblematical use in this context.

These difficulties and a host of difficulties like them make it doubtful whether the discourse used to spell out the reference range of "God" is sufficiently intelligible to make such God-talk coherent. An agnostic of the contemporary sort is a man who suspends judgment, oscillating between rejecting God-talk as an irrational form of discourse containing at crucial junctures incoherent or rationally unjustifiable putative truth-claims and accepting this discourse as something which, obscure as it is, makes a sufficiently intelligible and humanly important reference to be worthy of belief.

One reading of the situation is that the network of fundamental concepts constitutive of nonanthropomorphic God-talk in Judeo-Christianity is so problematical that the most reasonable thing to do is to opt for atheism, particularly when we realize that we do not need these religions or any religion to make sense of our lives or to buttress morality. But agnosticism, particularly of the contemporary kind specified here, need not be an evasion and perhaps is the most reasonable alternative for the individual who wishes, concerning an appraisal of competing world views and ways of life, to operate on a principle of maximum caution.

BIBLIOGRAPHY

Two extensive discussions are in Robert Flint, *Agnosticism* (London, 1903); and in R. A. Armstrong, *Agnosticism and Theism in the Nineteenth Century* (London, 1905). See also James Ward, *Naturalism and Agnosticism* (London, 1899). The central works from Hume and Kant relevant here are David Hume, *Enquiry concerning Human Understanding* (1748), and *Dialogues concerning*

Natural Religion (London, 1779): Immanuel Kant, *Kritik der reinen Vernunft (1781), and Die Religion innerhalb der Grenzen der blossen Vernunft* (1793). For the paradigmatic nineteenth-century statements of agnosticism see T. H. Huxley, *Collected Essays*, 9 vols. (London, 1894), Vol. V; and Leslie Stephen, *An Agnostic's Apology and Other Essays* (London, 1893), and *English Thought in the Eighteenth Century* (London, 1876).

The following works are central to the nineteenth-century debate over agnosticism: Sir William Hamilton, "Philosophy of the Unconditioned," *The Edinburgh Review* (1829); H. L. Mansel, *The Limits of Religious Thought* (London, 1858); J. S. Mill, *Three Essays on Religion* (London, 1874); and Herbert Spencer, *First Principles* (London, 1862). Noel Annan, *Leslie Stephen* (London, 1952); William Irvine, *Thomas Henry Huxley* (London, 1960); John Holloway, *The Victorian Sage* (New York, 1953); Basil Willey;, *Nineteenth Century Studies* (London, 1950); and J. A. Passmore, *A Hundred Years of Philosophy* (London, 1957), provide basic secondary sources. For material carrying over to the twentieth-century debate see R. Garrigou-Lagrange, *Die, son existence et sa nature; solution thomiste des antinomies agnostiques* (Paris, 1915); and J. M. Cameron, *The Night Battle* (London, 1962). For some contemporary defenses of agnosticism see Ronald W. Hepburn, *Christianity and Paradox* (New York, 1966); Bertrand Russell, *Why I am Not a Christian* (London, 1957); H. J. Blackman, ed., *Objections To Humanism* (London, 1963); *Religion and Humanism*, no editor, various authors—Ronald Hepburn, David Jenkins, Howard Root, Renford Bambrough, Ninian Smart (London, 1964); William James, *The Will to Believe and Other Essays* (New York, 1897), attacked agnosticism.

The following books by contemporary philosophers or analytically oriented philosophical theologians make arguments relevant to our discussion. A. J. Ayer, *Language, Truth and Logic* (London, 1935); Axel Hägerström, *Philosophy and Religion*, trans. Robert T. Sandin (London, 1964); John Hick, *Faith and Knowledge*, 2nd ed. (Ithaca, 1966); R. B. Braithwaite, *An Empiricist's View of the Nature of Religious Belief* (Cambridge, 1955); Diogenes Allen, *The Reasonableness of Faith* (Washington and Cleveland, 1968); Ninian Smart, *The Teacher and Christian Belief* (London, 1966); idem, *Philosophers and Religious Truth* (London, 1964); idem, *Theology, Philosophy and Natural Sciences* (Birmingham, England, 1962). Alasdair MacIntyre, *Secularization and Moral Change* (London, 1967); idem and Paul Ricoeur, *The Religious Significance of Atheism* (New York, 1969): H. H. Price, *Belief* (London, 1969); L. Susan Stebbing, "Critical Notice, *Language, Truth and Logic*," *Mind*, new series, 45 (1936); Kai Nielsen, "In Defense of Atheism," in *Perspectives in Education, Religion and the Arts*, eds. Howard Kiefer and Milton Munitz (New York, 1970); Paul Holmer, "Atheism and Theism," *Lutheran World*, 13 (1966); Alvin Plantinga, *God and Other Minds* (Ithaca, 1967); George Mavrodes, *Belief in God* (New York, 1970).

Some good critical and historical commentary on Hume occurs in Bernard Williams, "Hume on Religion," in *David Hume: A Symposium*, ed. D. F. Pears (London, 1963); in the essays by James Noxon, William H. Capitan, and George J. Nathan, reprinted in V. C. Chapell, ed., *Hume: A Collection of Critical Essays* (New York, 1966); and in Norman Kemp Smith's masterful *and indispensable introduction to Hume's Dialogues. See David Hume, Dialogues Concerning Natural Religion,* ed. and introduction by Norman Kemp Smith (Edinburgh, 1947). For Kant see W. H. Walsh, "Kant's Moral Theology," *"Proceedings of the British Academy,* 49 (1963).

5

In Defense of Atheism

I

Jews, Christians, and Moslems do not and cannot take their religion to be simply their fundamental conceptual framework or metaphysical system. Fundamental human commitments and attitudes are an essential part of being religious. The feeling of gratitude for one's very existence no matter what the quality or condition of that existence is at the very heart of religion. To be religious consists fundamentally in living in a certain way, in holding a certain set of convictions, in the having of certain attitudes, and in being a member of a distinctive confessional group.

Religious discourse reflects this. Religious utterances express our basic sense of security in life and our gratitude for being alive. Jews, Christians, and Moslems pray, and engage in rituals and ceremonies in the doing of which they use language in a distinctive way. In religious discourse, we give voice to our deepest and most pervasive hopes, ideals, and wishes concerning what we should try to be and what expectations we may entertain. If we really are religious and do not regard religion simply as "moral poetry" but use religious discourse seriously to make distinctively religious claims, we commit ourselves to what we as believers take to be a certain general view about "the ultimate basis of the universe." This is exhibited in the very use of certain religious utterances.

(1) God is my Creator to whom everything is owed.

Reprinted from *Perspectives in Education, Religion, and the Arts,* edited by Howard E. Kiefer and Milton K. Munitz, pp. 127-156, by permission of the State University of New York Press.

and

(2) God is the God of mercy of Whose forgiveness I stand in need.

are paradigms of the above mentioned use of religious discourse; they presumably are fact-stating uses of discourse, though this is not all they are, and they are closely linked with other uses of religious discourse. Such ceremonial and evocative talk as we find in Christianity could hardly exist if it were not for such uses of language as exhibited in (1) and (2). (1) and (2) are not theologians' talk about God but are sample bits of living religious discourse. Yet for believer and nonbeliever alike they are perplexing bits of discourse.

Wittgenstein and others have taught the importance of context. We must not examine religious utterances—especially those which appear to have a statement-making function—in isolation, but we should examine them on location as part of that complex activity we call "religion." To understand a religious utterance properly we must come to understand the topic or topics of our discourse and the purposes for which it is used.

Indeed, in using language we must not forget what Strawson has called the Principle of the Presumption of Knowledge or the Principle of Relevance. Of all speech functions to which this applies, it applies most appositely to the making of statements, which is indeed a central speech function if anything is. That is to say, when "an empirically assertive utterance is made with an informative intention" there is the standing presumption on the part of the speaker that "those who hear him have knowledge of empirical facts relevant to the particular point to be imparted in the utterance."[1] Moreover, statements have topics, they are in that sense about something, and reflect what Strawson calls a "centre of interest." To understand a statement we must understand the topic or center of interest involved in its assertion. We must not forget that we do not characteristically give out information or give voice to utterances in an isolated, unconnected manner; but only as part of some connected discourses. We need a Principle of Relevance to pick out, in terms of the topic in question, the proper kind of answer to what a statement is about. This is integral to our understanding of how to take (understand) the statement in question.

Take the classic example "The King of France is bald." We need a context, an application of the Principles of Relevance and the Presumption of Knowledge, to know how to take it. If our context is the present, and the relevant questions are "What is the King of France like?" or "Is he bald?" then neither "The King of France is bald" nor "The King of France is not bald" would be a correct answer, for the above questions in the above context are not to be answered, but are

are to be replied to by being rejected. The proper reply—a reply which rejects such questions—is: (De Gaulle notwithstanding) "There is no King of France." But if our topic is historical and, with some specific period in mind, we are asking, "What bald notables are there?"; "The King of France is bald" in such a changed context is an appropriate answer. And here it is a true or false statement.

"God," like "the King of France," is what Strawson calls a referring expression, though this shouldn't be taken to imply that it is *simply* a referring expression. In asserting that they are referring expressions, I am giving you to understand that presumably both expressions make identifying reference. Referring expressions may be names, pronouns, definite descriptions or demonstrative descriptions. In using referring expressions in identifying descriptions to make identifying references, e.g., "The Point Judith Ferry is White" or "Block Island is windy," we do not, Strawson points out, inform the audience of the *existence* of what our referring expressions refer to. Rather the very task of identifying reference can be undertaken "only by a speaker who knows or presumes his audience to be already in possession of such knowledge of existence. . . ."[2]

Similarly, when a religious man utters (1) or (2)—our paradigm religious utterances quoted above—there is the presumption that the speaker understands "God" and knows or believes in the reality of what is being talked about. The acceptance of the truth of (1) and (2) is partially definitive of what it is to be a Jew or Christian. In asserting (1) and (2), the religious man *presupposes* that there is a God and that this God has a certain character. The atheist, on the other hand, does not believe that (1) and (2) are true because he does not accept the presupposition on which they are made, namely that there is a God. He either does not accept such a proposition because he believes it to be false or because he believes the concept of God to be an incoherent concept. If he believes that the concept of God is incoherent, then he must also believe that the supposition on which (1) and (2) are based could not possibly be true. The agnostic, in turn, does not accept the presupposition on which (1) and (2) are built because he feels that he does not have sufficient grounds for accepting it even on faith, and yet he is not convinced that we have sufficiently good grounds to be justified in dismissing it as false or utterly incoherent.

As I remarked initially, Judaism, Christianity, and Islam are not by any means constituted by the making and accepting of certain statements. Rather the making of religious statements like (1) and (2) are the cornerstones on which all the other types of religious utterances in such religions depend; and they in return presuppose that the statement "There is a God" is true, and that in turn presupposes that "There is a God" is a genuine statement and that the concept of God

118 Atheism & Philosophy

is a viable concept. The most crucial question we can ask about Judaism, Christianity, and Islam is whether these religious presuppositions are justified.

It might be felt that I have already too much ignored context. In live religious discourse, it is sometimes maintained, questions about the existence of God or the coherence of the concept of God do not arise. It is only by ignoring the context of religious talk that I can even make them seem like real questions.

There are multiple confusions involved in this objection. First, believers characteristically have doubts; even the man in "the circle of faith" is threatened with disbelief. Tormenting religious doubts arise in the religious life itself and they are often engendered by some first-order uses of God-talk. "All my life I have lived under an illusion. There is no Divine Reality at all" is first-order God-talk and not talk about talk, e.g., "The word 'God' only has emotive meaning." The above first-order religious utterance has a natural context and topic for a religious man locked in a religious crisis. Most atheists and agnostics were once believers—in our traditions they were once Jews, Christians or Moslems—and they have a participant's understanding of these forms of life. Many of them, like Hägerström, Joyce or Sartre, have been caught up and immersed in such forms of life. They are not like anthropologists who in trying to gain an understanding that approximates a participant's understanding are trying to grasp how the discourses hang together. Moreover—to zero in on the critical objection about context—people who have a participant's grasp of the form of life in which (1) and (2) are embedded know how to use them and can readily, for certain purposes, prescind in reflecting about them from the context in which they are at home; for they know in what sort of linguistic environment they belong and to what sort of topics, centers of interest, they are directed. Reflecting about them in their religious context, we say that they presuppose the intelligibility and truth of "There is a God." Context or not, it is this traditional and central question that we need to face in asking fundamental questions about the Judeo-Christian tradition, though if we do not understand the environment in which the utterances which presuppose it are at home, we will not understand what is involved in such a question.

II

In pursuing this question let us start quite simply but centrally by asking: Why should anyone be an agnostic or an atheist? Why should this question about God be such a biting one? Formerly skeptical philosophers could not bring themselves to accept religious beliefs because they felt the proofs all failed, the problem of evil was intractable and the evidence offered for believing in the existence of God was inadequate. But contemporary philosophical disbelief cuts deeper and poses more fundamental problems, problems which challenge even the fideist who, *à la* Kierkegaard, would claim that the last thing a genuine knight of faith would want or should have is a proof of God's existence.[3] Ronald Hepburn succinctly states the sort of considerations that are involved in that "deeper ground":

> Where one gives an account of an expression in our language, and where that expression is one that refers to an existent of some kind, one needs to provide not only a set of rules for the use of the expression, but also an indication of how the referring is to be done—through direct pointing, perhaps, or through giving instructions for an indirect method of identifying the entity. Can this be done in the case of God? Pointing, clearly, is inappropriate, God being no finite object in the world. The theologian may suggest a number of options at this point. He may say: God can be identified as that being upon whom the world can be felt as utterly dependent, who is the completion of its incompletenesses, whose presence is faintly adumbrated in experience of the awesome and the numinous. Clear direction-giving has here broken down; the theologian may well admit that his language is less descriptive or argumentative than obliquely evocative. Does this language succeed in establishing that statements about God have a reference? To persons susceptible to religious experience but at the same time logically and critically alert, it may seem just barely to succeed, or it may seem just barely to fail. Some may even oscillate uneasily between these alternatives without finding a definite procedure of decision to help them discriminate once for all.[4]

An agnostic, abreast of contemporary philosophical developments, will indeed oscillate in this fashion. "God" is a referring expression whose referent obviously cannot be indicated by ostension. The agnostic clearly recognizes this and he also recognizes the need to exhibit an adequate nonanthropomorphic extralinguistic referent for "God." In essence his doubt comes to this: is the concept of God sufficiently coherent to make belief possible for a reasonable, nonevasive man? He knows that philosophically sophisticated, reflective Jews and Christians do not deny that the concept of God is a difficult, elusive, paradoxical concept. They stress that it could not be otherwise, but believe that it is not so elusive, not so ill-conceived, as to fail to make an intelligible and yet a religiously appropriate reference. In talking about God, a believer is committed to the belief that we are talking about a mystery, but while God, by common reflective consent, is indeed in large measure incomprehensible, the concept of God is not so utterly incoherent as to vitiate religious belief. This is the minimal commitment of a religious man; he may share much with the agnostic but this much he does believe; he *must* take his stand here.

I shall argue that both the agnostic and the believer are mistaken. Careful reflection on the use of "God" in the stream of Jewish and Christian life is enough to justify an atheism which asserts that the concept of God is so incoherent that there could not possibly be a referent for the word "God." I take it here that we are speaking of Jews and Christians who have advanced beyond anthropomorphism; Jews and Christians, who as MacQuarrie puts it, have revolted decisively "against the idea that the divine can be objectified, so as to manifest itself in sensible phenomena."[5] The Jew, Christian or Moslem who remains an anthropomorphite simply has false, superstitious beliefs. But I am concerned here with the Jew, Christian or Moslem who, consciously at least, is beyond anthropomorphism. I am maintaining against him that his belief in God is so incoherent that it could not possibly be true. If this controversial philosophical thesis is correct, it would have quite concrete normative consequences, for if it is correct, the rational thing to do is to reject belief in the God of the Jews, Christians, and Moslems.

III

In arguing that the concept of God is incoherent, I am not claiming that "God" is utterly meaningless. Surely "God" has a use in the language; there are deviant and nondeviant bits of God-talk. If I say "God is a ride in a yellow submarine" or "God brews good coffee" or even "God dieted," I have not said something that is false; I have not even succeeded in saying something blasphemous; I have rather indicated, if I make such utterances with a serious intent, that I do not understand God-talk. In saying something such as "God is a ride in a yellow submarine" I have said something closer to "Quite grounds calculated carefully" or "Elope sea with trigonometry." In short, my utterances are without a literal meaning. "God is a ride in a yellow submarine" could indeed be a metaphor. In the context of a poem or song, it might be given a meaning, but taken just like that it does not have a meaning. But even out of context—say in the middle of a commencement address—"Pass me a peanut butter sandwich" would be perfectly meaningful, would have a literal meaning, though the point, if any, of uttering it would remain obscure. However, "God brews good coffee," like "Elope sea with trigonometry," are immediately recognized as not even being absurdly false like "Humphrey walked on water" but as being without any literal meaning. "God is a ride in a yellow submarine" or "God brews coffee" is immediately and unequivocally recognized as deviant by people with a participant's grasp of God-talk, while other bits of God-talk are immediately recognized to be nondeviant and do in fact have a use in the language, e.g., "Oh God be my Sword and my strength" or "God so loved mankind that he gave to the world his only son." Even agnostics and atheists who understand how to use Jewish and Christian religious talk do not balk at such nondeviant utterances. If they are reading a religious novel or sermon, they keep right on going and do not balk at these nondeviant sentences, e.g., "God protect me in my need," as they would at "God lost weight last week." Philosophically perplexed as they are about nondeviant God-talk, they do not balk at it, while they do in a quite ordinary way balk at "Procrastination drinks grief" or "God makes good coffee." There are absurdities and absurdities. Thus it is plainly a mistake to say that God-talk is meaningless.

However, in saying that the concept of God is incoherent, I am saying that where "God" is used nonanthropomorphically, as it is in at least officially developed Jewish and Christian God-talk, there occur sentences such as (1) and (2) which purportedly have a statement-making function, yet no identifiable state of affairs can be characterized which would make such putative religious statements true and no intelligible directions have been given for identifying the supposed referent for the word "God." Religious believers speak of religious truth but "religious truth" is a Homeless Watson.

God, as Hepburn points out, cannot be pointed to but must be identified intralinguistically through certain descriptions, if He can be identified at all. But the putative descriptions Hepburn mentions will not do. If in trying to identify God we speak of "that being upon whom the world can be felt to be utterly dependent," nothing has been accomplished, for what does it *mean* to speak of "the world (the universe) as being utterly dependent" or even dependent at all? (And if we do not understand this, we do not know what it would be like to *feel* that the world is utterly dependent.) If we are puzzled by "God," we will be equally puzzled by such phrases. We know what it means to say a child, an adult, a nation, a species, a lake is dependent on something. We could even give sense to the earth's being dependent on something, but no sense has been given to the universe's being dependent on anything. What are the sufficient conditions for the universe being dependent? What would make it true or false or what would even count for the truth or falsity of the putative statement "The universe is dependent" or "The universe is not dependent"? To answer by speaking of "God," e.g., the universe is dependent because God is its final cause, is to pull oneself up by one's own bootstraps, for talk of the dependency of the universe was appealed to in the first place in order to enable us to identify the alleged referent of "God." And to speak of a *logically* necessary being upon whom the universe depends is to appeal to a self-contradictory conception, for only propositions or statements, not beings, can either be *logically* necessary or fail to be logically necessary. Yet to speak of a "factually necessary being" upon whom the universe depends is again to pull oneself up by one's own bootstraps; for what would count toward establishing the truth or falsity of a statement asserting or denying the existence of such an alleged reality? Nothing has been specified and no directions have been given for identifying "a self-existent being" or "a self-caused being" or "a necessary being" or "a totally independent being." All these expressions purport to be referring expressions, but no rules (implicit or explicit) or regulations have been discovered for identifying their putative referents. With them we are in at least as much trouble as we are with "God," and unlike "God," they do not even have an established use in the language. It is indeed true that Jews and Christians do not think of God as something or someone who might or might not exist. If God exists, He somehow exists necessarily. But given the self-contradictoriness of the concept of a logically necessary being or existent, it cannot be true that there can be anything which must exist simply because its existence is logically possible. Moreover, no sense has been given to the claim that there is something—some given reality—which categorically must exist.

It may well be that when believers use "God" in sentences like (1) and (2) they *feel à la* Otto as if they were in the presence of a reality which is awesome and numinous—an "ultimate reality" whose presence is but faintly adumbrated in experience. Yet if this numinosity is taken to be the God of the developed Judeo-Christian tradition, it is taken to be "transcendent to the world." But, while "transcendent to the world" is at best an obscure phrase, it should still be evident that "a transcendent X" could not be "an X whose presence was given in experience." Something given in experience would *eo ipso* be nontranscendent, for it would automatically be part of the spatio-temporal world. Believers, who in defending the coherence of this belief appeal to their experience of God, are pinned by a Morton's fork: on the one hand, it is not logically possible to encounter a "reality transcendent to the world" and, on the other, if our numinosity is not thought to be transcendent, we are no longer talking of the God of developed Judeo-Christianity.[6]

IV

The central beliefs of Judaism, Christianity, and Islam are indeed metaphysical beliefs since their scope purports to transcend the empirical world. If we are to come to grips with Judaism or Christianity there is no avoiding what Hägerström labelled "metaphysical religiosity." Such a metaphysical religiosity remains in even a minimal characterization of the common core of Judaism, Christianity, and Islam, for they all affirm the reality of one and only one God who is said to have created the universe out of nothing, and man, regarded as a sinful, creaturely being, is taken to be utterly dependent on this creator in whose purpose man is said to discover his own reason for living. To be a Jew, Christian or Moslem is to believe much more than that but it is to believe that, and it is here that we find, so to say, the basic propositions of faith upon which the whole edifice of western religiosity stands or falls. If in these religions there is to be religious truth, the statements expressing these core religious beliefs must be true, but, it should be objected, their meaning is so indeterminate, so problematical, that it is doubtful whether we have in them anything sufficiently coherent to constitute true or false statements.

To understand what it is to speak of the reality of God essentially involves understanding the phrase "creator of the universe out of nothing." Theologians characteristically do not mean by this that the universe was created at a moment in time. To speak of such a creator is to speak not of an *efficient* cause but of a *final* cause of the universe. It involves making the putative existential claim that there is an eternal, ever present creative source and sustainer of the universe. But do we really understand such talk? We understand what it is for a lake to be a source of a river, for oxygen to be necessary to sustain life, for the winning of the game to be the end for which it is played and for good health to be the reason why we exercise. But "the universe" is not a label for some gigantic thing or process or activity. It is not a name for a determinate reality whose existence can be sustained or not sustained. Moreover, what would we have to discern or fail to discern to discover or to "see" even darkly the end, the purpose or the meaning of the universe? A asserts the universe has a source or a sustainer and B denies it, but no conceivable recognizable turn of events counts for or against either of their claims; we have no idea what would have to obtain for either A's or B's claim to be so or even probably so. Yet both believe they are making assertions which are true or false. Plainly, language has gone on a holiday. We have bits of discourse which purport to be fact-stating but in reality they fail to come off as factual statements; that is to say, they do not function as fact-stating utterances. They purport to be fact-stating but they are not. But with a failure to make sense here, much more talk essential to the Judeo-Christian picture becomes plainly incoherent. Consider such key bits of God-talk as:

(3) God is wholly other than the world He made.
(4) God is the creator of the moral order of the universe.
(5) The universe is absolutely dependent on God.

In reflecting on them, we should not forget that "the world" (the "universe") does not denote a thing, an entity, process or even an aggregate which might be made or brought into existence. Moreover there is the ancient point that "to make something" presupposes that there already is something out of which it is made. If it is replied that I am forgetting my previous remark that God is taken to be the *final* cause and not the efficient cause of the universe and that "make" here means "sustain" or "order," then it should be noted that this still presupposes something to be sustained or ordered; there is no use for "ordering or sustaining out of nothing." Even if we try to give it a use by saying that the universe was chaotic until ordered by God or that unless the universe is a reality ordered by God the universe would be chaotic, we are still lost, for both "the universe is chaotic" and "the universe is not chaotic" are without a coherent use. Since the universe is not an entity or even a totality, there is no sense in talking of its being ordered or not ordered and thus, while we might speak coherently of "the moral order of his life" or "the morality of a culture or ethos," there is no coherent use for "the moral order of the universe," so (4) as well as (3) is nugatory. And again, considering (5), we have seen that no sense has been given to "the universe is dependent" so (5), to put it conservatively, is also conceptually unhappy, i.e., it purports to make a factual statement but we have no idea of what, if anything, could count for or against its truth or falsity.

Some theologians with an antimetaphysical bias would try to avoid treating (3), (4) or (5) as part of the corpus of Judaism or Christianity. If my argument has been correct, this is indeed an inadequate and evasive defense against skeptical criticism, but allowing it for the sake of the discussion and returning to (1) and (2), which are surely part of that corpus, with respect to those utterances, we still have overwhelming conceptual difficulties. Consider (2) "God is the God of mercy of Whose forgiveness I stand in need." This statement entails the further statement that God does or can do something, that God acts or can act in a certain way, for it is utterly senseless to speak of being merciful if one could not even in principle act, do or fail to do merciful acts. To recognize and accept this is not to be committed to reductionism or materialism. One might even argue, as Strawson does, that the concept of a person is a primitive notion not fully analyzable in behavioristic terms, but it does not follow from this that there can be "bodiless action," that we can understand what it would be like for a person to do something without making at least a tacit reference to his body, to a living, moving being with a spatio-temporal location. But God in developed Judeo-Christianity is supposed to be conceptualized as Pure Spirit. At the very least, He cannot be taken to be a reality with a body or as something with a spatio-temporal location. God is not a being existing in space. Some theologians have even wanted to deny that God is *a* being at all. Rather He is Being, but Being or a being, it is certainly evident that God is not conceptualized as a being existing in space. As the above arguments make clear, only something with a body could act, could do something, and thus trivially could act mercifully or fail to act mercifully. But if it is *logically* impossible for X to act or fail to act mercifully then it is also logically impossible for X to be merciful or fail to be merciful. Thus (2), a key bit of God-talk, is also seen to be an incoherent utterance.

To arguments of this sort it has been replied:

> Theists . . . are not people who misconceive action in applying it to God; they are simply people who employ this concept of action or agency in contexts where the nontheistic, or nonreligious do not. Which is to say no more than that they believe in God, while others do not. It is certainly not to say that their employment of the concept must be nonsensical.[7]

What is the argument for this? It is pointed out (1) that the language of action is logically distinct from that of bodily movement and that agency is logically distinct from spatio-temporal causation, (2) that there is no sharp distinction between the agent's body and the rest of his physical situation, and (3) that God is an agent without being a person.[8] I think all three of these claims are quite questionable to say the least. But even if we accept them, the argument can still be seen to be defective.

Consider how the argument runs: no matter how detailed our account of bodily movement, alternative descriptions of what an agent did would still always be possible. If my fist bangs against Jones's jaw in the water, this is quite compatible with any of the following three action descriptions (descriptions which in turn are arbitrarily selected from an indefinitely large number of apposite action descriptions of that bodily motion): I was trying to save his life, I was paying him back for an injury, I was trying to kill him. The conclusion which is drawn is that "an account of what is going on in terms of bodily movement, i.e., of spatio-temporal events causally connected, never tells us what the agent is doing."[9] But the acceptance of this argument does nothing at all to show that someone could possibly do anything without making bodily movements or without having a body. But this is what must be shown. A similar thing holds for both the claim that causal talk is not applicable to the language of agency and for the claim that no sharp distinction can be made between the agent and his physical environment. These claims might be accepted and it would still do nothing at all to show that it makes sense to say "action A occurred but nobody or nothing did it." To say "That was a merciful action," implies that some agent acted, but even though agency is hard to isolate from the rest of its physical situation and even if we cannot properly speak of the cause of an action, still typically an agent is a person and there can be no identifying a person and hence an agent except by reference to their bodies. A necessary condition for understanding the concept of action is the understanding of bodily movement.

However, in trying to resist such a conclusion it has been argued that God is not a person. We indeed, so the argument runs, cannot conceive of a person without a body, but we can, though characteristically we do not, think of agency without some idea of a bodily movement being involved. God, we are told, is to be thought of as an agent without a body; this "bodiless agent" acts without a body; he does merciful things without a body.[10]

I would counter that even when using a term such as "chemical agent"—where we refer to an active force or substance producing an effect—there is still a physically specifiable something which reacts in a determinate physically specifiable way. We have no idea of what it would be like for something to be done, for something to *do* something, for an action to occur, without there being a body in motion. In this connection we need to consider again "God is the God of mercy" ("God is love" would work as well); this means He (it) is conceived of as doing something or being able to do something, but we can only understand the doing of something if there is something identifiable which is said to do it. Moreover, X is only identifiable as an agent, and thus X can only be intelligibly said to be an agent if X has a body. For agency to be logically possible, we must have a discrete something specifiable in spatio-temporal terms. But the transcendent God of Judaism and Christianity is thought to be a wholly independent reality, wholly other than the world which is utterly dependent on this "ultimate reality" and is said to be ultimately unintelligible without reference to this nonphysical *mysterium tremendum et fascinans*. But then it is senseless to speak, as Jews and Christians do, of God as the God of mercy of Whose forgiveness man stands in need. Yet if this is so, it would appear to be the case that Judaism, Christianity, and Islam are incoherent *Weltanschauungen*.

V

A standard ploy at this moment in the dialectic is to maintain that utterances like "God is all merciful," "God is the Creator of the heavens and the earth" or "God loves all His creation," are symbolic or metaphorical utterances which manifest the Ultimate or Unconditioned Transcendent but are themselves not literal statements which could be true or false. They hint at an ineffable metaphysical ultimate which is, as Tillich put it, "unconditionally beyond the conceptual sphere.[11] The only thing nonsymbolic we can say about God is:

  (6) God is being-itself, the ineffable ultimate.
  (7) God is the Unconditioned Transcendent on which everything else is dependent.

On the remarkable assumption that such verbosities are helpful explications, some theologians, addicted to this obscure manner of speaking, have gone on to make remarks like (8) or (9).

  (8) Being-itself is not another being but the *transcendens* or *the comprehensive,* the incomparable and wholly other source and unity of all beings.
  (9) God is not a being, but Being-itself that wider Being within which all particular beings have their being.

Here "Being"—as well as "Being-itself" in (6)—purportedly functions as a name or some other referring expression; that is to say, as a word which supposedly denotes or stands for something. But to do this, that is, to function descriptively or designatively, "being" and "being-itself" must have an intelligible opposite. But in the above sentences it has no intelligible opposite. When we use "being," "being-itself," or "being-as-such," in sentences like (6) through (9) we are trying to catch the cognitive import of "God." We are trying to say that there is a realm of being as such over and above the being of individual objects. (The sense of "over and above" remains problematic. It is not a spatial sense, of course, but in what way it is "over and above" remains utterly mysterious.)

Such being is said to be neither a genus nor a property. But then we can scarcely avoid severe philosophical perplexity concerning its character and how, if at all, being is to be identified. To discover this, we would have to discover what it is not; we would have to discover its intelligible opposite; yet the opposite of "being" is "nothing." But "nothing," in ordinary discourse, does not function as a name or some other referring expression and if we try to regiment discourse and make "nothing" function as a referring expression then we are led to the absurdities that Lewis Carroll satirized in *Through the Looking Glass* when the Red King thought that if Nobody passed the messenger on the road then Nobody would have arrived first. To try to treat "nothing" as a name or referring expression is to get involved in the absurdity of asking what kind of a something, what kind of a being or what kind of being is nothing. It involves the incoherent reifying of nothing into a kind of opposed power to being and, at the same time, spoiling its supposed contrast with "being" by treating "nothing" as the name of a mysterious something, which makes it either identical with Being-itself or a being which has its being in Being. In either case we have an absurdity. But unless "Nothing" is treated as a referring expression, "Being," where we try to construe it as a referring expression, has no intelligible opposite and without an intelligible opposite "Being" lacks descriptive or designative significance and thus it is not, after all, as the Being-talk-man requires, a referring question. Superficially it appears to have that role but actually has no such use in the language. For (6), (8) or (9) to come off as intelligible factual assertions, "being" and "being-itself" must be genuine referring expressions with intelligible opposites. Unfortunately, for the theologian committed to such an approach, these expressions do not so function, and thus our sample sentences are not sentences with which we can make factual statements.

Basically the same difficulties apply to the terms in the above sentences which presumably are taken to be elucidations of "being-itself" or "being-as-such" by people who like to talk in this obscure and, I suspect, obscurantist manner. Consider such phrases as "ineffable ultimate," "Unconditioned Transcendent," "transcendens," or "the Comprehensive." They are not ordinary language expressions with fixed uses; that is, in order to try to understand them we must be given some coherent directions concerning their use. But we are hardly given any directions here. Presumably they are putative referring expressions, but how even in principle could we identify their referents? A says "There really is the Comprehensive" and B replies "It's a myth, there is no such reality." C wonders whether there really is an Unconditioned Transcendent, the transcendens or an ineffable ultimate and D reassures him that actually there are no such realities. Actually those who are hip on Being-talk never take such a matter-of-fact tone, but even if they did, it is evident that there is not only no way at all of deciding who is right, where such matter-of-fact-sounding questions are raised, but there is also no way of deciding which putative factual claim is the more probable. Nothing that we could experience now or hereafter, even assuming the intelligibility of "hereafter," helps us out vis-à-vis such "questions." But what then are we talking about if we try to question, affirm or deny that there really is an Unconditioned Transcendent? If, as it certainly seems to be, it is impossible to give an answer, then "being-talk" is only a less familiar and less evocative species of incoherence than God-talk.

At this point we are likely to hear talk about ineffability. To be so analytic, it will be contended, is appropriate to an examination of scientific discourse, but it is not appropriate to religious discourse. Such an analytic approach, it will be proclaimed in certain circles, ignores the existential dimension of man. Suffering from cultural lag, such an analytic approach, still too much in the temper of positivism, fails to take to heart man's existential encounter with Being, when the dread of non-being gives him a sense, scarcely characterizable in words, of his "total existence." Being-talk may indeed be so paradoxical as to be scarcely intelligible, but such concrete human experiences do lead to a confrontation with Being. And being-itself is indeed the Ineffable: that which is beyond all conceptualization. In our despair and estrangement we are led to an ineffable but supremely Holy something which can be experienced in a compelling manner but it can never be more than obliquely and metaphorically hinted at in words, symbols, and images. To gain insight here, we need to transcend our pedestrian literalness and acknowledge that there are some things which are literally unsayable or inexpressible but are nonetheless given in those experiences of depth where human beings must confront their own existence.

What is involved here is the claim that there are "ineffable truths" which cannot be put into words; religious truths—so the argument runs—are species of that genus. People with the proper experience and attitudes understand them; that is, they in a sense understand the concept of God, but what they know to be true cannot in any way be literally expressed. Our samples of being-talk haltingly and falteringly suggest these truths; they can awake in us the experience of such "ineffable truths" but they do not make true or false statements themselves. Instead they function evocatively to give rise to such experiences or expressively to suggest what cannot be literally stated. Given the proper experience, the reality they obliquely attest to will, while remaining irreducibly mysterious, be humanely speaking undeniable.

Such doctrines of the Ineffable are incoherent and will not enable us to meet or resolve religious quandaries legitimately. To hold such a doctrine is to be committed to the thesis that, though there may be something appropriately called "God," "Being-itself" or "the Unconditioned Transcendent," in reality nothing literal, or at least nothing affirmative, can be said about God. That is to say, no sentences about God or sentences in which "God" occurs literally express a fact or make a true or false assertion. Thus, on such a reading of God-talk, "The world is dependent on God" or any other God-sentence cannot literally make a true or false statement, assert something that is so or is not so, though such sentences are not without sense for they have a metaphorical or symbolic use. But if an utterance P is metaphorical, this entails that it is *logically* possible for there to be some literal statement G which has the same conceptual content. "Metaphorical," or for that matter "symbolic" or "analogical," gets its meaning by being contrastable with "literal." There can be no intelligible metaphorical or symbolic or analogical God-talk if there can be no literal God-talk. Thus the ineffability thesis is internally incoherent.

However, it might be replied that the above argument does not touch the most fundamental core of the ineffability thesis, namely, that the man of faith can know what he means by "God" though he cannot, literally or even obliquely, say what he means and what he means cannot in any way be expressed, even if it is given in an ecstatic encounter or confrontation with Being or an Unconditioned Transcendent. The latter part of this is nonsense, for, as I have already pointed out, a reality transcendent to the universe could not be encountered or confronted; only some being in the world could, logically could, be encountered or confronted.

We are however, still on slightly peripheral ground, for the major claim in the ineffability thesis is that one can know what P means even though P cannot even in principle be expressed or publicly exhibited. One can know that there is a God though the concept of God is inexpressible and our talk of God is nonsensical.

What makes this maneuver seem more plausible than it actually is, is its easy confusion with the rather ordinary experience of knowing very well what something is (say a bird one sees) and yet being at that time quite unable to *say* what it is. One looks at the bird and recognizes it but one cannot remember its name. In this context we should also call to mind that we have a whole range of "Aha!-experiences." But the ineffability thesis under examination maintains something far more radical than would be encompassed by a theory which took into account, as it indeed should take into account, the above straightforwardly empirical phenomena. The ineffability thesis commits one to the belief that there are things one can know which are *in principle* impossible, that is, logically impossible, to express or to exhibit in any system of notation. In this way "a true religious statement" or "an expressed religious truth" would be self-contradictory.

It is tempting to take the short way with such a thesis and reject it on the following grounds: (1) If one knows P then P is true, since "I know it but it isn't true" is a contradiction. Thus, since only statements are literally true, there could be no inexpressible knowledge. (2) Reflection on "means" also establishes that there could be no such "ineffable understanding." For something to have a meaning or to have meaning, it must have a use in a language or in some system of notation. This partially specifies what it means for something to have a meaning or have meaning even when we speak of the meaning of a concept, for we use "concept" to signify what is expressed by synonymous expressions in the same or different languages or systems of notation. But only if something has meaning or has a meaning can we understand what it means, so we cannot understand something which is inexpressible *in principle;* there would be nothing to be understood, for there would be nothing that is meaningful.

However, some might think, mistakenly I believe, that some of these premises make unjustified and question-begging assumptions. Rather than extending my argument for them here or entering into complicated questions about so-called "private languages" and the like, I shall see if there are still simpler considerations that can probably be utilized to refute or render implausible the ineffability thesis. (Keep in mind that the job of challenging premises can always go on and on; the most we can hope for in philosophy is to give from the alternatives available the most plausible perspicacious representation of the conceptual area in question.)[12] First, take note of the platitude that if you know something that is literally in principle unsayable, inexpressible, incapable of being shown or in any way exhibited, then there trivially can be no communicating it. You cannot justifiably say it is *God* you experience, know, encounter, love or commit yourself to in utter trust; you, on your own thesis, cannot significantly say that if you do such and such and have such and such experiences, you will come to know God or come to be grasped by God. "What is unsayable is unsayable," is a significant tautology. Only if one could at least obliquely or metaphorically express one's experience of the Divine could one's God-talk have any significance, but on the present *radical* ineffability thesis even the possibility of obliquely expressing one's knowledge or belief is ruled out. So, given such a thesis, there could be no confessional community or circle of faith; in fine, the thesis is reduced to the absurd by making it impossible for those who accept such a thesis to acknowledge the manifest truth that the Judeo-Christian religion is a social reality. On this simple consideration alone, we should surely rule out the ineffability thesis. Thus Dom Illyd Trethowan is wide of the mark when he remarks: "Flew and Nielsen . . . are asking for a description of God. And the believer, again if he knows his business will reply . . . that God cannot be described. God is the Other.[13] If we try to take this claim of Trethowan's literally, then the word "God" is surely not just the vehicle for an incoherent concept, but "God" is *meaningless* for we cannot even say *that* something is if it is indescribable. What is indescribable is also unintelligible.

Three reminders here: (1) In asserting that nonanthropomorphic concepts of God are incoherent and according to some theological construals of "God" even meaningless, I am not merely giving you to understand that skeptics (atheists and agnostics) do not understand

God-talk. Rather, I have been contending that, the believer's beliefs
about his beliefs notwithstanding, the concept of God in developed
Judaism and Christianity is an incoherent one and neither believer
nor nonbeliever understands what they are talking about when they
talk about God or attempt to talk to God. I am not simply urging that
the believer make his beliefs meaningful to the skeptic, I am asking
that he show how God-talk is a coherent form of language, period.[14] (2)
I do not accept either the Wittgensteinian assumption that every form
of discourse is all right as it is and that the only thing that could be
out of order is the philosophical talk about the talk or the further and
related Wittgensteinian claim that philosophy can only relevantly display the forms of life and not relevantly criticize them or assess them.
Not only God-talk but also Witch-talk and talk of fairies have their
own distinctive uses and even within our culture once constituted a
discourse and were embedded in a form of life. But all the same such
forms of life were open to criticism and came gradually to be discredited as they were recognized to be incoherent. Indeed in *many
cases* first-order discourse and the beliefs embedded in them are beyond philosophical reproach and it is merely the characterization, the
second-order discourse, that is troublesome. Thus if someone tells you
that you never see tables or chairs and that you do not have a mind,
that is a bad joke, but if someone tells you that you do not have a soul,
you just think you do, it may very well engender a live dispute or a
live worry if you are a traditional Christian. Where God-talk is involved, both the first-order and the second-order discourse are problematical.[15] (3) The acceptance of even a thorough-going fideistic point
of view will not protect the believer from my critique. If we understood
what it *meant* to assert or deny "And God shall raise the quick and
the dead" or "God is the creator of the Heavens and the earth," we
might accept them humbly on faith. We might, out of our desperate
need to make sense of our lives, accept them *de fide.* But we can only
do that if we have some understanding of what they *mean.* If I ask
you to believe in *Irglig,* you cannot believe in *Irglig* no matter how
deep your need because you do not know *what* to take on faith (on
trust). Faith presupposes a *minimal understanding* of what you take
on faith, and if my arguments are correct, we do not have that understanding of a nonanthropomorphic concept of God.[16]

VI

It might be contended that I have so far ignored the major and most
obvious objection to my procedure. I am, it is natural to say, being a
philosophical Neanderthal, for my arguments rest too exclusively on

verificationist principles and by now it is well known that the verifiability principle is plainly untenable.[17]

I, of course, agree that it is certainly plainly evident that it is not true that a sentence is meaningful only if it is verifiable. In fact, I would go further and claim that such a claim is itself incoherent. It is sentences, not statements, which are meaningful or meaningless and it is statements, not sentences, which are confirmable or infirmable, true or false. Questions of meaning are logically prior to questions of verification; in order to verify or confirm a statement we must already know what it means. Moreover, many sentences which are plainly meaningful, e.g., "Pass the butter," "Oh, if this agony would only end," "Will the weather change?" do not even purport to make statements, let alone statements of fact which are confirmable or infirmable. It is by now crystal clear that the verifiability principle will never do as a *general* criterion of meaningful discourse.[18]

There are two points, however, that should be made here: (1) it is less evident that some form of the verifiability criterion is not correct as a criterion of *factual* significance and (2) that many of my key arguments do not even depend on or presuppose such a criterion of factual significance. The second point alone is enough to free me from the charge that I am entangled in a thoroughly discredited "logical empiricist metaphysics" but I would like, in what I fear is too brief and too brusk a manner, to defend my first point, for it may seem obscurantist.

Do we have, for the many and varied types of meaningful utterance, a criterion in virtue of which we can decide which of them are fact-stating? I maintain that we do, for a statement has factual content only if it is in principle testable or, to put it differently, for a sentence to function in a discourse as a factual assertion, it must make a statement which it is logically possible to confirm or infirm. If anything can give us "some insight into the ultimate nature of things"—to utter a tantalizing obscurity—it will be factually informative statements, i.e., statements which give us knowledge of what is-the case. To have insight into "the ultimate nature of things" would-be at least to have some reliable beliefs about what *in fact* the universe is like. That is, we would gain some information about some very fundamental facts. I do not say this is all we would need but we would at least have to have that. But *factually* informative utterances must, in principle, be verifiable. To put the point more exactly, a statement has factual significance only if it is at least logically possible to indicate the conditions or set of conditions under which it could be to some degree confirmed or infirmed, i.e., that it is logically possible to state evidence for or against its truth.[19]

Certainly my claim here is a controversial one—a claim that many analytic philosophers would reject on the grounds that it blurs too many distinctions and relies on too many vague claims. I have already met some of the usual criticisms through the very specification of its actual scope. Beyond that, all I can do in the space available here is to use Hume's method of challenge and to ask you if you can think of a single unequivocally factual statement—a statement that all parties would agree had factual content—that is not in the sense specified above verifiable (confirmable or infirmable) in principle. If you cannot—and I do not think you can—is it not reasonable to believe that my demarcation line for a statement of fact is justified?[20]

Indeed this gauntlet has been taken up, but the most usual and sophisticated of the alleged counterexamples to my claim are of the following two sorts, neither of which seem to me genuine counter-examples: (1) "Every human being has some neurotic traits," and (2) "My head aches." As Hempel and Rynin have pointed out, statements of unrestricted generality with mixed quantification are not decisively confirmable or infirmable and we cannot even state a precise probability weight for their confirmation or disconfirmation.[21] But this does not mean that in a weaker and less precise sense we could not give perfectly empirical evidence for or against their truth. Since language is not like a calculus, we should not continue to believe that it will function like one. If we continue to discover neurotic traits in all the people who are so examined and if some independently testable personality theory gives us reason to believe, say, that the very growing up in a family always leads to some neurotic stress, the generalization has some confirmation. On the other hand, if we find a human being who does not, so far as we can determine, behave neurotically at all, the generalization is slightly weakened. The same thing is true for other statements involving mixed quantification which might be plainly thought to have factual content, e.g., "Every substance has some solvent" or "Every planet has some form of life."

"My head aches," or "I have a headache," poses different problems. From the period of *The Blue Book* on, Wittgenstein thought that such utterances do not have a verification. Malcolm points out that in his *Philosophische Bemerkungen* Wittgenstein thought that they could be verified, but after 1932 his recognition that they were avowals rather than statements of fact led to his "turning away from the full-blown verification theory of meaning."[22] However, it is just this conception of avowals that is important for my case. I do not verify, "My head aches," or "I have a headache." After all, in normal circumstances I, by my very utterance, simply avow that my head aches. I am not, Wittgenstein argued, trying to state a fact but to give expression to how I feel.

If you reply—and I for one have considerable sympathy with that reply—that this is too extreme, for "head aches," in "My head aches," when uttered by Nielsen, has factual content, note that it has the same factual content as "Nielsen's head aches" and that this statement is perfectly open to confirmation by what I say and do. What makes "Nielsen's head aches " true or false is exactly what makes "My head aches" true or false, where the utterer of this last utterance is Nielsen. So we still have no genuine example of a factual statement which is not verifiable. Either we drop the claim that "My head aches" is true or false, in which case no issue arises about it being a factual statement or about how we could come to know that it is so, or we allow it is true or false, in which case we come to know that it is true or false, that it is verified, in the same way that we come to know or verify that "Nielsen's head aches" is true or false. When I utter "My head aches" and Jones utters "Nielsen's head aches," both these claims are, to use a slightly outmoded and pleonastic terminology, intersubjectively verified in the same way to the extent they are verified or are known to be true or false at all.

There are those who think that behind my talk of "factual significance" and the verifiability principle there lurks a series of false dichotomies such as "factual meaning"/"emotive meaning," "cognitive meaning"/"metaphorical meaning," "literal meaning"/"nonliteral meaning" and the like. I do not think any such "multiplication of meanings beyond need," is involved in what I have argued, but for those who remain unconvinced and suffer from the anxieties described above, I want to stress that what is most essential to my argument about fact-stating discourse can be put in this way: If a sentence is used to make what is thought to be a factual statement and yet the statement made by its use is neither confirmable nor infirmable even in principle, then the statement in question actually fails to come off as a factual statement, i.e., it fails to assert a fact and thus is not a genuine bit of fact-stating discourse. An utterance that comes off as a statement of fact must be verifiable in principle.

To sum up. Judaism and Christianity are thought by Jews and Christians to involve an entry into a relationship with a being transcendent to the world or at least with a creative and gracious "world ground" which is distinct from the world and upon which the world is dependent. Thus we face what for the Jew or Christian is an awkward fact, namely, that while being a Jew or Christian consists in much more than believing that certain allegedly factual statements are true, it does, in an utterly irreducible manner, involve the acceptance of what are taken by the faithful to be certain factual beliefs. And these purportedly factual beliefs are often of vast scope; they are not only ordinary empirical beliefs such as Jesus was born in Bethlehem. The expression of such "cosmic factual beliefs" results in the making of religious or, if you will, theological statements, e.g., "There is an infinite, eternal Creator of the world" or "There is an ultimate loving reality in which all men find their being," and these statements are taken by the faithful to be factual statements. Yet they are neither directly nor indirectly confirmable or infirmable even in principle and thus are in reality, as many nonbelievers have suspected, devoid of factual content.[23] They purport to be factual but fail to behave as factual statements. We have no idea of how to establish their truth or probable truth, or their falsity or probable falsity. We have no conception of what it would be like for them to be true (or probably true) or false (or probably false). Yet they are supposedly expressive of factual beliefs. But such a statement which is in no way confirmable or infirmable even in principle is not a factual statement. To make sense of such utterances on their own terms, and not just the sense a Santayana or a Feuerbach would make of them, believers must believe that these key bits of God-talk are fact-stating, but these utterances fail to come off as bits of fact-stating discourse. So here we have at the very foundation of such faiths a radical incoherence which vitiates such religious claims.[24]

It might be countered that "Every human being is dependent on an infinite 'world ground' transcendent to the universe," is factually intelligible because it is after all weakly confirmable or infirmable in a manner similar to the way "Every human being has some neurotic traits," is confirmable or infirmable. There is weak verification in each case. Feeling dependent and morally insufficient counts weakly for the truth of the putative theological assertion; making sense of one's life and of morality independent of any reference to religion and overcoming feelings of utter dependency counts against its truth. But this is deceiving, for atheists can, and *some* do, agree that human beings pervasively have these feelings of dependency and moral insufficiency and still these atheists can make nothing of nonanthropomorphic talk of God or an infinite "world ground" transcendent to the universe. The believer cannot legitimately respond that he is simply talking about such feelings and *nothing more* for then his belief would be indistinguishable from atheism. But it is his alleged "something more" that does not make a verifiable difference even in the weak sense. "God is wholly Other," is, taken by itself, nonsense for it is an incomplete sentence: in order to understand it, we need to know "a wholly other *what*." The alleged answer frequently comes by talk of "Being-in-itself," "Unconditioned Transcendent," "Being transcendent to the world" and the like, but, as we have seen, though they are purportedly referring expressions, no intelligible directions have been given as to how to identify the supposed referents of such referring expressions. The affirmation and denial that there are such "realities" is equally compatible with anything and everything that could conceivably be experienced. Such nonanthropomorphic God-talk does not make verifiable sense.

VII

Such is my argument about God-talk. There are three morals I wish to draw from this, one religious and ideological and the other two about philosophical methodology.

To put the religious or ideological point bluntly: If my central arguments are essentially correct, one should not be a Jew, Christian, Moslem or any kind of theist. To be any of these things involves having beliefs "whose scope transcends the empirical world." More specifically, it involves believing in the reality of God as a creator of the universe. But, if my arguments are near to their mark, such a belief is utterly incoherent. That is to say, with nonanthropomorphic conceptions of God there is nothing intelligible to be believed, so atheism (a reasoned rejection of belief in God) becomes the most reasonable form of life. If beliefs are persisted in where there are no *reasons* for holding them, we should look for the *causes*: look for what makes people believe as they do; belief in God is absurd, but, as Feuerbach, Santayana, and Freud have shown, the psychological need for this construct of the human heart is so great that in cultures like ours many people must believe in spite of the manifest absurdity of their belief. They can see and accept this absurdity in the religious beliefs of other tribes and sometimes, as with Hamann and Kierkegaard, they can partially see it and accept it in their own tribe, but the acceptance is not unequivocal and the full absurdity of their own belief remains hidden from them.

There are multiple confusions here. I am philosophically conservative enough to believe, Searle and Black to the contrary notwithstanding, that categorical normative conclusions are not entailed by any set of purely non-normative premises. But even if I am right about this and there is such an is/ought divide, it does not at all follow that normative claims are not supported or justified or at least weakened or strengthened by non-normative claims. After all, entailments are not the only conceptual connections.[26] And this is all I am maintaining. In other words I am only maintaining that, if my arguments about the concept of God are accepted, it would be unreasonable for those who accept them to remain Jews, Christians or Moslems. Moreover, in such a circumstance it would be more reasonable to be an atheist than an agnostic. There are in such considerations crucial normative implications about how to live and die. The clickety-clack of linguistic analysis has human implications.

I want to turn for a moment to J.C. Murray's dichotomy for it is a false dichotomy. Atheism, like Christianity or any other way of life, does, of course, involve a normative stance, a option about how to live. But it is by no means a matter of the godless man of the academy or the marketplace simply willing or opting "to understand the world without God." Any way of acting which reflects deliberation involves the decision to act in a certain way; and to act deliberately in a certain way is part of what it is to live in accordance with norms. That is to say, my remarks here are conceptual remarks or what Wittgenstein, with a considerable stretch of "grammatical," called "grammatical remarks." Between men of God and atheists there is indeed the clash of affirmations. But it is not *simply* a clash of affirmations or even in *the last analysis* simply a clash of affirmations. Atheism involves a decision about how to live, but it also involves an intellectual understanding of what our world is like; and the decision to reject religious belief would not be made without a certain intellectual understanding of the situation.

My concluding remarks about philosophical methodology are not unrelated to what I have just maintained. For anyone at all knowledgeable about philosophical analysis, for anyone touched by the work of Moore, Wittgenstein, and Austin, it is natural, when faced with my arguments, to assert that something must have gone wrong somewhere. Philosophical analysis is normatively and, if you will, ideologically or metaphysically neutral. It is tempting to maintain that when anyone claims to have drawn such vast ideological conclusions as I claim to have drawn form philosophcial analysis, you can be quite confident that he is unwittingly sneaking some nonanalytical element into his philosophical analysis—that somewhere, somehow some special pleading has occurred—for philosophical analyses are ideologically neutral.

There is an ambiguity in the phrase "philosophical analysis is neutral" which once exposed will undermine this argument. Philosophical analysis is neutral in the sense that, *independently* of one's normative, ideological, or metaphysical view of the world, it either does or does not follow that to say X ought to do Y presupposes X can do Y, or to say that X knows God is to give one to understand that X loves God, or to say that X believes *in* God presupposes that X believes *that* God exists. These relationships are logical or conceptual, and they either hold or fail to hold, and what in this way holds or fails to hold here is not a factor of one's ideological commitments. In this important sense philosophical analysis is ideologically neutral. If this were not so, philosophical dispute would degenerate into a clash of rival unarguable affirmations. In a very important sense it would cease being *philosophical* and philosophy would itself be impossible.

However, there is another sense in which philosophical analysis is not normatively or ideologically neutral. In carrying out a philosophical analysis, we attempt, through a description of the uses and the unscheduled inferences of philosophically perplexing terms and utterances, to gain a perspicuous representation of the discourse in question. If, after a careful analysis of "can," one concluded that "I can," in moral contexts typically and irreducibly functioned categorically and that these uses of discourse were essential to the understanding of human action, it would be unreasonable to be a soft determinist; if, after a careful analysis of "good," "right," and "ought" in moral contexts, it became apparent that "good" was never equivalent to any term or set of terms standing for purely empirical characteristics or relations, it would be unreasonable to be an ethical naturalist; similarly it would not be reasonable to remain a Jew or a Christian if careful elucidation of "God" and God-talk indicated that, while believers took "God" to be a referring expression, "God" actually functions neither as a name nor as a definite or indefinite description and that there are no directions in the discourse concerning how to identify God so that we could have some idea of what we are talking about when we speak of God.

It is evident in such a situation vis-à-vis soft determinism, ethical naturalism, and theism, that certain results of philosophcial analysis indicate that a given ideological position is not tenable.[27] In this respect philosophical analysis is not ideologically neutral. But if it were not philosophically neutral in the way I first characterized, analysis itself would be impossible and there could be no philosophically relevant grounds for accepting or rejecting any of these ideological positions.

This leads me to my last point which is a general one about the nature of philosophy. It is tempting to remark that in proceeding as I have in this essay, I have been trying to do something that cannot be done: I have in effect tried to give philosophy a task which cannot be its own; I have implicitly described what activities, what forms of life, are legitimate or rational and what usages, reflecting these forms of life, are coherent, when in actuality philosophy can only legitimately clearly display the actual structure of the discourse embedded in these activities. Again we are back to a very Wittgensteinian point. The claim is that the philosopher's sole legitimate function is to describe our discourse so as to dispel conceptual perplexities engendered by a failure properly to understand the workings of our language.

Certainly such a Wittgensteinian stress is an understandable and justified reaction to the kind of *prescriptivism* which would persuasively redefine "knowledge," "proof," "explanation," "evidence," and

the like in such a way that most of the things commonly called such
are not real knowledge, proof, explanation, evidence and the like.
Moore, Wittgenstein, and ordinary language philosophers have amply
demonstrated the barrenness of such philosophical rationalism. But
such a descriptivism can throw out the baby with the bath and utterly
lose one of the deepest rationales for doing philosophy, namely, that
of criticizing received opinions and more generally and uniquely of
providing a critical discussion of critical discussions and forms of life.

These are grand old phrases, it might be replied, but they remain
empty: what exactly is this critical discussion of critical discussions
and what Archimedean point can the philosopher possibly attain
which would enable him legitimately to criticize whole forms of life?
The very concept of rationality is itself a deeply contested and context-
dependent concept.

In considering this, let us start with one of the less contested
points first. "Rational" and "rationality" are indeed used eulogistic-
ally, but we should be aware of concluding that they are just emotive
labels or that they are so essentially contested as to be thoroughly
subjective. Translation into the concrete should make this evident,
though it will not, of course, provide us with an elucidation of the
concept of rationality. A man who never listens to others and always
shouts others down is not rational; it is also irrational to persist in a
practice which gives rise to vast human suffering when this could be
avoided by adopting another practice that would achieve much the
same thing as the first practice but would cause much less suffering;
finally, to point to a specific kind of behavior, to believe in witches or
fairies is also irrational if one is a tolerably well-informed Westerner
living in the twentieth century. "Rational," whatever its precise analysis, is not so vague that it does not have an established use and
evident paradigm cases. Moreover, activities or forms of life are not
neatly isolated activities with their own distinctive criteria. There is,
for example, no such thing as "religious language," though there are
religious discourses carried on in English, Swedish, German, French,
etc. And even in these discourses the criteria of relevance, the use of
"evidence," "rationality," and the like are not utterly unique to the
discourse in question. It is just not so that God-talk is a self-contained
form of language or form of life, though it does have its distinctive
topics and centers of interest.

The very criticisms I have made of religious beliefs, if they are on
the whole correct, constitute a *reductio* of the Wittgensteinian thesis
that philosophy can only be descriptive. To this it might be replied
that since philosophy can only be descriptive there must be something
basically wrong with my arguments about religious belief. Forms of
life are immune from anything but piecemeal criticism; there can be

no incoherent forms of language or irrational forms of life. But remembering the very different things that philosophy has been throughout its long history, and keeping in mind the immense variety of types of investigation that have gone on under the name of "philosophy," and the precariousness and contested nature of generalizations about the nature of philosophy, is it not—I put it to your reflective consideration—more reasonable to doubt the descriptivist thesis as a completely adequate account of the proper office of philosophy, than to reject my arguments *simply on the grounds that they fail to square with a thesis in the philosophy of philosophy?*

Wittgenstein generalized primarily from reflecting on epistemology, the philosophy of mind, and mathematics. There his descriptivist thesis seems to me thoroughly plausible; but he may, to turn his own phrase against him, have suffered from a one-sided diet. Religion is a form of life that may indeed be given, but it is still not beyond the pale of relevant philosophcial criticism.

This essay might have been entitled "A refutation of Theism" or "A Refutation of Judeo-Christianity." Until and unless specific arguments can be provided to show that my criticisms fail, it is more reasonable to accept them and reject such a form of life than to maintain, on the basis of a general and disputed thesis in the philosophy of philosophy, that such arguments must be mistaken. Even if some—or worse still all—of my criticisms fail, unless criticisms of such *a general type* can be shown to be irrelevant, there is no reason to assume that the descriptivist thesis must be so and that "A Philosophical Refutation of Theism" is a conceptual anomaly.

I admit that the concept of such a type of critical assessment (a "criticism of criticisms" or "a critical discussion of forms of life and of critical discussion") is itself a disputed concept expressive of a controversial thesis in the philosophy of philosophy and that it is in need of a careful elucidation and defense.[28] But *ambulando* what I have done here vis-à-vis religion and what Ronald Hepburn did in *Christianity and Paradox* and Antony Flew did in *God and Philosophy* are examples of what I have in mind. We have learned from Moore and Ryle that we can typically do with words what we may not in fact be able on demand to characterize adequately.

It is also well known that "What is philosophy?" is itself a deeply contested philosophical problem and many men—past and present—who considered themselves philosophers and who are generally considered philosophers have thought they could provide disciplined, rational criticism of ways-of-life. Moreover, they thought they were doing this in the course of philosophizing and not as an activity that was ancillary to their philosophizing.[29] I have tried to do just that for a family of ways-of-life, namely, Judaism, Christianity, and Islam, by exhibiting the incoherence of absolutely central beliefs they hold in common. Most of my arguments are fairly specific exercises in philosophical analysis. Unless they and arguments like them fail, we have good grounds for believing that it is not the case that philosophy properly done must always be purely descriptive. So my exercise gives rise to two important general claims: it challenges Judeo-Christian belief at its very heart and it also challenges a fashionable thesis about the nature of philosophy.

One final salvo of I hope not too homiletic a nature. People who try to apply the techniques of linguistic analysis are still frequently accused of engaging in trivial endeavors and with what has been called "an abdication of philosophy." But note this: whatever else may be wrong with what I have argued here, it remains one example of analytic philosophy that cannot be so criticized. What the critic must do is to show that my arguments are mistaken and not complain that they are trivial because they do not touch fundamental problems of human existence.

NOTES

1. P. F. Strawson, "Identifying Reference and Truth-Values," *Theoria* XXX (1964, Part 2): 115.

2. Ibid., p. 101.

3. This view is well expressed by Alasdair MacIntyre in his *Difficulties in Christian Belief.*

4. Ronald Hepburn, "Agnosticism," Vol. I, *Encyclopedia of Philosophy,* Paul Edwards, ed. (New York: Macmillan & Co. and The Free Press, 1967), pp. 58-59.

5. John MacQuarrie, *God-Talk* (New York: Harper & Row, Publishers, Inc., 1967), p. 176.

6. See John Hick, "Christianity," Vol. II, *Encyclopedia of Philosophy.*

7. W. D. Hudson, "Transcendence," *Theology* LXIX (March, 1966): 104.

8. Ibid., pp. 103-4.

9. Ibid., p. 103.

10. Ibid.

11. Paul Tillich, "The Religious Symbol," in *Religious Experience and Truth,* Sidney Hook, ed., p. 303.

12. This conception of philosophy as resting on considerations of plausibility is well expressed by J. J. C. Smart in his *Philosophy and Scientific Realism* (New York: Humanities Press, 1963), pp. 12-13, and in more detail in his "Philosophy and Scientific Plausibility," in Feyerabend, Paul K. and Maxwell, G. E. (eds.) *Mind, Matter, and Method, Essays in Honor of Herbert Feigl* (Minneapolis, MN: University of Minnesota Press, 1966).

13. Illyd Trethowan, "In Defense of Theism—A Reply to Professor Kai Nielsen," *Religious Studies* 2 (1966): 39.

14. So Trethowan is again wide of the mark when he remarks: "Nielsen will be entitled to say that he can make nothing of it, but (I submit) he will not be entitled to say that there is anything logically the matter with it. He seems to think that a believer is not logically entitled to regard his beliefs as meaningful unless he can make them meaningful to an unbeliever." Ibid., pp. 38-39. Generally, it seems to me, Trethowan's defense of theism and criticisms of my arguments are ineffective.

15. I have stated this rather bruskly and perhaps in a dogmatic sounding way. I have argued for it in some detail in my "Wittgensteinian Fideism," *Philosophy* XLII (July, 1967), in "Language and the Concept of God," *Question 2* (January, 1969): 36-40, in "God and the Forms of Life," *Indian Review of Philosophy* 1 (January, 1972): 45-66, and in my book *An Introduction to Philosophy of Religion* (London: The MacMillan Press Ltd., 1982), pp. 43-139.

16. I have argued the ins and outs of this in my "Can Faith Validate God-talk?" *New Theology No. 1*, Martin Marty and Dan Peerman, eds. (New York: Macmillan & Co. and The Free Press, 1964) and in my "Religious Perplexity and Faith," *The Crane Review* VIII (Fall, 1965).

17. The application of these considerations to religious discourse have been succinctly stated by Alvin Plantinga, "Analytic Philosophy and Christianity," *Christianity Today* (October 25, 1963): 75-78, and by George L. Mavrodes, "God and Verification," *Canadian Journal of Theology* 10 (1964): 187-191. But see my response "God and Verification Again," *Canadian Journal of Theology* XI (1965): 135-141.

18. These and other closely related points have been decisively argued by G. J. Warnock, "Verification and the Use of Language," *Revue Internationale de Philosophie* 17 (1951); J. L. Evans, "On Meaning and Verification," *Mind* LXII (1953) and *The Foundations of Empiricism* (Cardiff, 1965); Paul Marhenke, "The Criterion of Significance," *Proceedings and Addresses of the American Philosophical Association*, 1950; and R. W. Ashby, "Verifiability Principle," Vol. 8, *The Encyclopedia of Philosophy*.

19. Some contemporary philosophers have tried to take up this challenge and show how certain key religious utterances are verifiable. I examine their arguments and attempt to show *that* they fail and *how* they fail in my "Christian Positivism and the Appeal to Religious Experience," *The Journal of Religion* XLII (October, 1962); "Eschatological Verification," *Canadian Journal of Theology* IX (1962), and "On Fixing the Reference Range of 'God'," *Religious Studies* (October, 1966).

20. I argue for this in detail in my "Metaphysics and Verification Revisited," *The Southwestern Journal of Philosophy* 6 (1975).

21. Carl Hempel, *Aspects of Scientific Explanation*, Chapter IV (New York, The Free Press, 1965) and David Rynin, "Vindication of L*G*C*L*P*-S*T*V*SM," *Proceedings and Addresses of the American Philosophical Association*, 1957.

22. Norman Malcolm, "Wittgenstein's *Philosophische Bemerkungen*," *The Philosophical Review* LXXVI (April, 1967): 225.

23. This cannot be taken as evidence that we have statements which are plainly factual but still not verifiable, for the examples themselves do not have an undisputed factual status. Many nonbelievers and even some who call

themselves believers (Hare, Braithwaite, and Miles) do not regard them as factual statements. Moreover, they do not all make this assumption because they assume the verifiability criterion of factual significance but some do so because they think an examination of the use, the depth grammar, of key religious utterances will show that they have a very different function than do statements of fact.

24. I am not asking that religion become what it plainly is not, i.e., science. There are plenty of fact-stating discourses which are not scientific. Man did not have to wait for the rise of science before he could start stating facts. I am also not ignoring context, for these presuppositions operate in religious contexts. See Crombie's remarks on this in the opening pages of his "The Possibility of Theological Statements," in *Faith and Logic*, Basil Mitchell, ed. (London, Allen & Unwin, 1957), pp. 31-33.

25. John Courtney Murray, *The Problem of God*, p. 84.

26. Stephen Toulmin argues this point very effectively in his *The Uses of Argument* (Cambridge: Cambridge University Press, 1964). I have tried to sustain the is/ought divide in my "On Deriving Ought From Is," *The Review of Metaphysics* 32 (March, 1979): 487-514.

27. It might be objected that this does not hold for ethical naturalism, for ethical naturalism is itself a meta-ethical theory and not a normative ethical theory. That it is a meta-ethical theory is indeed so, and I would further agree that this distinction in ethical theory is an important one. But meta-ethical theories themselves have normative implications. It would be unreasonable for a man not to take the dictates of his own society as normative for his behavior within that society, *if* he believed that "One ought to do *Y*" *meant* "*Y* is a dictate of one's society." For a discussion of the normative implications of meta-ethics see my "Problem of Ethics," Vol. 3, *The Encyclopedia of Philosophy*, pp. 119-124.

28. What I have said in the last few pages has been influenced by the views of John Passmore; see his essay "Philosophy" in Vol. 6, *The Encyclopedia of Philosophy*, pp. 216-226. I have tried to say something about philosophy as a criticism of criticisms in my "John Dewey's Conception of Philosophy," *The University of Massachusetts Review* II (Autumn, 1960).

29. A powerful case for such ideological considerations being ancillary has been made by Anthony Quinton in "Philosophy and Beliefs," but in line with the point I have been making, note the powerful counter thrusts of Stuart Hampshire and Isaiah Berlin. See A. Quinton, S. Hampshire, S. Murdoch, and I. Berlin, "Philosophy and Beliefs," *The Twentieth Century*, Vol. CLVII (1955), pp. 495-521.

6

Religion and Commitment

The end of ideology has been proclaimed. Whether or not it will come to an end is hard to predict. We do not know whether with our present understanding of ideology intellectuals will finally cease making claims that in reality are only empty rhetorical flourishes but are intended by their authors and taken by some of their hearers—hearers taken in by the ideology—to be grand cosmological claims about the nature and destiny of man.[1] But it is plain enough that a *philosopher ought not* as a philosopher to be an ideologist. Many think that philosophy, as conceptual analysis, should place itself quite modestly with the rest of the academic disciplines and renounce all claim to giving us reasoned insight into the human condition. Philosophers should not even seek to discover certain general principles, as Aristotle, Descartes, and Hegel did, but they should limit themselves to conceptual analysis or, if you will, pure description of those fundamental concepts that perplex us. It is often maintained that it is *not* a philosopher's job to propose general theses, to discover general principles, and above all it most certainly is not his job to be a sage or an ideologist. That is to say, it is not his job to tell his fellowman what his nature and destiny is or give him a blueprint of the good life. Any such attempt would be both absurd and unbelievably pretentious; his proper scholarly niche is to clear up the confusions that arise when we do not properly understand the workings of our language in certain very crucial areas, e.g., in talk about "time," "good," "God," "cause," "freedom," "truth," and the like.

Now I am ambivalent about this. I most certainly do not want, as

From *Religious Languages and Knowledge*, edited by William Blackstone and R. H. Ayers, © 1972 by The University of Georgia Press. Reprinted by permission of the publisher.

a philosopher, to be an ideologist and I don't want other philosophers to be ideologists either. Ever since I was a graduate student, I have been distressed at the hollowness and the ideological character of traditional philosophers' talk about the nature and destiny of man. Much of what they have said about the nature of the good life has seemed to me ideological—empty obscurantist rhetoric passed off as statements of general principles about the ultimate nature of reality. Philosophers from Plato to Royce, and even down to such obscurantist mystagogues as Heidegger and Tillich, have indeed upon occasion said penetrating things about life. But, as John Passmore has perceptively noted, exactly the same thing can be found in the great novelists and dramatists.[2] The difference presumably is that the philosopher, unlike the sage, has *thought through* his principles; he doesn't *simply rely on insight* but also upon argument and reason. He doesn't seek simply to be perceptive but to give grounds for his insights. But the arguments one finds such philosophers using to support their insights are very obscure and often incoherent, and the metaphysical machinery is not infrequently scarcely intelligible. Increasingly with philosophers such as Heidegger, Sartre, and Jaspers, one gets what is in effect a contempt for closely reasoned argument. They dish out the dark, yet sometimes insightful sayings and you can either take them or leave them. They are not to be argued about and no serious attempt is made to reason for them. I suspect what attracts nonphilosophers to Plato, Spinoza, or Sartre is not their towering metaphysical systems but their sage remarks about life. The strictly philosophical superstructure is not understood by them, but they feel that in some way—which they as neophytes do not understand—these philosophers' insights are supported by their obscure metaphysical superstructures and that people with a thorough training in philosophy can and do, if they are wise and deep men, understand this obscure talk and that perhaps they too could come to understand it, if only they would study it hard enough and long enough. But if even a little bit of what we have learned from analytic or linguistic philosophy is correct, these philosophical superstructures are in Wittgenstein's celebrated phrase "houses of cards." Such philosophy is ideology and a good philosopher should expose it for what it is, e.g., he should show how disguised nonsense is patent nonsense.

Rightly or wrongly, I believe that this low estimate of the metaphysical claims and systematizings of much of traditional philosophy and contemporary continental philosophy is on the whole just. Yet, as I have said, I am ambivalent, for while I want nothing of such metaphysics or such philosophical systems, I am also unhappy just doing analysis, *if* this somehow is taken to *deny* that the *end* of a philosopher's activity should be to give insight into the problems of life, though most certainly insight supported by argument. I very much feel about the force of Austin's remark that we don't yet have enough clarity in philosophy and that it will be time enough to say that clarity is not enough in *philosophy* when we have achieved a tolerable degree of that. But I remain obstinately concerned with the question *"Clarity for what?"* and, like Wittgenstein, I am concerned to "assemble reminders for a particular purpose." I remain, if I dare put it so naively, concerned with trying to understand the concept of truth and the concept of knowledge; and I find I am interested in them because I am vitally interested in trying to know what, if anything, it is possible to know about what sort of life a man ought to lead, what would be a good life and what would be an ideal society; and I very much want to know what, if anything, this has to do with God, freedom, and immortality. My activities as a philosopher center around this enterprise, but I most certainly do not want to be simply a sage, simply an undisciplined, free-floating intellectual, journalist or publicist and most certainly I do not want simply to be an ideologist. But I am prepared to argue for philosophical theses, though I am concerned with the soundness of these theses and the necessity of giving clear and convincing arguments for them. If I can bring this off, I should hope and expect that it would have an important bearing, directly or indirectly, on how a man should live his life and how we should order society. I remain ambivalent about this; the fox in me warns me how difficult it is and how pretentious it is. Yet it seems to me a task that people should, though with fear and tremblng, address themselves to.

But enough of such program constructing, enough of such grandiose talk. Let me tie what I am trying to say to an example by saying something of religion. I shall also illustrate, by way of examples, (1) what I mean by holding philosophical theses, for which I am prepared to give arguments, and (2) to illustrate how these theses, if sound, would be of considerable importance for our lives. It has long been a conviction of mine—a conviction that has survived several changes in philosophical orientation—that there is no reason, no intellectual justification or moral need to believe in God. I am convinced that religious beliefs should belong to the tribal folklore of mankind and there is no more need to believe in God than there is to believe in Santa Claus or the Easter Bunny. We do not need such beliefs to give our lives meaning or to undergird the moral life, and such beliefs are not essential for an understanding of the nature and destiny of man. The great religions do indeed contain bits which can serve as aspirational ideals, but in this respect there is nothing there that is not perfectly available to the atheist. That is to say, for *some* people religion may be of value as a kind of "moral poetry," but even in this way, it is not something essential to the human animal. Some people can get on very well without it. Man, I believe, should prize truth and should try to live according to what Freud called "the reality principle." But if he is to do this, he must reject the claims of religion. Here is my commitment. Let us have a look at how I can support it.

Let me state this conviction a little more fully and a little more exactly in the form of three philosophical theses. I shall then defend them and illustrate how I use philosophical analysis in their defense.

1. The ultimate basis or rationale of our morality cannot be grounded in our belief in God or in our belief that ultimate reality is being itself (whatever that may mean) or in anything of that order. In fact, just the reverse is the case, only if we already have some moral understanding, some *knowledge* of good and evil, could we ever come to believe that there is a God or properly understand what people are talking about when they speak of God.

2. When religious people talk of the love, mercy, and the omnipotence of God or even of His reality, they make statements which are either patently false, most probably false, or are, in a significant sense, unintelligible. Furthermore, modern theologians such as Buber, Tillich, Robinson, and Bultmann are no improvement on the traditional supernaturalists, for they either say, in extravagant Hegeloid jargon, something that is identical with what an atheist would or could consistently say or they engage in a kind of obscurantist gobbledygook that is as unintelligible as anything traditional supernaturalists tried to say. "There is a God" like "There is a Santa Claus" is a bit of mythology for it is either patently false, grossly improbable, or without the significant factual content it purports to have.

3. The claim, so characteristic of modern apologetics, that atheists are really believers in disguise, is not correct. Furthermore, there need be nothing either shallow, confused, or back-woodsy about atheism, and atheism is not itself, as such apologists claim, another religion. It is not even an *Ersatz*-religion.

Let us, in examining my first thesis, have a look at a fairly orthodox characterization of God. I take it from Pope Pius XI's Encyclical *Mit brennender Sorge*. In 1937, addressing himself to German Catholics, Pius XI first tells us what God is not:

> Take care, Venerable Brethren, that above all, faith in God, the first and irreplaceable foundation of all religion, be preserved in Germany pure and unstained. The believer in God is not he who utters the name in his speech, but he for whom this sacred word stands for a true and worthy concept of the Divinity. Whoever identifies, by pantheistic confusion, God and the Universe, by either lowering God to the dimensions of the world, or raising the world to the dimensions of God, is not a believer in God. Whoever follows that so-called pre-Christian Germanic conception of sub-

stituting a dark and impersonal destiny for the personal God, denies thereby the Wisdom and Providence of God. . . .

Whoever exalts race, or the people, or the State, or a particular form of State, or the depositories of power, or any other fundamental value of the human community—however necessary and honorable be their function in worldly things—whoever raises these notions above their standard value and divinizes them to an idolatrous level, distorts and perverts an order of the world planned and created by God: he is far from the true faith in God and from the concept of life which that faith upholds.[3]

Then Pius goes on to tell what God really is. "Our God is the Personal God, supernatural, omnipotent, infinitely perfect, one in the Trinity of Persons, tri-personal in the unity of divine essence, the Creator of all existence, Lord, King and ultimate Consummator of the history of the world, who will not, and cannot, tolerate a rival god by His side." Orthodox Christians—Catholics and Protestants alike—have, until recently at least, all been asked to believe in such a God; and if we delete the part about the trinity of persons, we have a concept of Deity that is also integral to Judaism and Islam. There is much more to these religions than the asserting of certain dogmas, but one thing integral to these religions is just such a belief in God. It is presupposed in all the rest that a Christian and Jew does; it is presupposed in the rest of their religious activities. The core notion of such a Deity can be briefly put as follows: "God is the sole, supernatural, omnipotent, infinitely perfect creator and director of all finite existence." Now, in order to examine my first thesis, let us assume—what surely is to assume a lot—that such a statement is perfectly intelligible and a tolerably adequate characterization of God and let us also assume that there in fact is such a reality. In order to appraise my first thesis, let us now consider the relations between this God and morality. For a bit let us neglect, in asking this question, the phrase "infinitely perfect" in this characterization of God. Just consider (1) "There is a single, supernatural, omnipotent creator and director of all finite existence." What follows from this about what we *ought* to do and what would be good to do and what things, actions or attitudes, if any, are of *ultimate value?* The answer is nothing: (1) purports to be a factual statement and from a purely factual statement or from a set of factual statements no normative conclusions can be deduced. One cannot get a normative statement, directive of human behavior and/or attitudes, from purely non-normative statements.

To this it may be replied that while we cannot derive an *ought* from an *is,* we can and do all the time use factual statements to support our normative judgments. This is indeed true. Furthermore the existence of a single, supernatural, omnipotent creator and director of all finite existence would be a fact of great relevance to a believer. Given that fact (assuming now that it is a fact) and given the further fact that this Being commands a certain thing, a believer would most certainly judge that he ought to do what this being commands. But why, we might very well ask. His being creator of man and all finite existence, his being the omnipotent director of all finite existence does not *prove* or in any way establish his goodness, does not show that He is *worthy* of being obeyed. He might, with those attributes, even be a malevolent deity. After all, what did Job learn when God spoke to him out of the whirlwind but that God was marvelously powerful, that God was his creator and the like? Given God's behavior to Job and given God's pact with Satan, it would have been more reasonable for Job to have concluded with Schopenhauer that God is evil. How does power, intelligence, and creativity by itself show goodness?

If the Christians' picture of the world is true, we ultimately owe our existence to God and, given that we *prize* our existence, we should be glad of that. But this surely does not exhibit His goodness any more than the fact that we proximately owe our existence to the hot night of our father's desire exhibits our father's goodness. Given God's power and intelligence, it is certainly prudent to follow the commandments and directives of God. No one wants to suffer. But, in the heyday of their power, it would also have been prudent to follow the directives of a Hitler or a Stalin if you were under their hegemony. But these are prudential reasons for acting in one way rather than another. We have not yet found any *moral* reason for doing as God commands.

Well, we should do what God commands for God is all wise and perfectly good. It is only by dropping part of the Pope's characterization of God that we made difficulties for ourselves here. The Pope, as all believers do, conceives of God as being infinitely perfect.

Granting this conception, as surely we must, let us now ask: how do they or how can we come to *know* that God is infinitely perfect? Granted that a believer assumes it or presupposes it, why does he? What reasons does he have for his presupposition? And how could the man without faith come to know that God is infinitely perfect or even good?

Suppose we say: "Here is where we need Revelation, the Bible and an awareness of the concrete actions of God. Here is where our knowledge of Jesus is essential. Jesus the mediator through his moral perfection teaches us something of the infinite perfection of God. We see in gentle Jesus wisdom and goodness and thus we come to know the little we can know of the infinite goodness of God."

Now one might dispute about Jesus' perfection: one might wonder why *this* Bible, *this* putative revelation rather than that? Why the Bible rather than the *Koran* or the *Upanishads*, the *Kaevala*, the

Bhagavadgita or the *Lotus of the Good Law*? But all such questions aside, let us for the sake of the argument assume that Jesus is perfect and the Old and New Testaments are the sole ultimate source of genuine revelation, still it is we finite creatures who saw in Jesus' behavior perfection and goodness. Using our own finite moral powers, we recognized that Jesus was this moral exemplar pointing to the infinite perfection of God; beyond that we also recognized that the parables of the Bible were so *noble* and *inspiring* that the Bible *ought* to be taken as our model in moral matters. But these things show, as clearly as can be, that in making these moral assessments we already have a moral criterion, quite independent of the Bible, God, and Jesus, in virtue of which we make these moral judgments.

The believer should say, I think, if he has his wits about him, that he doesn't have and can't have *reasons* for his assertion, anymore than I can have reasons for my assertion that all bachelors are males for, "God is infinitely perfect" is true by definition. It is, in the language of modern philosophy, analytic and this is why it is not open for the believer to question the goodness or perfection of God. Nothing within Christian and Jewish discourse would be called "God" unless it were also called "all good" and "infinitely perfect." This requirement is built into the very logic of God-talk and thus there can be no justification of it or no question of giving evidence for it. Believer and nonbeliever alike must recognize that within such religious discourse "God is *not* infinitely perfect" is a contradiction.

But doesn't this show, as clearly as anything could, that my first thesis is unsound? Not in the slightest. I can most economically show this in the following way: "God" in such discourses functions as a proper name, though indeed, like "Churchill" and "Mussolini" and unlike your names and mine, a name that takes certain fixed descriptions. Now as a proper name it must make reference, it must denote, it must stand for something that at least conceivably could exist. Now when we say something is good or bad, perfect or imperfect, we are not simply applying a certain descriptive predicate to it. We are not just characterizing it as having a certain property that could, directly or indirectly, be discovered by observation. What we are doing when we ascribe value to something is very difficult to say; sometimes we are expressing our approval of it, taking some interest in it, commending it and the like, but one thing is clear: "Good" or "perfect" are not property words like "red" or "hard." We could not discover some action or person to be good by simply observing it quite independently of any attitudes we might take toward it. Now in considering the concept of God think for a moment only of what the term "God" purports to refer to. From what we observe in the world what could be given in an encounter with God or what could be postulated as actual characteristics of the deity? That is, we note our finitude and dependency and this leads us to conceive of a nondependent, infinite being. Considering only this—considering that infinite but unique nonspatio-temporal individual that is supposed to be the *denotation* of our word "God"—how do you know, from simply in some way being aware of the reality of that entity, that this individual is good or infinitely perfect? How can you know, except through your own limited, finite, fallible moral judgments concerning any X whatsoever that it is infintely perfect or for that matter even perfect or good, where X is simply a force, creator, first cause, ground of being, whether spatio-temporal or nonspatio-temporal, finite or infinite? The answer is that you can't and thus in the most fundamental respect your moral judgments can't be derived from or based upon the fact that there is or is not a reality, some force or supernatural being or ground of being, whom some people call "God." "X is a powerful creator of everything other than himself, a director and sustainer of the universe but all the same X is evil" is perfectly possible. That such a Being *says* he is good, *says* he is infinitely perfect does not prove that he is, even if he is omniscient and omnipotent. How can we know or have reason to believe, except by making up our own minds that he or it is perfect or good? Fallible though our insight is, we must rely on it here.

When we decide to use the label "God" for this alleged Power or, if you will, this ground of being, we imply that this reality is infinitely perfect, but we are able to do this only because we have a prior and logically independent moral understanding that could *not* have been derived simply from discovering that there is a reality transcendent to the world, a reality that created man and sustains him, or from discovering that there is some being *as such,* some ground of being, that is the dimension of depth in the natural. In this crucial way morality, even Christian morality, must be independent of religion. In fact just the reverse is the case, for before we can intelligibly decide that some reality is worthy of worship and thus properly called "God" or some reality is ultimately gracious, to use the obscure talk of MacQuarrie and Robinson, and thus our God, we must have some independently arrived at concept of worthiness or graciousness. Thus in a very crucial sense religion presupposes a moral understanding that is logically independent of religion and not, as Brunner, Kierkegaard, and Barth would have it, just the reverse. To say this is not an expression of human hubris, but simply a matter of logic.

Someone might very well accept this *logical* point and still insist that I miss an important *psychological* point about how religions reinforce the moral beliefs of many people. I recall a psychiatrist once saying to me, after I had given a lecture on psychoanalysis and religion, that while he didn't need religion, while many people didn't need religion, a significant number of people who came to him for help very much needed their religion to attain psychological stability. Their chance of finding any significance in their lives, and no doubt their ability to hold onto any effective moral orientation, was tied for all practical purposes to their holding onto their religious beliefs. But he also agreed that if they had been differently indoctrinated, soberly educated without these religious myths, they would not need this religious crutch. Yet his central point was that if we look at the actual, concrete situation, it is manifest that many people need their religion to give meaning to their lives. Many men know what they should do, but can't bring themselves to do it, many need the moral imagery, the parables, the stories of their religions; and they very much need the solidarity, the sense of belonging, that religion gives them. Without their religion they would as a matter of fact lose their aspirational ideals; their capacity for moral endeavor would be blighted. In a word, they need religion to put their heart into virtue.

Nothing I have said was calculated to deny this or even underplay it, though I should not like to see it apologetically overplayed into the Pascalian theme that *all* men need religion to give significance and moral orientation to their lives. But a recognition of this psychological truth does nothing to show how our knowledge of good and evil does or even can rest on our belief in God or in our knowledge that such a reality exists. It only shows how some men with an understanding of good and evil need a *prod* and *crutch* to continue to act as moral agents.

No doubt most people, in point of origin, get their moral beliefs from their religion in the sense that moral talk for many is first introduced in the context of religious talk, and later, psychologically speaking, they need to associate difficult moral endeavors with these religious pictures. But questions of *validity* are independent of *origin*. Such a psychological account says nothing whatsoever about how we can justify moral beliefs or about our *knowledge* of good and evil. This, as I have shown, is independent of religion. Furthermore, it does not show that all people need such images or that moral belief and significant moral endeavor could not survive and would not have a point in the twilight or even in the complete absence of the gods.

I shall now support my second thesis. Religion, as Hepburn has wisely reminded us, should not be identified with its doctrinal formulae; furthermore the great religions of the world have a unity, amidst a very considerable internal complexity, that makes it difficult to understand their central doctrinal claims in isolation.[4] Yet in stressing this, one must make a new "myth of the whole," one must not neglect the fact that presupposed in these religions are certain very mysterious allegedly factual claims. And if they are truly factual claims, as they appear to be, they must have a certain logical character. For any statement p to be a bona fide factual statement the assertion and denial of p must *not* be equally compatible with any conceivable observation that might be made. If p and not-p have exactly the same empirical consequences, if everything that is logically possible for us to experience is equally compatible with the truth and falsity, or the probable truth and falsity, of p and not-p then p and not-p are *not* factual statements, whatever p and not-p may be. This, of course, does not mean that in every respect they are meaningless. (In fact the ability to deny p implies that in some sense p is intelligible.) But what I have said above does show that p and not-p are devoid of factual significance or intelligibility if such conditions obtain. In short they could not be statements of fact.

Religious people, however, do believe that certain of their very central religious doctrines are statements of fact. They presuppose "There is a God"—that they do not utter it very often is logically irrelevant—and they believe "God created the world." Both of these statements they take to be factual statements.

A sufficiently anthropomorphic believer—someone who thinks that in *some way* it is literally possible to see God—might well use these statements as bona fide factual statements. For him God would be very much like the Homeric gods except that his monotheism commits him to taking God to be a loner and not the head of a clan of gods. But it is simply superstitious to believe in *such* a god. What evidence do we have for such a god up there or out there?[5] Who has observed him under controlled conditions? Why is it that the Eskimos see Sedena, a female God, who lives in the sea and not on the land and who controls the storms, the weather, and the sea mammals, while the Israelites with a very different family structure and very different problems see Yahweh, a God of the desert and a ferocious male God who protects the Israelites from alien peoples? The Alaskan Eskimos by contrast have their risks in the winter sea mammal hunting; here they meet some of the crucial crises of their lives. The anthropomorphic deities of the various cultures are tailor-made projectively to meet the anxieties and emotional needs of their members.[6] It isn't a question of first seeing or somehow apprehending Sedena or Yahweh and then making certain claims. It is rather a matter of projecting certain needs onto the universe and then making up stories about the deifications. Our divinities are fashioned projectively to fit our cultural preoccupations.

Even more fundamentally—all questions of origin apart—who has seen or in any way apprehended Sedena, Yahweh, Zeus, Wotan or Fricka? We have no good evidence for their existence. Belief in such anthropomorpohic deities is intelligible enough. "Fricka exists" or "There is a God" are in such a context something we can understand. But to believe that there are such anthropomorphic divinities is just a bald superstition. To believe that there are such gods is like believing that there is a Santa Claus or that there are fairies.

But sophisticated believers and, I believe, even most plain believers for a long time have ceased believing in such anthropomorphic gods. God is neither up there, down there or out there in any literal sense. God is not a reality you can see or even apprehend. God is thought to be transcendent to the whole cosmos, the creator and sustainer of this cosmos, but He is still somehow a person, an individual—though an infinite individual—who is nonidentifiable, non-spatio-temporal, and in no spatio-temporal relation with the world.[7] The object of our discourse when we discourse of God—when we talk *to* as well as *about* God—is taken to be an infinite, nonspatio-temporal particular named by the name "God." But given this sophisticated use, "There is a God" or "God created the world" are not false but unfalsifiable statements, completely incapable of being confirmed or disconfirmed. No matter how much order we see in the world, the nonbeliever can deny what the believer affirms with as much and with as little plausibility. He can quite consistently, after taking note of this order, assert that there is no God and that the observed order is just a natural part of the world; likewise no matter how much evil and disorder there is, the believer can speak of man's corruption and God's inscrutable grace. The believer can and does go on making his affirmations, no matter what happens and the nonbeliever can and does make his denials no matter what happens. Try this little experiment for yourselves: if you think of yourselves as believers, what *conceivable* turn of observable events would make you say you were mistaken or probably mistaken in holding that belief; and if you think of yourself as an atheist or as an agnostic try this experiment on yourself: what *conceivable* turn of observable events, if only you were to observe them, would make you say you were mistaken or probably mistaken in denying or doubting that it is true or probably true that there is a God? If the God you believe in, deny, or doubt, is anything like the nonanthropomorphic God I have just characterized, I predict you will not be able to answer that question. But if this is so, and I think it is, then your alleged God-statements "There is a God" or "God created the world" are devoid of *factual* significance. They are then equally compatible with anything and everything that the believer and non-believer alike can conceive as being experiential. This being the case, they are no more saying anything that is in reality incompatible, than the American is asserting anything that the Englishman is not when the American calls all those things and only those things ele-

vators that an Englishman calls lifts. The man, in such a circumstance, who says "There is a God" is not asserting anything incompatible with or even different from the statement of a man who says
"There is no God." But this shows that neither statement has factual
content; neither succeeds in asserting or denying the existence of the
peculiar reality that they were meant to assert or deny. Belief, para-
doxically enough, becomes indistinguishable from atheism. But this,
in effect, shows that such a believer has not succeeded in showing how
he can make a claim to reveal a reality or reveal some level of reality
that the nonbeliever does not grasp. The realm of the supernatural
remains unrecognizable.

We are no better off, if like Tillich and Robinson, we reject super-
naturalism and claim that to speak of God being transcendent to the
cosmos is to speak metaphorically or that to speak of the creation of
the world by God is to speak metaphorically, for we are still saddled
with very similar difficulties. Consider the following sentences, sentences that are used to make central claims within their theologies:

1. There is being itself.
2. There is a creative ground of being and meaning.
3. The *agape* of the Cross is the last word about Reality.
4. Reality is not ultimately impersonal or neutral; it is ultimately
   gracious.
5. God is the beyond in the midst of our lives.

Apply the same tests to these statements. What conceivable experiences
would lend probability to any of these statements, would make it
more or less reasonable to believe them to be true? What would confirm or disconfirm them where they are taken to affirm something
incompatible with what a nonbeliever could say? These obscurantist
statements are no more capable of supporting belief than are the familiar claims of traditional theism. You are being deluded if you think
people like Tillich, Bultmann or Robinson will take you beyond the
chains of illusion. All you are doing is substituting an unfamiliar
absurdity for a familiar one.

There is an important objection to my arguments that deserves careful
attention. Such an objector agrees "There is a God," is intended, when
believers use it in typical contexts, to assert a fact.[8] He would stress,
as I would, that it most certainly is not intended simply to express a
person's attitude toward the world or simply to guide conduct or alter
behavior. But, he would add, we must not forget there are all kinds of
assertions and many kinds of factual statements. By taking "There is
a God" to be a contingent factual statement asserting a contingent
fact or a "contingent state-of-affairs" one distorts the actual logic of

God-talk. We must not violate the integrity of God-talk by forcing upon it alien rules or alien criteria. If we, as we should, consider how "God" and "There is a God" are actually used in religious contexts, we will come to see that the existence of God cannot be taken to be a "contingent fact," and if "There is a God" cannot be taken to be "a contingent fact" then the proposition which asserts the existence of God cannot, it is argued, be a contingent proposition. "There is a God" must be taken to be logically or necessarily true.

This being so, it, of course, makes no sense to ask how "There is a God" can be verified or falsified, confirmed or disconfirmed, for it is a mark of a logical or necessary truth that it is true a priori. The man who asks for some contingent, empirical state of affairs to verify an a priori or logical statement merely shows that he does not understand the statement in question.[9] He shows by his very request, that he doesn't understand what an a priori statement is. Given that "There is a God" is logically and thus necessarily true and that God, the superlatively good and only adequate object of worship, necessarily exists, my request for confirmation or disconfirmation is utterly inappropriate.

But why say God's existence is necessary and that "There is a God" is a logical truth or necessarily true? A crucial and typical employment of "There is a God" is to assert that there is a being, superlatively worthy of worship, who is the sole adequate object of the religious attitude of worship. But an adequate object of such an attitude could not be a being who just happens to exist, or might come to exist or cease to exist or upon whom other beings just happen to depend.[10] Such an object of worship, that is God, must be a being whose nonexistence is wholly unthinkable in any circumstance. There must be no conceivable alternative to such a reality. Since, by definition, God is said to be that reality upon which all other things depend for their very existence, we could not, of course, state even a conceivable state of affairs that would be incompatible with His existence for, for any X if some conceivable state of affairs Y is incompatible with the existence of X, then X by definition could not be God, for Y would attest to the fact that there was something whose existence did not depend on X. Similarly since God's nonexistence is unthinkable under any circumstance (including any conceivable circumstance), God's existence is necessary and "There is a God" is logically true and asserts a "logical fact."

There are a host of objections that can and have been made to arguments of this sort, but I shall here, so as to not go too far afield, limit myself to one.[11] The crucial point I want to make here is just this: in asserting that in calling something "God" we must also say about that object of our discourse that its existence is necessary, its nonexistence wholly unthinkable, it is not at all necessary to construe "necessary" or "the necessity" here as "logically necessary" or "logical necessity."[12] The model term "necessary" has many uses. As Anscombe and Geach point out "since what is 'necessary' is what 'cannot' not be, to say that 'necessary' can only refer to logical necessity is equivalent to saying that whatever cannot be so, logically cannot be so—e.g., that since I cannot speak Russian, my speaking Russian is logically impossible: which is absurd."[13]

It is true that if something is appropriately designated by the word "God," it cannot not exist. But it doesn't at all follow from this, what is prima facie implausible, that "There is no God" is a contradiction and "There is a God" is a logical truth. This would only follow if the "cannot" in "cannot not exist" were a logical cannot, but what evidence do we have that this is so? Surely it looks as if we could significantly deny that there is a God.

That God couldn't just happen to exist, come to exist, cease to exist, if He exists at all, establishes that we conceive of God as an eternal being, but that "God is eternal" is analytic does not at all prove that an eternal being exists or that there are eternal beings. God couldn't come to exist or cease to exist, but it might be the case that there is no God.

That "God" is so defined that other beings are said to be completely dependent on God and that this dependence is not merely fortuitous does not prove that "There is a God" is logically necessary. "There is no completely independent being upon whom all things depend" or "There is a reality whose existence is necessary for all other being" can be significantly denied.

God's existence is thought to be necessary; but there is no good reason at all for thinking His existence is *logically* necessary or "There is a God" is logically true; and there is prima facie, though perhaps not decisive evidence, for asserting that God's existence is not logically necessary, namely that existential statements do not appear to be logical truths and that more specifically, "There is no God" does not at all appear to be self-contradictory or in any way contradictory. When believers say, as many of them do, that God's nonexistence is wholly unthinkable in any circumstance, they need not be taken to be holding a theory about the logical status of "There is a God," namely, that it is self-contradictory to deny that God exists. They can be taken to be asserting that the presence of God is so evident to them that, given their conception of Him as an eternal being, they could not, as a matter of psychological fact, in any way find it thinkable that God should not exist. God's actuality is so vividly present to believers that they could no more, except in a purely logical sense, come to doubt for one moment the reality of God than I could doubt that the earth has existed for many years and that I have been on or near to the surface of that earth during my life. I recognize that I can significantly deny these propositions (after all they are not analytic) but, like Moore, I am quite certain of them and I find it quite unthinkable that they might be false. When certain believers tell us that the nonexistence of God (that reality given to them through faith) is quite unthinkable, it is very plausible to take them to be making such an assertion.

God's existence is thought to be necessary; that is, if God exists the existence of God is without beginning or end and without dependence for existence upon any reality other than himself. But this necessity is not a logical necessity but the *aseity* of the scholastics, of what Hick calls a factual necessity.[14]

Thus it will not do to try to evade my contention that, given an nonanthropomorphic conception of God, "There is a God," is not an intelligible factual statement by claiming "There is a God" is logically true and asserts a "logical fact." There is no convention in English or logical rule which makes "There is no God" a contradiction. One might, by suitable stipulations and a little ingenuity, set up an artificial "ideal language" in which, given certain stipulative meaning-postulates, "There is no God," when interpreted by that "language," would be a contradiction, but this would only prove that certain people with certain needs and a certain amount of logical ingenuity had constructed such an artificial language. It would show nothing at all about whether "There is no God," which after all is part of the corpus of English, or its German, Spanish, or Swahili equivalents, is used to make a contradictory statement. In short, it would be of absolutely no avail in showing that the statement that there is no God is a contradiction and its denial a logical truth. Thus there are good grounds for thinking that "There is a God" is *not* a logical truth and there are no good grounds for thinking that it is; but, as even Clarke (a defender of the above view) insists, "There is a God" is surely taken to assert something and it is a statement around which ultimately all theistic discourse revolves.[15] It is not a logical statement asserting a "logical fact"; it is rather intended by believers as a factual statement asserting what, logically speaking, is a "contingent fact." But then our initial questions about confirmation and disconfirmation are perfectly relevant and this criticism of my argument fails. Consider the following: (1) there is a God; (2) there is an eternal being; (3) there is an infinite, nonspatio-temporal individual who never began to exist and never shall *cease* to exist and upon whom all other beings depend. When (1) and (2) are asserted by nonanthropomorphic believers and when (3) is asserted, their asserters do not know what, even in principle, would confirm or disconfirm these putatively factual assertions. Since this is so they are bogus, pseudo-factual statements, devoid of the kind of intelligibility that believers rightly demand of them.

Once we leave a simple but false or highly improbable anthropomorphic theism, we find that the key claims of nonanthropomorphic truly transcendent theistic beliefs are thought by those who accept these beliefs to be beliefs which are expressed in mysterious yet genuinely factual, nonanalytic statements; but these key theological statements, unfortunately, are not factual claims for, being unverifiable in principle, they are devoid of factual significance. In short, key doctrines of Judaism, Christianity, and Islam, doctrines without which these religions would be radically transformed and thoroughly undermined, are confused beliefs, parading as factual beliefs but actually functioning as bits of ideology that distort our understanding of the world and give a delusory support to certain peoples' basic commitments by making them appear to be based on facts, written so to say in the stars.[16] If what I have said in this essay is generally correct one ought to be an atheist and reject religious belief, anthropomorphic or nonanthropomorphic, as irrational and unnecessary.

This brings me to my third and final thesis, namely, my thesis about atheism. Kierkegaard and Tillich and many like them claim atheism is impossible. Atheism, in their view, is something like a contradiction for, in this very seriousness, in their very concern to destroy idols, atheists exhibit their belief, i.e., exhibit that in a profound sense they are *not* atheists. There is, as I shall show, an inordinate amount of confusion in such a claim. Atheism is not a kind of religion: it is not incoherent or contradictory; it is a reasonable belief that we all ought to adopt.

But before I go into that there are some important terminological distinctions that ought to be made. The first I owe to my colleague Paul Edwards and the second to the British philosopher Alasdair MacIntyre. Edwards points out that there are two ways in which the word "atheism" is used. Sometimes when a man maintains that there is no God he *simply* means that "There is a God" or "God exists" is false. This rather traditional atheism, as Ayer noted long ago, runs into the difficulty that the putative statement "There is a God" is factually meaningless when "God" is used in its straightforward religious ways. Since this is so there is an important respect in which such putative factual statements are unintelligible. But if "There is a God" is so unintelligible the parallel statement "There is no God" is likewise unintelligible. It does not express a false factual statement. Such an atheism is as nonsensical as such a theism! But, Edwards reminds us, there is a second way in which "atheism" is used, and this use of "atheism" is not entangled in these difficulties: ". . . a person is an atheist if he *rejects* belief in God, regardless of whether his rejection is based on the view that belief in God is false."[17] I think of myself as an atheist in this broader sense. To put the matter more precisely, "God exists" seems to me, depending on how "God" is used, either absurdly false, of such a low order of probability that belief in such a being is superstitious or, in its more characteristic uses, it is devoid of factual content and is thus in a significant sense unintelligible and unworthy of belief. To reject the concept of God for any of these reasons is to be, in this second broader sense, an atheist.

Yet even, acknowledging this important distinction, there are atheists and atheists. As MacIntyre points out, atheism of any of the above types tends to be what he calls a speculative atheism; that is to say its interests are theoretical: it is concerned with pointing out the fallacies in arguments for the existence of God, the unintelligibility of God-talk and the like. Its patron saints are Hume, Russell, and Ayer. But there is another kind of practical-activist atheism, an atheism that *presupposes* the truth of some form of speculative atheism, but goes far beyond it. We indeed must, such atheists argue, remove the mask of supernaturalist error, but, as Nietzsche and Feuerbach stressed, we must also transform man. We must develop the vision and the intelligence to live in a world without God; we must come to understand in some concrete detail how to give significance to our lives in such a world.

We need to see more clearly than most speculative atheists have that it is not argument or speculative wonder that stokes religion in the first place; rather it is emotional need that fathers religious belief. "Religion," as MacIntyre puts it, "is misunderstood if it is construed simply as a set of intellectual errors; it is rather the case that in a profoundly misleading form deep insights, hopes, and fears are being expressed."[18] We must cure man of his need for religion, and not just show the intellectual absurdity of it. We must, as Feuerbach and Marx stressed, transform society so that men will no longer need to turn to religious forms to give inspiration to their lives. We must show how men's visions and aspirations can be demythologized, can be embodied in purely secular *social forms*. We must, as Feuerbach, the greatest of all these activist atheists, puts it, change "the friends of God into friends of man, believers into thinkers, worshippers into workers, candidates for the other world into students of this world, Christians, who on their own confession are half-animal and half-angel, into new men—whole men." The patron saints of this kind of atheism are Feuerbach, Marx, Nietzsche, David Strauss, and Freud.

I count myself as such an atheist too—though certainly not as a patron saint. I hope in defending and advocating atheism, without personally engaging in any ideology or propagandistic moves, to establish the theoretical untenability of theistic beliefs, to show we do not need them to justify our moral convictions or to give significance to our lives, and to show that there are other ways of life, other ways of thinking and acting, that are more desirable, more admirable, more *worthy* of allegiance than our religious ways of life. In carrying out this last task, a philosopher must indeed do a little normative ethics and he must dirty his hands with a few empirical facts, but I see no reason why he should do these things, if only he does not confuse normative ethics with meta-ethics.[19] In this essay I have tried to do something toward establishing the first two points. To establish the third point, one must go into the nasty detail of normative argument and into an examination, in some concreteness and with some honesty, of the messy details and harassments of living.

Now I am in a position to examine the rather frequent charge that such atheism, and sometimes indeed all atheism, is not a denial of religion, but in effect and in reality its affirmation, an *Ersatz*-religion of its own.

Will Herberg, reasoning much as Kierkegaard, Tillich, Bultmann, and Bishop Robinson do about these matters, stresses the fact that we should see the "problem of God" not as a speculative affair but as an existential concern. Viewed in that way, he argues there are "on the existential level . . . no atheists."[20] Why not? Because, according to Herberg, "the structure of a human being is such that man cannot live his life, or understand himself, without some ultimate concern that he takes as the that-beyond-which-there-is-nothing of this world. That is indeed his god, and the articulation of his life in terms of it his religion. . . . In this sense every man, by virtue of being human, is *homo religiosus;* every man has his religion and his god. On the existential level, then, the question is not god or no god, religion or no religion; but rather: what *kind* of god? What *kind* of religion?" [21] Luther remarks that "whatever your heart clings to and confides in, that is your god." And Robinson and Tillich tell us that belief in God is a matter of what you take seriously without any reservation. That which ultimately concerns us, that which we finally place our trust in, that is our God. But since every man, and the atheist most fervently, places his trust in something, has some intimate and ultimate concern, no man is *existentially* an atheist or, if you would rather talk that way, atheism is a religion or at the very least an *Ersatz*-religion. "The atheism," Herberg argues, "of a Feuerbach or a young Marx was existentially not atheism at all, but the deification of Man; just as the 'atheism' of the later Marx, and so many Marxists, was actually a quasi-Hegelian deification of the Dialectic of History."[22]

There is a whole evening's worth of confusion in these Kierke-gaardian-Tillichian arguments. I shall only have time to expose a few of them, but that will be quite enough.

1. How do we know, or do we know, that all men or even most men

have these *ultimate* concerns? It is truistic that human beings care about things, if only booze, the opposite sex, and getting a new sports car. But does such a concern count as an ultimate concern? Well if it does we are well on our way to making "All men have ultimate concern" stipulatively, but arbitrarily, truistically true. If we do not play with words in this way, we certainly need a little raw empiricism, a little sociological and anthropological evidence, that all men have such *ultimate* concerns and thus man is *homo religiosus*. But these religious apologists do not give us such evidence.[23]

2. Let us, however, suppose we have such evidence. Let us suppose that all men everywhere have their ultimate concerns, have something they are deeply devoted to, committed to and finally put their trust in, it still does not follow at all that all such men are religious, that all such men believe in God, have a god, some sense of a *numinous* reality, or a sense of the divine or anything of that sort. We should beware of essentialist definitions of "religion."[24] Theravada Buddhism, a religion of spiritual liberation, has no God or object of worship and devotion.[25] To achieve nirvana (literally the "going out" as of a flame) is to finally achieve liberation (*moksa*) from the endless series of rebirths of a life that is full of suffering. But the goal of this religion is also a spiritual one; nirvana is a very different concept than God, but like the concept of God it is a transcendental concept, e.g., the Buddhist faithful will not allow that naturalistic accounts of it can be fully adequate. In this way, all religions, besides being matters of ultimate concern, have some concept of the sacred or some concept of spiritual reality. But the atheist repudiates nirvana as fully as God; he rejects thinking in terms of sacred, divine, or spiritual realities. If like Nietzsche, Feuerbach, and Freud, he is what I have called an active atheist, he too has his commitments, has his vision of what a good world would be like, has—if you will—his ultimate concerns. But this does not make him religious, except in the perfectly trivial sense that to be religious about anything is to be deeply involved with it and the like; it does not give him a religion or a god, except in another *metaphorical* sense. To place your trust in something, to be ultimately concerned, to be concerned about the meaning of your existence is at best a *necessary* but most surely not a sufficient condition for being religious or having a religion. To have a religion is to have a distinctive ethical outlook, to accept a certain *Weltanschauung*, but the converse need not be the case. Ethics is not religion and religion is not simply ethics, or ethics touched with emotion, or associated with parable. A practical activist atheist has a normative view, a *Weltanschauung*, but no religion. "A religious way of life" is not a redundancy; "a religious *Weltanschauung*" is not a pleonasm and "an antireligious or areligious ethic or way of life" is not a contra-

diction, a logical oddity or a deviation from a linguistic regularity.

Herberg argues that on the existential level there are no atheists for atheism is itself a religious affirmation. He has not shown how this is the case and I have given good reasons for denying that it is the case. But Herberg goes beyond this, for according to him atheism is not only religious, it is an idolatrous religion for it deifies man, the dialectic of history or the state. Herberg again confuses having a certain way of life, having a set of ethical and aspirational ideals, with having a religion. But I think it must be admitted that *some* atheists, not sufficiently emancipated from religious thinking, did stupidly deify man. Comte and Saint-Simon are offenders here, and this most surely is ideological thinking and ought to be resisted most strenuously. But no atheist *must* think this way; no atheist should think this way; and most atheists do not think in this confused way. Commitment yes; ideology and religion no. A commitment to a way-of-life need not be a religious commitment or an ideological commitment.

How this is so can be brought out most economically by contrasting a remark Herberg makes about Christianity with a remark I would make about religion. Herberg remarks that "the fundamental conviction of Christianity is the belief in the insufficiency, nay impotence, of man to straighten out his life or achieve anything worthwhile through his own powers and resources, without reliance on the God beyond."[26] Now I am perfectly aware that there is corruption in the palace of justice; all my life I have felt keenly in myself and in others the deeply perverse Dostoevskian ambivalences of the human animal. Man is, in Pascal's magnificent phrase, but a frail reed; however, I would still reply to Herberg that it is either false or factually meaningless to assert that there is "a God beyond" as the ground of being and meaning, or as the reality transcendent to the cosmos. Such beliefs are ideological and mythological, and man, frail though he be, has no such reality to place his trust in or to rely on. Furthermore, man does have some knowledge of good and evil that not only is but must be independent of any knowledge of a transcendent reality, being-as-such, or a ground of being. Some men have straightened out their lives, given meaning to their own existence and helped to give meaning to the lives of others by using their own puny powers and the help of others similarly situated. To believe that this is so for some men, to *hope* that it may be so for others, and to work to bring about social and psychological conditions under which this will be so for as many as possible is not to engage in ideology, to *deify* man, or to make for oneself an idolatrous religion, an *Ersatz*-religion, or for that matter any religion at all.

NOTES

1. These remarks about ideology were occasioned by a reading of Henry Aiken's perceptive essay "The Revolt Against Ideology," *Commentary* 37 (1964): 29-30. For an exact account of the nature of ideological statements see my "On Speaking of God," *Theoria* 28 (1962): 118-125.

2. These remarks were made by Professor Passmore in a lecture "What Is Philosophy?" given to the New York University Philosophy Club during the spring semester of 1964.

3. Anne Fremantle, ed., *The Papal Encyclicals* (New York: New American Library, 1956), p. 25.

4. Ronald Hepburn, "A Critique of Humanist Theology," in *Objections to Humanism*, ed. H. J. Blackham (Philadelphia: Lippincott, 1963), pp. 52-54.

5. Some of the difficulties, evasions, and obscurities are brought out in Robinson's somewhat sensational book *Honest to God* and in the subsequent volume *The Honest to God Debate.*

6. Weston LeBarre, "Religions, Rorschachs, and Tranquilizers," *The American Journal of Orthopsychiatry* 29 (1959): 688-698.

7. This is most clearly put by I. M. Crombie in his "The Possibility of Theological Statements," in *Faith and Logic,* ed. Basil Mitchell (London: George Allen and Unwin, Ltd., 1957), pp. 31-83.

8. The views I have in mind are clearly expressed by Bowman L. Clarke in his "Linguistic Analysis and the Philosophy of Religion," *The Monist* 47 (Spring 1963): 365-386; and Charles Hartshorne, *The Logic of Perfection* (La-Salle, IL: The Open Court Publishing Co., 1962).

9. J. N. Findlay, "Can God's Existence Be Disproved?" in *New Essays in Philosophical Theology* (New York: The Macmillan Co., 1955), pp. 47-57.

10. Ibid., p. 52.

11. Terrence Penelhum's essay "Divine Necessity," *Mind* 69 (1960): 175-186, the essays in response to Malcolm's defense of the ontological arugment by Allen, Ableson and Penelhum, *The Philosophical Review* (January 1961): 56-92; Robert C. Coburn's, "Professor Malcolm on God," *Australasian Journal of Philosophy* 41 (1963); John O. Nelson, "Modal Logic and the Ontological Proof for God's Existence," *The Review of Metaphysics* 17 (1963); and Adel Daher, "God and Logical Necessity," *Philosophical Studies* (Dublin, Ireland) 18 (1969) all raise effective arguments against some facets of such a position.

12. This is nicely shown by John Hick, "Necessary Being," *Scottish Journal of Theology* 14 (1961): 355-369 and Alvin Plantinga, "Necessary Being," in *Faith and Philosophy,* ed. Alvin Plantinga (Grand Rapids, MI: Wm. B. Eerdmans Co., 1964), pp. 97-108.

13. G. E. M. Anscombe and P. T. Geach, *Three Philosophers: Aristotle, Aquinas and Frege* (Oxford: Oxford University Press, 1961), p. 114.

14. John Hick, p. 365.

15. Bowman Clarke, p. 376.

16. Attention to my remarks about ideological statements will help make the nature of such claims clearer.

17. Paul Edwards, "Some Notes on Anthropomorphic Theology," in *Religious Experience and Truth,* ed. Sidney Hook (New York: New York Uni-

versity Press, (1961), p. 242. See also my "On Being an Atheist," *The Personalist* (Winter 1970).

18. Alasdair MacIntyre, "God and The Theologians," *Encounter* (September 1965): 3.

19. For some of the crucial distinctions here and for some of the ways in which we may do normative ethics see my "Speaking of Morals," *The Centennial Review* 2 (1958): 414-444 and Hans Albert, "Ethik und Metaethik," *Archiv für Philosophie* 2 (1961): 28-63.

20. Will Herberg, "God and The Theologians," *Encounter* (November 1963): 57.

21. Ibid., p. 56.

22. Ibid., p. 57.

23. I have said something more about this in my "Is God So Powerful That He Doesn't Even Have to Exist," in *Religious Experience and Truth*, pp. 270-282.

24. Ninian Smart, "Numen, Nirvana and The Definition of Religion," *Church Quarterly Review* (April-June 1959): 216-225.

25. Ninian Smart, "Buddhism and Religious Belief," *The Humanist* 76 (1961): 47-50. See also his *A Dialogue of Religions* (London: 1960).

26. Will Herberg, p. 57.

7

The Burden of Proof
and *The Presumption of Atheism*

I

The Presumption of Atheism is a well-made selection of Antony Flew's essays on the grand Kantian trio consisting of God, freedom, and immortality. It is a collection that is to be welcomed, for, while some of the essays are plainly occasional pieces, others, such as the title piece "The Presumption of Atheism," "The Free Will Defense" and "The Identity of Incorporeal Persons" are central contributions. Moreover, the essays taken together constitute a lively and well-integrated effort aggressively to articulate on these topics, much in the tradition of Flew's hero Hume, updated through Russell and Ayer, a rationalistic empiricist posture. Flew does not mince words; he has a sound streak of common sense and is usually (though often at the crucial point with too great a penchant for brevity) clear. *The Presumption of Atheism* should be required reading for all ministers, theologians and theology students.

I am going to concentrate on the central essays on God in Part One and most particularly on the key methodological challenge laid down in the presumption of atheism. I do this because we have here, in part supplementing and in part replacing his earlier famous Falsification Challenge, an absolutely crucial challenge to theistic religions, which, if the case can be justifiably conducted on Flew's terms, will provide a distinctive and very powerful defense of atheism and thus a ground for rejecting Judaism, Christianity, and Islam.

From the *Religious Studies Review* 3 (1977): 144-150. Reprinted by permission of the publisher.

II

A very crucial and not easily settled point in almost any important philosophical discussion concerns where the burden of proof lies. Whether a consideration of it surfaces or not, a decision over such a matter will deeply affect the whole perspective. And this remains as true when the decision is an "in effect decision" not made reflectively or rationally as when it is a decision made under those constraints. Antony Flew is very conscious of this and that is why he very explicitly conducts the argument the way he does in *The Presumption of Atheism*. Flew's thesis is that the burden of proof lies with the Christian or Jew "first, to introduce and to defend his proposed concept of God; and second to provide sufficient reason for believing that this concept of his does in fact have an application" (p. 15).[1]

Flew goes on to remark that it is the first stage of this two-stage contention that needs most to be emphasized. In this way "God" is unlike the "Loch Ness Monster" or the "Abominable Snowman," where it is tolerably clear what it is we are asking about. In the case of "God" it cannot be taken for granted that a Jew or a Christian, most particularly a reasonably orthodox Jew or Christian, is "operating with a legitimate concept which theoretically could have an application to an actual being" (p. 15).

Flew defends this procedure by claiming (a) that it is in an important sense neutral, for in adopting it we make, he claims, no substantive assumptions about God or about what there is or is not or can or cannot be, and (b) it forces the parties to the dispute, including the Jew, Christian or Moslem, to begin at the beginning and to deploy arguments "to ensure that the word 'God' is provided with a meaning such that it is theoretically possible for an actual being to be so described" (p. 16).

In stating his case Flew stresses that the presumption of atheism is a methodological presumption and not an assumption or a presumptuous preconception (pp. 13-14 and 31). It is through and through defeasible (defeatable) and, like the presumption of innocence in English law, can be defeated. Though, unlike particular cases of the law, Flew believes that the presumption of atheism has in fact never been defeated. However, in both cases the presumption is a procedural device designed, in the conduct of their respective inquiries, to provide as fair and as impartial an outcome as is possible. In this way they both resemble procedural justice.

In the God case it indeed throws the burden of proof on the believer, where the word "proof," quite properly, is "being used in the ordinary wide sense in which it can embrace any and every variety of sufficient reason." But the Christian, by accepting this procedural framework, is, Flew would have it, no more betrayed or trapped than is a party to a trial in accepting the procedural framework in which the accused is presumed innocent until proven guilty. The adopting of such a procedure does not at all preclude all the parties to the dispute from having very deeply embedded and deeply felt convictions concerning the substantive question of the existence of God. There is nothing, Flew contends, in the procedural commitments that denies the believer the right to affirm the reality of God or even suggests that in coming to have such beliefs the believer must be or is likely to be behaving irrationally: "the context for which this particular procedure is being recommended is that of justification rather than of discovery" (p. 25).

III

Flew's lead essay "The Presumption of Atheism" first appeared in *The Canadian Journal of Philosophy* in 1972 and is reprinted in *The Presumption of Atheism* "with comparatively minor revisions" (p. 8). When it first appeared in *The Canadian Journal of Philosophy,* Donald Evans responded that Flew's supposedly neutral procedural device was in reality anything but neutral. Without doubt that is a natural suspicion to entertain. And with that in mind, I want to follow but, in the light of the extended arguments in the whole of Flew's book, the central arguments about this in the exchange between Flew and Evans. I want to see if we can ascertain where the truth lies.

Evans is quite aware that the intent and indeed the actual function of Flew's allegedly purely procedural presumption of atheism is to leave quite intact whatever religious or areligious convictions the parties to the dispute may have. Why then does Evans believe the procedure is inextricably skewed in favor of atheism from the very beginning? One central reason is that Evans believes that there is "a hidden substantive element in Flew's proposal."[2] To smoke out what this may be, ask this question: why should the theist accept Flew's proposed procedural rule for debating theism/atheism, granting to the atheist the burden of proof is on him as a believer to produce to the nonbeliever or even to an impartial spectator good enough reasons for believing?[3] The hidden substantive assumption, answering this question and used to justify Flew's stance, is, according to Evans, that the "only reasonable position for anyone is to be 'completely noncommital' concerning God unless and until good enough reasons are produced" for religious belief. However, the believer, Evans claims, knows, or at least should know, beforehand, that if he starts a debate on theism/atheism with a skeptic, from the procedural base of atheism, that he will probably lose. In speaking of God, we are speaking of what the believer takes to be an ultimate mystery. A reflective believer, if he is philosophically literate, knows very well the concept of God—the concept of such a mysterious ultimate reality—is only partially intelligible to him and is likely to be through and through unintelligible to the skeptic. Given this state of affairs, it is very unlikely that it will be the case that the believer can produce good enough reasons to convince the skeptic that this procedural presumption of atheism has been defeated and that it is not unreasonable to believe in God.

Moreover, the dispute between believer and skeptic is so deep and so, at least, apparently intractable that the dispute will in large measure turn on "what counts" in such a domain "as a a good enough reason," and there may even be—Evans thinks there actually are—"differences in criteria of intelligibility and rationality between theist and atheist."[4] In making background assumptions of a fundamentally empiricist and rationalistic sort, such as his Agnostic Principle (i.e., "that we ought always to proportion our belief to the evidence"), a principle which Flew says he cleaves to throughout, Flew assumes a very contestable and indeed problematic conception of rationality. A ruling assumption of Flew's is that reasonable people will, if philosophically sophisticated, reason according to the Agnostic Principle, will be aware of the problematic nature of the concept of God, and will know that there is no good evidence for (or a sound argument for) the claim that God exists. In such a situation they will not believe or at least they will not take belief in God to be justified until grounds that would convince informed, impartial, and rational persons can be produced. But here, Evans argues, in these assumptions about reasonability, we have a cluster of interlocking substantive conceptions, which (a) would be a trap for the believer to accept, (b) would very definitely deflect the debate in favor of the skeptic, and (c) which make tendentious assumptions about rationality.

Evans sets out another argument for questioning the neutrality of the presumption of atheism. Flew conceives of God as an alleged entity sufficiently similar to the theoretical entities of science to admit of the relevance of raising questions about applying Ockham's razor. But Flew is also perfectly aware that the question of the existence of God, like questions concerning freedom and immortality, are questions of very considerable human import, deeply affecting people's conceptions of themselves. Where such a situation obtains, Flew stresses, it is very important to have adequate grounds for belief. But is it not, given the immense human importance of the issue involved, equally important to have adequate grounds for disbelief? If we start with the presumption of atheism we are not likely to acquire such grounds. If we still cleave, as Flew does, to the presumption of atheism, and to the Agnostic Principle as well, are we not in effect at least assuming "that an uncommitted stance on matters of grave import where there is a paucity of universally-accepted reasons/or evidence is always morally superior"?[5] We can weaken that, as I believe we should, to "usually/or generally morally superior" and still reasonably ask whether reason commits us to any such thing. It seems to me very questionable, to put it minimally, that it does, and yet it appears (a) to be a background assumption of Flew's and (b) it seems to be required if we are going to accept his procedural assumption of atheism. Moreover, someone might be thoroughly convinced by Flew's arguments against Pascal's wager (chapter 5) and against Tolstoy's arguments that without belief in God and immortality life is meaningless (chapter 12) while still, as is Evans, being quite unwilling to make that very strong but still crucial background assumption. At the very least we need further argument from Flew on this point.

Flew, in briefly responding to Evans, revealingly avoids either argument or concession concerning this last issue.[6] Flew responds to Evans by remarking that the crucial issue is not whether a believer or a skeptic thinks there are or are not good reasons for belief in God but whether there really are. The "procedural presumption of atheism is recommended as the right one for an inquiry directed to discovering whether there are in fact good reasons for believing. . . ."[7] The question about the rational or moral integrity of a certain person—say Evans or Nielsen—believing a certain thing is a quite different matter. That latter question can be answered by finding out whether the person, after "the most searching examination of which he is capable," still believes that the reasons he is in this way acquainted with are sufficient, everything considered, for belief.[8] But, Flew stresses, this leaves open the question of whether there are in fact good reasons for that belief (in this case belief in God) or whether what that person reasonably takes to be good reasons are in fact good reasons for belief.

To Evans's unargued assumption that criteria of intelligibility and rationality differ between skeptics and believers and across domains of discourse, Flew responds, predictably and reasonably enough, by challenging that assumption. He does not deny that in some cases it may be true but "before we accept so depressingly divisive a conclusion" we should, Flew argues, "surely first explore very thoroughly the alternative possibility, that our disagreements arise instead from differences over the correct application of the same criteria."[9] Moreover, as he has argued elsewhere, for there to be two different concepts of rationality between two groups indicates that there must also be a "considerable coincidence between one and the other" such that the differences between them cannot be so unbridgeable that no argument is in order.[10] They must, Flew claims, share some common criterion or otherwise we would not be able correctly to speak of them as being two concepts of *rationality*.

However, Evans could reply by accepting Flew's point that there are very abstract and general criteria, such as Flew alludes to, and such as have been set out by Hollis and Lukes against Winch's partial attempt to make relative the criteria of rationality.[11] He could accept all this and still reasonably argue that between believers and skeptics in moral and religious domains, as between the participants of different cultures—say Westerners and the Azande disagreeing over magic—there remain deeply embedded partially differing criteria of rationality with no bases in the agreed upon criteria in virtue of which we could reduce disagreement over such matters and show which groups exemplified most fully what it was to be rational and had the best reasons for believing as they did. Flew rightly distinguishes between truth and rationality and between being deluded and being irrational. A "militantly secular historian who makes no bones about his conviction that the distinctively religious beliefs of all parties were uniformly delusions" could still consistently argue that certain people—say Müntzer more than Luther—were more consistent and, given their conceptions, attended more adequately to the evidence, and thus were more rational than other people operating within the same framework.[12]

Flew wants us to use this distinction to beat back what he regards as the false and dangerous contention that "which beliefs count as delusions is a matter of the standards of a given time and place."[13] Flew remarks that "what truly is determined by such relativistic standards is: not what is really a delusion; but which delusions are recognized as such."[14] But the recognition of this conceptual distinction is cold comfort if, over convictional and ideological matters, standards of rationality do in fact differ and there seem, at least, to be no agreed upon criteria across cultures, and between believers and skeptics, as to what, in such domains, counts as a delusion and what does not.

Evans thinks that this is the way believers and skeptics are divided over fundamental questions of religious belief. If that in fact is the situation, then it is not at all clear that there is, over fundamental disputes concerning religious belief, the background agreement in judgment and in criteria of rationality in virtue of which there could be any rational agreement between believers and skeptics such that we could settle what, through and through, are not only thought to be good reasons but really are good reasons for such beliefs. If this is the case, it is not at all clear that Flew has shown to Evans or any other reflective believer that he should make the presumption of atheism and that in accepting this presumption he is accepting a neutral procedural device that will not trap him. At the very least, Flew must do more than he has done hitherto to elucidate and defend an objective and unitary conception of rationality and perspicuously to exhibit its relation to what we can reasonably believe and do. He must give us, to make his position convincing, good reasons for believing that we have a common concept of rationality with strong enough criteria to give us grounds for assessing the comparative rationality of the commitments of believers and skeptics. Without such an articulation and defense there will be a large question mark before Flew's presumption of atheism.

IV

The above assumptions about rationality are not the only assumptions that make problems for Flew's presumption of atheism. To make the others more pointed and to lay out the rationale for the arguments pro and con around Flew's defense of his case, it is important to flesh out a little more fully how Flew does defend his methodological tack in philosophical theology. His claim, as we have seen, is that in debates over atheism and theism "the onus of proof must lie upon the theist" (p. 14). Yet, the procedural commitment to atheism is not the positive claim either that there is no God or that the concept of God is incoherent; rather it is the negative one that is simply not taking a theistic stance and that one does not make the assumptions of theism. Flew calls this "negative atheism" and while this is a minimal position, it is, when compared with what by now is commonly regarded as agnosticism, a very bedrock position indeed, for the negative atheist has not even conceded that we have "a legitimate concept of God," which may or may not have an application, such that there is or at least could be "ultimate reality" which answers to that concept or—perhaps more adequately—conception (p. 14). Flew regards it as a very important matter that we do not take it "for granted that even the would-be mainstream theist is operating with a legitimate concept which theoretically could have an application to an actual being" (p. 15).

Flew goes on to argue that the general reason the presumption of atheism matters is that "its acceptance must put the whole question of the existence of God into an entirely fresh perspective" (p. 15). We no longer, as so many theologians do, start with the assumption "that there is a Divine Being, with an actual nature the features of which we can investigate" (p. 15). Here a contrast between *The Presumption of Atheism* and I. T. Ramsey's *On Being Sure in Religion* would be very instructive indeed. Flew's methodological gambit, if accepted, forces the "theist who wants to build a systematic and thorough apologetic . . . to begin absolutely from the beginning" (p. 16). He will have "to ensure that the word 'God' is provided with a meaning such that it is theoretically possible for an actual being to be so described" (p. 16).

Flew recognizes and indeed seems to welcome the fact that acceptance of the presumption of atheism makes "the whole enterprise of theism" appear "even more difficult than it did before" (p. 16). It is not, he continues, that in accepting that procedural framework any substantive assumptions are made either for or against theism. Still it is the case that theism is now thrown into a more problematic light. There is, if we proceed in this way, the recognition of "the imperative need to produce some sort of sufficient reason to justify theist belief" (p. 16). And certain difficulties, which from a fideistic methodological stance, for example, are thought to be rather peripheral or even factitious now stand out as fundamental (p. 16).

In accepting this presumption of atheism, Flew claims, there is no more a precluding or even a prejudicing of the theist's case than the presumption of innocence in law precludes a verdict of guilty or prejudices the case in favor of the innocence of the accused. A prosecuting attorney may be through and through convinced of the guilt of the defendant; yet in accepting the procedural presumption of innocence built into English law, he does not betray a trust or trap himself such that he cannot establish guilt. Similarly the theologian conducting counsel for theism need not at all modify his perhaps unshakable belief in God or preclude the possibility of conducting a successful defense of theism by accepting the procedural presumption of atheism. He can, Flew argues, in "good conscience allow that a thorough and complete apologetic must start from, meet and go on to defeat, the presumption of atheism" (p. 18). There is here no presumption or assumption of the substantive beliefs of Stratonician atheism, namely, that we "must take the Universe itself and its most fundamental laws as themselves ultimate" (p. 52). Nor is there the assumption of the Principle of Sufficient Reason, namely, "that there has to be a sufficient reason for anything and everything being as it is, was and will be. . . " (p. 52). Flew indeed thinks, as is apparent in his *God and Philosophy*, that Stratonician atheism is true but he does not assume it in his arguments for the presumption of atheism; concerning the Principle of Sufficient Reason, Flew believes that T. M. Penelhum has shown this principle to be demonstrably false (pp. 55, 171). But for us, the crucial thing is to see that we do not need to presuppose any of these substantive claims or their denials to make the presumption of atheism.

Why, it is natural to ask, should the burden or onus of proof be on the theist rather than the negative atheist? This question, Flew remarks candidly, cannot be answered without an appeal to the scale of values involved for the people making the argument anymore than the presumption of innocence in our legal system can be justified as superior to the presumption of guilt in some other legal systems without reference to the comparative value of the aims built into either presumption. If, for example, "for you it is more important that no guilty person should ever be acquitted than no innocent person should ever be convicted, then for you a presumption of guilt must be the rational policy" (p. 21). What is irrational to believe and do cannot be specified independently of the scale of values or the reflective preferences of the people involved. The same is true about the presumption of atheism.

It is the value we place on knowing or at least having good grounds for what we believe that tips the scale in favor of the presumption of atheism. (We may call this, following Flew's own manner, Flew's Rationalistic Principle.) It is not reasonable or desirable to believe where we have no grounds for belief. If we are to reasonably (justifiably) believe that there is a God, we must have good grounds for a belief that that is so. In all sorts of matters—say that a friend of ours has been accused of something discreditable—we must be scrupulous in not asserting that he did so act or that he did not so act, unless we have grounds sufficient to warrant that claim. If this is so here, it is even more evident that, on the weighty questions of life and death, it is "scandalous . . . to maintain that you know either on no grounds at all, or on grounds of a kind which on other and comparatively minor issues you yourself would insist to be inadequate" (p. 22). In short, there is, Flew maintains, this inescapable and perfectly plausible demand for grounds for belief. Beliefs must be shown to have grounds to be reasonably believed. So it is perfectly in order and nonprejudicial to demand that of the believer, particularly when the belief is that this exhibiting of grounds is just what cannot be done for certain fundamental religious beliefs. So, Flew reasons, given that reasonable demand for grounds, the presumption of atheism is justified (pp. 21-22). Until and unless some grounds "are produced we have literally no reason at all for believing; and in that situation the only reasonable posture must be that of either the negative atheist or the agnostic" (p. 22).

This is in essence how Flew conducts his case. However, there are at least two very fundamental objections that should be made to Flew's account. The first harks back in part to the objection of Evans's. If there is an understandable human need (motive) to believe in something where that something is (a) of grave human import and (b) where it is generally accepted that there is a paucity of universally

acceptable reasons for even the probable truth or probable falsity of
the claim in question, to claim, without some additional and independent grounds, as Flew in effect does, that to be reasonable a person
should remain uncommitted (here be a negative atheist) is at best an
arbitrary claim.[15] Why is it not reasonable to accept God on *faith* in
such a circumstance? (One need not make claims about knowing that
God exists or having some esoteric grounds for believing that God
exists.) This need not be a failure of nerve if one admits that if evidence were forthcoming which tipped the evidential scales reasonably
decisively in favor of positive atheism, that then one would abandon
one's faith. But (or so it could be claimed), as things stand, one lives
by faith and does not make the presumption of atheism. Why should
one assume one's faith is unjustified if there is a human rationale for
it in making sense of our tangled lives?[16] And what is unreasonable
about it if one accepts it understanding full well that one is not believing on the basis of evidence?

There is indeed here no evidence for one's belief, but, as Flew
stresses himself, we should distinguish between *reasons as evidence*
and *reasons as motives*. Here we still have reasons as motives. Moreover, we can appeal to them without making Pascal's desperate wager
or Pascal's or Tolstoy's extreme claim that life is meaningless or morality is groundless without belief in God. Rather the claim is that
religion meets needs that are not satisfied by a purely secular view of
the world and that, since this is so, one has a rational motive (a rationale) for believing in God and not making the presumption of atheism even when there is no universally acceptable *evidence* for the
probable truth of theism.

To accept Flew's rationale for the acceptance of atheism is just to
ignore or groundlessly override such considerations in favor of purely
cognitive interests. It is, that is, to cleave groundlessly and at least
apparently arbitrarily to the Rationalistic Principle. What Flew must
do to justify his procedure here is to establish at least one of the
following: (a) that it is false that religious belief meets genuine needs
that cannot be met by a purely secular view of the world, (b) that one,
even when one has a rationale rooted in human need, should not believe anything unless one has some generally acceptable evidence for
its truth, for "we ought always to proportion our belief to the evidence" (p. 7).

Flew, as far as I know, has not tried to establish the truth of (a)
though it is by no means clear that (a) could not be justified. Still it is
fair enough to say that a case needs to be made for (a). For (b), however, we should say that it is in effect thought to be justified by what
Flew calls the Agnostic Principle. However, it is just here where my
second objection to Flew's defense of his presumption of atheism

would be made. It is wildly unrealistic and indeed actually an unreasonable demand to require that all one's reasonable believing must have grounds and that the strength of our belief should be proportional to our evidence for that belief. There are many things we reasonably believe which we do not believe for a reason and it is even true, as Wittgenstein and Malcolm powerfully argue, that it is difficult for us to realize the extent of our groundless believing. There are the subtly and extensively developed arguments of Wittgenstein in *On Certainty* which show that without a whole battery of beliefs which we as a matter-of-course hold without grounds, and indeed often have no idea at all what it would be like to have grounds for them, we would not be able to know anything or base anything on evidence or on grounds. This conception, earlier articulated by Pierce in his assault on Cartesianism, need not involve the claim that there is any single belief for which, in certain contexts, it would not be legitimate to ask on what grounds it is held, while still claiming that at any time there must be a multitude of beliefs which are held without grounds.

If there is a positive and specific need to request grounds because there is reason to think the specific belief is false, or perhaps even incoherent, then it is reasonable to request grounds for that belief. But to do that for belief in God is to go beyond the methodological limits Flew imposed on himself and to make substantive claims via theism, e.g., to claim that there are some at least *prima facie* good positive reasons for believing theistic claims are either false or incoherent. Flew actually has or believes he has such reasons, but in his modest proposal for the procedural presumption of atheism he was determined to bypass such substantive assumptions, but it is just this that he cannot do *and* justify his distinctive presumption of atheism.

Flew cannot evade this objection by maintaining that, like Aquinas and Ockham, he is merely following, in justifying his presumption of atheism, the quite innocuous procedural policy of postulational economy, for if he makes that appeal, it can be immediately pointed out that the conception here is that we are not to multiply the postulation of entities *beyond* need and that difficulty is, as has often been brought out, in the appeal to need (pp. 27–30). Whether there is indeed a need for such a postulation cannot be decided independently of those very contestable substantive considerations that divide believers and skeptics. It will, that is, bring in those very considerations that Flew was trying to avoid taking sides on in making what he hoped would be his neutral and modest methodological proposal for the presumption of atheism.

Flew might in turn respond that I am forgetting that his presumption of atheism is being recommended in the context of *justification* rather than *discovery* and that it was not designed to show that for a religious conviction to be respectable it must have been *first* "reached through the following of an ideally correct procedure" but rather that it must be able to withstand in debate such a procedural challenge if it is to be reasonably believed (p. 25). But the context of my discussion has been a justificatory one. I have been concerned to argue that the insistence on this presumption as the correct procedure for conducting the debate between theism/atheism rests, in a way Flew tries unsuccessfully to deny, on disputable claims which are themselves substantive, and unless and until Flew can justify them there is no reason that the believer, Flew's fellow atheists (of which I count myself one) or an impartial observer of the actual (if such there be) should follow him in such a presumption of atheism.

V

What he says in chapter 2 about "The Principle of Agnosticism" and in chapter 6 about the Falsification Challenge reinforces the above conclusion. The picture Flew paints is that it is best to accept the Falsification Challenge, the Presumption of Atheism, and the Principle of Agnosticism, if one wants, as a reasonable, reflective person, to face the problems of life with an open mind and a commitment to clarity. Flew believes that these conceptions nicely mesh together to define an undogmatic posture toward questions of religious belief (pp. 31, 76–77). They will be the conceptual equipment of the person who follows reason as far as it can take one and their acceptance is the hallmark of the reasonable human being. There is no space fully to argue here but all these claims need a thorough challenging and there are evident objections to his underlying commitments, which Flew does nothing to counter. The most obvious difficulty is in his unequivocal commitment to the Agnostic Principle "that we ought always to proportion our belief to the evidence" (pp. 7, 32, 35). As Wittgenstein has shown, there are many beliefs which a reasonable person holds (if he is a twentieth-century Westerner)—that he has two hands, a head, that things don't just disappear without cause, that if he puts a book in a drawer it really stays there, that the earth has existed for over a hundred years, that Mont Blanc is 4000 meters high, that there are radio waves that pass through plate glass, that there are germs that cause diseases, and that there are subatomic particles—that he does not believe, if he is at all a typical Westerner, because he has grounds for them. He simply has been taught them or has in some less didactic way been socialized into them. He could check *some* of them and he could, and I believe should, say with Pierce that, if the specific need actually arises, there is nothing impossible or wrong about subjecting any of them to critical inspection. But, as Pierce also recognized, and as Wittgenstein stressed even more, in order to scrutinize any one belief masses of others would have to stand fast and remain unscrutinized. And no good reason has been given, *à la* Descartes, to try to scrutinize them all and rank them in believability by the amount and quality of evidence we have for them. Indeed, to do so is an impossibility.

It is, as Wittgenstein put it, "difficult to realize the groundlessness of our believing." Yet it is a pervasive fact of our lives that many deeply embedded but ungrounded beliefs remain thoroughly reasonable to believe and indeed, if they were not believed, it would hardly be possible to carry out the kind of critical inquiry that Flew recommends.

Flew, solidly in the Enlightenment Tradition, argues that it is essential that our opinions be suitably grounded, if they are to be rated as items of knowledge, or even probable belief; of belief in God in particular, he stresses that there is an "imperative need to produce some sort of sufficient reason to justify theist belief" (pp. 23 and 16). But, if for all of us and unavoidably there is this massive background of quite mundane, groundless beliefs which are still reasonably believed, Flew's demand for grounds comes to seem very quixotic and unrealistic indeed. It very much appears at least to be the case that Flew needs, if his presumption of atheism is to have any force, to show how groundless religious beliefs are different and require justification before they can be reasonably accepted.

VI

Finally, I shall set out two more important ways in which Flew makes assumptions, essential for his defense of atheism, which he makes no attempt to defend and whose acceptability is in doubt. Flew claims that "it cannot be taken for granted that even the would-be mainstream theist is operating with a legitimate concept which theoretically could have an application to an actual being" (p. 15). But Flew just assumes, and without benefit of any developed theory about this, that we can recognize when we do and do not have a *legitimate concept*. Yet he rejects those positivist and later Wittgensteinian doctrines which might give us some inkling of when we do or do not have a legitimate concept (pp. 36–37 and 76–77).

However, without a "general doctrine about meaning," Flew is still willing to hold forth on what are and what are not legitimate concepts. But different philosophers, whether believers or not, might differ very much here and many would no doubt say that, given the state that theories of meaning are in, the question could hardly be profitably broached let alone answered. There is little reason to think that a believer should believe that he should take such a claim, without much added argument from Flew, as rationally constraining. Why should he accept the challenge to prove his concept of God a legitimate concept when we have not been shown that we have any reasonable understanding of what is and what is not a legitimate concept?

Flew also claims in his latest word about the Falsification Challenge that a putative religious claim can hardly be a substantial claim with any "explanatory or predictive or retrodictive power unless it carries some consequences about what has occurred, or is occurring, or will occur" (p. 77). I, as those who have read my essays on the philosophy of religion know, am very partial—perhaps overly partial— to that claim, but it is a claim which has been subjected to severe and varied sorts of criticisms from some very tough-minded philosophers. What bothers me is that Flew keeps trying to assert it as the most obvious bit of common sense and insists on defending it without developing anything like a general doctrine of either meaning or of factual significance (pp. 77-78). But that, as Flew likes to remark, surely will not do in view of the state of play of arguments about the Falsification Challenge.

Given the way that not just the Plantingas have challenged it but the Davidsons as well, a reflective theist might very well be excused for wondering whether Flew is here being as open-minded and undogmatic as he likes to take himself to be.

VII

The thrust of this critical review might come as quite a surprise to those who know how deeply I have been influenced by Flew's views about the Falsification Challenge and Theistic Identification. Part of it emerges from my own chastening realization that I know less now than I used to think I knew; but part of it springs, as well, from a belief that things are usually more complicated than Flew allows and that more acknowledgment should be made to Wittgenstein than Flew's rather rationalistic empiricism allows. Nonetheless, and for all of that, the Falsification Challenge and the problem of Theistic Identification still seem to me important instruments in philosophical theology. However, they need sustained and systematic defense and explication, and they need placement in a philosophical theory.

Flew, perhaps out of fear of being caught up in the errors of positivism, and perhaps because of a not unhealthy skepticism about philosophical theories, refuses to develop such a defense and yet without such a defense his Falsification Challenge has little force. Flew wants, without Wittgenstein's "obscurantism," to remain securely fixed in a sturdy, very English commonsense posture, muddling through without grand theories which may turn out to be grand ideologies. Earlier, with his Falsification Challenge, and now with his Principle of Agnosticism and methodological presumption of atheism, Flew wants to develop a simple set of instruments that will undermine, in religion and in other domains of ideology, extravagant metaphysical claims. He understandably wants to entrench himself "behind certain impregnable defenses," but neither the world nor human reaction to the world is that simple and his critical thrusts over the great topics of God, freedom, and immortality, tend to die the death of a thousand qualifications.

However, I would not close on a sour note. I think, perhaps mistakenly, that Flew's work has its severe limitations and indeed a certain rationalistic shallowness which he confuses with a commitment to clarity. Yet, I invariably learn from Flew and find, again and again, his views challenging and enlightening. And I too would defend something bearing a family resemblance to his presumption of atheism, only it would quite explicitly make substantive assumptions and would not think for a moment it could sustain itself as a neutral procedural device. Like Flew, I would start (or try to start) with as few tendentious epistemological, semantic, and metaphysical theses as possible, and I would make much of Pierce's point, mentioned in passing by Flew, that "one positive reason for being especially leery towards religious opinions is that these vary so very much from society to society; being, it seems, mainly determined, as Descartes has it, 'by custom and example' " (p. 24). But more of that on another occasion.[18]

NOTES

1. Antony Flew, *The Presumption of Atheism*, (New York: Barnes and Noble, 1976). Currently published by Prometheus Books under the title *God, Freedom, and Immortality* (1984).

2. Donald Evans, "A Reply to Flew's *The Presumption of Atheism*," *Canadian Journal of Philosophy* (September, 1972): 48.

3. Ibid.

4. Ibid., p. 49.

5. Ibid., p. 50.

6. Antony Flew "Reply to Evans," *Canadian Journal of Philosophy* II (September, 1972): 51-3.

7. Ibid., p. 51.

8. Ibid.

9. Ibid., p. 52.

10. Antony Flew, "Anthropology and Rationality," *Question* (January, 1972): 95-6.

11. See the essays by Winch, Lukes, and Hollis in *Rationality*, Bryant R. Wilson (ed.) (Oxford: Basil Blackwell, 1970) and see, as well, my "Rationality and Relativism," *Philosophy of the Social Sciences* (1974) and "Rationality and Universality," *The Monist*, (1976).

12. Antony Flew, "The Ideologist Behind the Mask," *The Humanist* 87 (February, 1972): 59-60.

13. Ibid., p. 60.

14. Ibid.

15. Donald Evans, op. cit., p. 50.

16. I am thinking here of the kind of arguments made from rationales given by Diognes Allen in his *The Reasonableness of Faith* (Washington-Cleveland: Corpus Books, 1968).

17. Ludwig Wittgenstein, *On Certainty* (Oxford: Blackwell, 1969), p. 35.

18. For one such occasion see the final essay in this volume.

8

The Primacy of
Philosophical Theology

I want to develop and defend what once was a rather traditional
position about the relation of philosophy to both religion and theology
and to refute what has become a widely accepted view of the relation
of philosophy to theology, on the one hand, and to Jewish or Christian faith, on the other. Put bluntly the claim I shall be concerned to
undermine is this: "It does not belong to the business of philosophy to
construct or justify . . . theological systems" or to criticize and refute
them either. Neither such systems nor the Christian faith itself are
legitimate objects of philosophical assessment, for philosophy is a
conceptual inquiry and, if the philosopher is aware of what philosophical analysis may properly do, he will be aware that it is a
second-order inquiry which must be normatively and ideologically
neutral.[1] It cannot assess the truth of theological claims but can only
elucidate their logic. Philosophical analysis itself properly understood
gives us a solid intellectual ground for rejecting the dominance of
philosophy over religion and theology and for rejecting as incoherent any attempt to set forth a philosophically grounded negation of
all theology.

In addition, if Christian claims are being considered, it is utter
hubris and a bit of incoherence as well to think of justifying belief in
Him who has revealed Himself as man's savior and judge, the reality
upon whom man is utterly dependent. Religious "Truth has to do, in
the first place with encountering God in Jesus Christ. Truth is our
relationship with God in Christ. Christ is the truth. It is amazing
nonsense to think we can justify this truth by philosophy."[2]

From *Theology Today* 27 (July 1970): 155-169. Reprinted by permission of the publisher.

It is natural to take such a remark to be a claim that philosophy cannot legitimately assess fundamental religious claims or at least fundamental Christian claims. A good philosophical analysis, we are given to understand, must be theologically and religiously neutral.

This is the view I want to give rationally persuasive reasons for rejecting. What alternative view do I want to elucidate and defend? The center of theology, I shall argue, is philosophical theology, i.e., philosophcal analysis of fundamental religious concepts and claims. Whether there can be any revelation, general or special, and which putative revelation or revealed theology, if any, is genuine must be settled by reference to philosophical criteria.[3] Whether the very concept of God itself is a coherent concept such that there could be revelation, a legitimate object of faith and a source of religious truth, must be made out on philosophical grounds. (I do not say, as I shall explain later, that *only* philosophical considerations are revelant.) The critical question is: can philosophy justifiably be the kind of arbiter I am maintaining it can? In the remainder of this article I shall wrestle with this question.

I

Antony Flew in his *God and Philosophy* and Paul Edwards in his "Difficulties in the Idea of God" have argued for the incoherence of a central concept of God embedded in the Judeo-Christian tradition.[4] If the concept of God is actually incoherent (not that we just mistakenly think it is), we have decisive grounds for not believing in God and thus Christian and Jewish theology and their respective faiths as well would be utterly undermined by philosphical reasoning.

So it is of considerable moment to try to determine whether this important concept of God is incoherent. Some of the central reasons given for making the claim that it is incoherent are that when "God" occurs in a biblical sentence such as "But God showed his love for us in that when we were yet sinners Christ died for us" that (1) God is not identifiable, (2) it is senseless to maintain that such a being can love or fail to love and (3) there is operating here a sense of "Creator" which is self-contradictory.

In arguing for (1), Flew points out that God is conceived as an incorporeal individual who is not taken to be a part of the universe but as maker and preserver of the universe. The whole universe is said to be dependent upon this individual. The problem, however, is: we have no idea at all of how to identify or pick out a Being so characterized. We have no way of knowing whether or not such a concept has or could have an actual application.

Even if we can put aside that consideration and admit the unique-
ness of God—His radical difference from dependent creation—He must
be at least in principle identifiable. But there is no understanding of
what it would be like to identify such a putative individual. We have
no idea of what, now or hereafter, we would have to encounter to
encounter God. Yet an individual who in principle is not identifiable is
a contradiction in terms, and if we have no idea what in principle or
in theory it would be like to identify or fail to identify such an alleged
individual, then the concept of such an individual is so problematic as
to be incoherent. Flew maintains that this is the pickle we are in
about God.

The second point is also forcefully argued. Edwards points out
that we can indeed conceive of a loving God with a body, but by
contrast an incorporeal, utterly spiritual reality loving or failing to
love is a very problematic notion indeed. In support of this contention,
Edwards argues that "psychological predicates are *logically* tied to
the behavior of organism."[5] He is not claiming that a person is just
his body but that "however much more than a body a human being
may be, one cannot sensibly talk about this 'more' without presup-
posing (as part of what one means, and not as a mere contingent fact)
that he is a living organism."[6] God by definition is alleged to be
without any local existence or bodily presence. But what would it be
like for an X to be just loving without doing anything? One is at a loss
here. And what would it be like for an X to act lovingly without
behaving in a certain way? Surely no sense is attached to "acting
lovingly but not doing anything" and surely "to do something," "to
behave in a certain way" is to make—though this is not all that it
is—certain bodily movements. Thus if "love" is to continue to mean
anything at all near to what it actually means, it is meaningless to
say that God loves mankind. Similar considerations apply to the other
psychological predicates tied to the concept of God. Such considerations about these predicates give us further evidence for believing that
the concept of God is incoherent.

It is not my task in this essay to attempt to appraise such philosophical theses about the coherence of the concept of God, but to
show what the implications would be if either such a position or some
reasoned rejection were right. First, if Flew and Edwards are right,
the Jewish and Christian theologian plainly ought to close up shop. If
by contrast the Flew-Edwards case is undermined by philosophical
criticisms this very undermining gives us some evidence, though
hardly sufficient evidence, for the belief that philosophy is logically
prior to theology; for then it is philosophical analysis which shows
that it has not been established that the concept of God is incoherent.[7]
Finally, if it is not clear whether or not the concept of God is in-

coherent, it is philosophical analysis which shows that we do not know whether the concept of God is coherent or incoherent. Thus whatever we decide here it looks as if it is reason which is sovereign.

It is natural to make moderate fideistic objections at this point. That is to say, a non-Kierkegaardian fideist who believes his faith is acceptable only if it is not in conflict with the observed facts or with what is securely established by sound arguments still could plausibly respond that given the human importance of the Jewish and Christian faiths and the important role of biblical theology in elucidating and sustaining those traditions, it is more reasonable to rely on the revealed word of one of those religious traditions than on anything so problematical as a philosophical argument. Even if questions of philosophical analysis about the coherence of the concept of God are *logically* prior to Christian theological questions or Jewish theological questions, it does not follow that they are *humanly* prior or that people should refrain from giving answers to religious and theological questions until they are answered.

This seems to me the crucial objection to what I have been saying and I want to develop it and exhibit its full force and ramifications before I attempt to reply to it. It seems to me that it is here where we are likely to get a fruitful dialogue between philosophy and theology.

II

There are several reasons proffered for not putting such a considerable trust in philosophical reasoning and for relying on what is said to be divine revelation instead.

There is first the difficulty stemming from a consideration of philosophy itself. The core of it is to maintain that since philosophy does not have objective and agreed on answers to the fundamental questions with which it concerns itself, including the questions common to philosophy and theology, that philosophy can hardly be a trustworthy base for rejecting the claims of religion. Consider the contemporary situation in philosophy. There is in philosphy a confusing plethora of styles of philosophizing—styles that are often radically different in scope, method, conception of subject matter and judgments concerning what is important. Meta-philosophical discussions about the concept, scope, and proper office of philosophy abound, are at least seemingly intractable, and are deeply disconcerting to our rational desire to attain objectivity and truth (surely one of the things that drove us into philosophy in the first place). And while this situation may be exacerbated in contemporary philosophy, it is a situation which has repeatedly occurred where there is anything approximating cultural complexity. Moreover, while philosphers do not like to be reminded of the nonrational influences on their thought, it is patently obvious that their particular styles of philosophizing are not unrelated to their cultural backgrounds. Philosophical analysis is the dominant mode in the Anglo-Saxon countries and in Scandinavia; in West Germany, France, and Italy varieties of phenomenology and existentialism hold sway; and in East Germany and Eastern Europe generally Marxism in various forms is dominant. Even among analytic philosophers and those rather more traditional philosophers such as Hall, Blanshard or Hartshorne, who are in a somewhat sympathetic reaction to them, there is a wide variety of philosophical approaches. And even these analytical and quasi-analytical approaches are often in fundamental conflict. (Compare Tarski's method with Toulmin's.) Even more extreme differences obtain between analytic philosophers, on the one hand, and existentialists and phenomenologists, on the other. They are so fundamental that it is difficult to see for example how anyone who has ever studied carefully and has taken to heart the work of Austin or Wittgenstein could find much of value in Heidegger or Tillich or, to switch to another obscure metaphysical manner, the later metaphysical work of Whitehead. And the reverse would no doubt be true. Indeed there are those who make the effort and it is an effort that should be made, but usually the results of these cultural forays consist in showing, often in a rather patronizing way, that where there is anything of value in the other tradition it is that they say in an obscure and misleading manner what is better said from within one's own tradition. It is not simply or basically a matter of being provincial or narrow-minded but that the approaches and intellectual values are so different that an active philosopher (someone concerned not just with the history of ideas but with philosophizing himself) standing within one of these traditions can hardly be anything other than distressed or bored by the work of philosophers from *radically* different traditions than his own. There is indeed room for discussion and argument between traditions, but when the differences are as great as those between an Austin and a Maritain there is not much room for creative dialogue though perhaps sometimes sharp confrontation will clear the air. Even among men of a similar age, philosophical culture, and set of philosphical interests, there exist very fundamental philosophical disagreements with no obviously agreed upon set of standards for resolving these differences. As Malcolm Diamond has rightly pointed out, "even among analysts, who do pretty much adopt the same premises and standards of argument, the central doctrines of one generation have proved to be the scornfully rejected dogmas of the next."[8]

Such a philosophical situation has led to the theological ploy that philosphers, as well as theologians, have their indemonstrable absolute presuppositions and articles of faith too. Philosophy, it is often maintained, is such an essentially contested concept and there are such radical and unsettled and perhaps irresolvable conflicting claims in philosophy—so rooted in cultural and subjective differences—that any philosophical claim to have established that the concept of God is incoherent is much less trustworthy than central and fervently held religious and theological principles, which conflict with that philosophical claim, and which are part of an established religious tradition. At least it is not at all evident—given this extensive and fundamental conflict within philosophy itself—that it is more reasonable to accept such a radical and basic philosophical claim than it is to accept the claims of Jewish and Christian revelation.

In addition to this skepticism about philosophy, there is a further and distinct line of argument relevant here that theologians should and many would utilize in arguing against my claim for the primacy of philosophical theology. The counter would be that, in arguing as I do, I fail to take properly into account the nature and import of Christian revelation. Christian theology, as N. H. G. Robinson has put it, operates under "obedience, from first to last, to divine revelation."[9] Christians who operate within the theological circle and, as they must as Christians, within the context of their confessional group and worshipping community, believe in an invisible unbounded reality which reveals himself in the Old Testament as the absolute master of being.

Reason may or may not—theologians differ about this—be of some aid in coming to know this incomparable, radically alive, unabounded reality, but it is God's self-revelation in Christ which is, reason to the contrary notwithstanding, the decisive thing in man's knowledge of God. It is through revelation—God's self-disclosure to man—that genuine religious understanding and knowledge is attained. As Brunner puts it in his *The Philosophy of Religion from the Standpoint of Protestant Theology*, "theology has to do not with religion but revelation" and it is essential for such a theology to stress "that the living and personal God can be known only by a personal meeting, through His personal word, through that special event to which the Bible alone, bears witness, and the content of which is Jesus Christ." There are some Christian theologians who in contrast to Brunner would maintain that we have some natural knowledge of God, but where what is taken to be such knowledge conflicts with revelation, revelation must be normative for Christian belief. It is revelation which is the fundamental thing. We do not—so the argument runs—need philosophical analysis to understand the concept of God, for God describes himself in the Scriptures. And in talking in an appropriate manner about faith we must remain within this closed circle of faith, for a "faith appropriate to revelation can be understood only by revelation. . . ."

A philosopher listening to this for the first time, is likely to be utterly amazed. The natural rather untutored response is to ask: why believe this is so? There are many putative or candidate revelations. Why believe in this particular putative revelation? More fundamentally still, why believe in any revelation or even believe there can be any revelation at all? What criteria can be given for accepting what an individual or confessional group maintains as revelation is indeed revelation or The Revelation?

Gordon Kaufman in an important essay, "Philosophy of Religion and Christian Theology," tries to show us a way around such difficulties.[10] From the fact, Kaufman argues, that one is committed to the Christian framework it follows that one is committed to the claim that there can be no human perspective higher than or superior to revelation in accordance with which revelation can be judged. To give up that commitment is in effect to cease to be a Christian. One cannot be a believer in Christian revelation, one cannot remain within the Christian framework, and admit that there is a human point of view external to and apart from revelation which can understand and investigate revelation and assess its truth. To think that there is or could be such a position is itself (among other things) to fail to understand the concept of Christian revelation. It is as senseless to say that revelation can be assessed by human standards as it is to say that a bachelor can be married. Anything that could be so assessed would *not* be revelation.

In further explicating the concept of revelation, we come to see that a revelation is not a discovery. It is not something we can gain through scientific investigation, intuition or mystical insight, but is something *not otherwise accessible* to man which *God chooses* to reveal to man. It is something that suddenly and inexplicably comes to man from beyond him and not something that he comes to understand from the normal exercise or even the abnormal exercise of either his cognitive faculties or his affective capacities. In speaking of revelation, we are speaking of something *essentially* unpredictable that must come from beyond all human capacities. It is something that God simply chose to reveal to man. It is something that is hidden from man if God does not act to reveal it. Thus the term *revelation* "refers first and foremost to *God's act,* not man's." It refers to something which, apart from God's grace, "is in principle accessible only to God and not to man and which therefore only God can make known to man."[11]

In considering what we can know or understand or what we can accept as sound reasoning, we inescapably must operate with the

canons of validity, intelligibility, and truth that human beings have
or might devise. Revelation, Kaufman argues, necessarily is not
accounted for by these canons and would from such an exclusively human point of view "have to be regarded as absurdity or illusion. . . . "[12]
Revelation is that which is not assessable in human categories or
predictable through human imagination. It is God's free self-disclosure
of something which otherwise is utterly hidden from man. We cannot
expect anything which is to count as "revelation" to fit in with our
conceptions of knowledge; "anything that did fit in with these canons
could be known *ipso facto* not to be revelation. . . . "[13] To argue,
Kaufman continues, that revelation is "illogical or irrational, or something which we cannot reasonably accept on the basis of what we
know of human experience" is not to have actually said anything
destructive of the notion, but to have unwittingly shown that one does
not understand the concept of revelation.[14] In short

> that through which revelation is recognized to be valid—as well as the
> content of the revelation itself—must be given in the revelation: revelation
> must be self-confirmatory or self-validating in order to be revelation. The
> marks by means of which revelation is recognized to be true revelation
> could not be determined or expressed before or apart from the revela-
> tion itself.[15]

This is why we cannot, if we understand what we are doing, argue
whether revelation is an actuality, for if there is revelation it is precisely something that could not be validated or in any way assessed
or decided on by an appeal to human criteria of truth, validity, rationality, intelligibility, and the like. All recipients of the alleged
revelation can reasonably do is confess their faith, proclaim the truth
and in an analytical fashion block misunderstandings of what con-
stitutes a revelation.

Given the above explication, Kaufman argues, it should no longer
seem "so arbitrary that (1) no other criteria are allowed sufficient
validity to judge revelation" and (2) that the Christian theologian will
refuse to give philosophy or what I have called philosophical theology
primacy over theology or, at a more fundamental level still, that he
will, and indeed must, refuse to give the canons of human reason
primacy over the commitments of Christian faith. The theologian "is
operating under the peculiar compulsion to take his final norms from
the specific event or series of events which he refers to as revelation"
and he cannot "accept the philosopher's work as in any real sense
normative or definitive for his own work, however conclusive it may
seem to be as a work in philosophy."[16] The philosopher, by contrast,
whether he conceives his work solely as conceptual analysis or not,

must be prepared to follow the argument where it will go. If analysis shows that the concept of God or revelation is self-contradictory or incoherent, then this is what he must, *qua* philosopher, believe. The theologian, however and by contrast, must believe that "revelation necessarily stands as a judgment over every form of human activity" and this the philosopher, at least as a philosopher, cannot believe.[17] *In philosophy and theology there are rival basic criteria for the fixation of belief* and while "each point of view finds it possible to deal with the other in its own terms; neither is in a position to assert with finality the error of the other and the truth of itself."[18]

III

In the last section I have tried to state the core of the case for a theological view, which, if one stands within the Christian tradition, is a point of view that may come to seem compelling. If I were a Christian, I would be tempted to try to hole up here too and adopt this attitude about the relation of philosophy to theology: an attitude that categorically rejects my claim about the primacy of philosophical theology. But I shall argue that argument is still possible here and that it actually cuts in my favor.

We should ask whether the concept of revelation is a coherent concept. The viability of theology and indeed even the viability of the Christian faith and other faiths as well hang on its being a coherent concept. If it is not, the whole edifice comes down.

Attention to our language and an attempt to be very literal-minded is important here. Ask yourselves quite literally what we are talking about when we talk of God's self-disclosure to man, or God's descriptions of himself to man, or the self-revelation of the Lord of all being? Try very carefully to confront what is being said with care. Let us assume for a moment that we can make sense of some tolerably orthodox conception of God. Let us, that is, assume we do not find utterly incoherent Karl Rahner's conception of God as "the being who keeps himself absolutely and essentially distinct from the world, although he is the abiding, all-pervading principle and ground of the world, conserving all things in their own being."[19] Still, how are we to understand the remark that such a being utterly distinct from the world *describes* himself? What is meant by that? Does he do it in a very loud voice in English, Swahili, Hindi or Esperanto or alternatively in all languages of the world? We are assured that to ask these questions with serious intent is utterly to misunderstand what is meant. And indeed this seems to be so. But then how are we to understand it? If the above is a misconstrual, what counts as a correct construal of such talk? And if God's describing himself is a metaphor or a symbolic utterance what is it a metaphor of or what is it symbolic of? What are we talking about here? If God in His grace were to speak to you, what would you expect to happen? Have you any understanding at all of what you would have to have or fail to have to become aware that God was *describing* Himself to you? I do not think that you do and if you do, it surely must be something you could in principle at least describe, for what is utterly indescribable is not understandable.

The same considerations apply to "self-disclosure" or "self-revelation." You have an understanding of what would have counted as a self-disclosure or self-revelation of even such illusive people as Eliot, Hammarskjöld, De Gaulle, or Austin. But what counts as a self-revelation or self-disclosure of the transcendent creator of the world? If you have any understanding at all of these phrases, you must have some idea of what it would be like to have such a disclosure, otherwise such talk is so problematical that we do not understand what is being said; and if there is a logical ban in describing what it would be like to have such a disclosure, then nothing is being asserted when we use these words. But ask yourself quite honestly and quite literally what it would be like. Do you have any idea at all what would constitute such an experience or occurrence?

No answers have been given that have not involved concepts equally as problematical as the concepts self-disclosure and self-revelation, which, when used in such a *religious* environment, originally produced the difficulty. What, if anything, is meant here is utterly opaque. Language, seems at least, to have gone on a holiday.

It is not fair to retort that I am invoking "positivist dogmas," some narrow kind of verificationism or any kind of verification at all. I am simply making the conceptual point—indeed a truism—that to believe is to believe in something and that if there is anything that one believes in, it ought in some way or other to be possible to say what the difference is between what one believes being true and what one believes being false, for to understand a proposition or a statement is to know what is the case if it is true or at least what counts for and against its being true. I did not say that one must know what sense experiences or observable states of affairs count for or against its truth. (I did not deny it either; but my above point about understanding such conceptualizations of "revelation" is independent of that point.)

Furthermore, it is of no avail to say that while these words, e.g., "God's self-revelation," are meaningless to human beings now, we still believe that sometimes when they are appropriately employed what they say is true and moreover we believe that there could come a time, due to the action of God, in which we could come to understand them, but now we just accept them on faith (on trust) even though we have no understanding of what they mean.

This is a rather natural defensive stratagem but a confusion all the same. Unless we understand at least in some minimal sense what it is we are to believe, it is logically impossible for us to either believe or disbelieve them. I cannot believe or even fail to believe p unless I understand at least to some extent the meaning of p. I could, however, in a sense accept p, not understanding what p means, on someone else's authority. I trust this other person in every respect and thus, though I do not understand what he is saying when he uses p, I trust that what he says is so. In one way, I should add, I cannot trust what he says because I do not understand what he says but I can trust what he says in the sense that I trust him even when he utters what seem to me to be meaningless phrases. Such trust without understanding is quite possible. But at least he or someone else taken as an authority in this domain must understand these phrases, if they are to be intelligible bits of human discourse. They cannot be meaningless to us all or even *in principle* be meaningless to anyone. Someone—some human being—must understand them, if they are intelligible bits of human discourse, and this means that it must be at least logically *possible* for someone to give an account of what they mean—including what, if anything, they assert—and this in turn involves showing their truth conditions. But this has not been done.[20]

There is, however, another defensive stratagem for someone trying to maintain the coherence of the concept of revelation that merits consideration. Dialectical theologians maintain that the "marks by means of which revelation is recognized to be true revelation could not be determined or expressed apart from the revelation itself."[21] Otherwise revelation would have checks external to it and thus it would not be revelation. "The only basis in terms of which anyone could speak of the truth of revelation would be in the awareness of the actuality of the revelation itself."[22]

There are two essential points to keep in mind in considering this rebuttal. First, we should beware of confusing "revelation" with revelation or confusing the concept of revelation with the putative reality it is supposed to signify. We must have some human criteria—indeed, that sounds odd doesn't it—for "revelation," including human criteria for the application of the term, or we could not even converse or think about the subject. There is no choice here but to define it "in terms of possibilities of knowledge open to man."[23]

However, to utilize an analogy, if no one can give an intelligible description of what is meant by "a tok" it does no good to say "You will recognize a tok upon encounter," for if I have no idea of what is meant by "tok" I have no idea what I must encounter to encounter one. Similar things surely hold for "revelation." If I have no idea of what counts as "a revelation," I have no idea of what I must have to have what is called pleonastically a self-confirmatory revelation. If I have no understanding of "tok," I cannot know or directly grasp that I have had a tokish encounter. If I have no understanding of "revelation," I cannot know or directly grasp that I have received God's gracious self-disclosure.

If, as Kaufman claims, theology "is attempting to deal with that which is really humanly inexpressible," then it must be an *Ersatz* discipline for what is literally inexpressible cannot even be understood much less known to be or even taken on faith to be true. Since it is human beings who are involved in theology and if what theology deals with is humanly inexpressible, it follows that the very subject matter of theology is and must remain unintelligible to human beings and we should indeed say with Feuerbach that "nonsense is the essence of theology. . . .

These defensive theological moves have now been knocked down (or so it seems to me) and it most certainly appears at least to be the case that we have very good reasons for believing the concept of revelation is incoherent and thus we have a very good *a priori argument* against the actuality of revelation, namely, that there are no revelations, for, given the incoherence of the concept of revelation, it is not possible that there could be a revelation. After all, what is not possible cannot be actual.

Some may counter—in reality shifting the grounds of the argument—that I have mistakenly talked about revelation apart from Scripture and the authority of the church to *authorize* who can speak for God. But here to break out of what seems to be an almost inevitable theological ethnocentrism, we must in turn ask *which* Scripture—and there are many Holy Writs—on *whose* interpretation and which church? To give a respectable answer that would justify making one claim rather than another, we would have to be able to answer the question: *who is justified in speaking for God?* (After all God plainly does not actually speak for himself. Recall Rilke's quip: And does God speak Chinese too?) More fundamentally still, a decent answer here would require our answering the question: how can we know or have good reason to believe that anyone speaks for God? There is, as Kierkegaard points out, no learning to speak for God. Christians indeed do believe that God is the ultimate authority and that He chooses those to whom He will reveal Himself and that Christian theology must remain obedient from first to last to what it takes to be Divine Revelation. But why should we believe that what these men, i.e., Christians *take* to be Divine Revelation *is* Divine Revelation or that *their* Scripture is the *True* Scripture: the central document in which God reveals himself to man? And if a man happens to be a Christian why should he remain one and continue to believe these things are so? Answers are not forthcoming here. Rather there is a retreat to the allegedly self-validating, self-confirming nature of Divine Revelation. But it was because of difficulties with such conceptions that we were led to appeal to Scripture and the church. Now we are back where we started. Furthermore—and independently—Christian theology to establish itself as a viable enterprise must presuppose answers to these questions. But these questions are basically philosophical questions. Thus we have still another reason to believe in the primacy of philosophical theology.

NOTES

1. William Zuurdeeg, "Implications of Analytical Philosophy for Theology," *The Journal of Bible and Religion* (July, 1961): 208.

2. Ibid. But see in this context the remarks of Jerry H. Gill, "Talk about Religious Talk," *New Theology No. 4*, Martin E. Marty and Dean G. Peerman (eds.), (New York: 1967), pp. 101–108.

3. Most of my references will be to Christianity or to Christian theology since I know it best. But this self-imposed limitation is incidental. Most of what I have to say here could equally well be said about Judaism or Islam and their respective theologies.

4. Paul Edwards, "Difficulties in the Idea of God," in Edward H. Madden, Rollo Handy and Marvin Farber (eds.) *The Idea of God*, (Springfield, IL: C. C. Thomas, 1968).

5. Ibid., p. 45.

6. Ibid., p. 48

7. The need for arguments of this sort is powerfully argued by Ninian Smart in his *Philosophers and Religious Truth*, (London: 1964) and in *Secular Education and the Logic of Religion*, (London: 1968). Note also the review by G. Stuart Watts, *Australasian Journal of Philosophy* (May, 1969).

8. Malcolm L. Diamond, "Contemporary Analysis: The Metaphysical Target and the Theological Victim," *The Journal of Religion* (July, 167): 227.

9. N. H. G. Robinson, "Faith and Truth," *Scottish Journal of Theology* 19 (June, 1966): 145.

10. Gordon Kaufman, "Philosophy of Religion and Christian Theology," *The Journal of Religion* XXXVII (October, 1957).

11. Ibid., p. 235.

12. Ibid., p. 236.

13. Ibid.

14. Ibid., p. 237.

15. Ibid.

16. Ibid.

17. Ibid., p. 242.

18. Ibid.

19. See the selection from Rahner in John Bowden and James Richmond (eds.), *A Reader in Contemporary Theology,* (London: 1969), p. 63.

20. For a development and further qualification and defense of this see my "Can Faith Validate God-talk?," *Theology Today* (July, 1963) and "Religious Perplexity and Faith," *The Crane Review* (Fall, 1965).

21. Gordon Kaufman, op. cit., p. 237.

22. Ibid., p. 238.

23. Ibid., p. 237.

9

Religious Ethics
Versus Humanistic Ethics

I

I shall look critically at some "foundational accounts" of the religious moralities that emerge from the main doctrinal stream of Western culture, namely, the moralities of our three sister religions, Judaism, Christianity, and Islam. I shall put my argument principally in Christian terms in elucidating and critiquing the Thomistic tradition of the natural moral law and the Protestant reformationist tradition of the morality of Divine Commands. But this is incidental; very similar arguments could be put in Judaic or Islamic terms. Vis-à-vis these religions my account is religion-specific only in vocabulary. It challenges the common core of claims of these religions to provide the sole adequate foundation for the moral life.

I should add, however, that a secular humanist critique of attempts at a religious grounding for morality could also be put in terms of the other great world religions but there the arguments would not be so very similar to the ones I shall make here, though again the main thrust would remain against the need for and indeed the very possibility of a cosmic underpinning for morality.

I will first state and then critique the traditional Thomistic account of the natural moral law, an account finding its classic statement in the medieval theologian and philosopher St. Thomas Aquinas—an account that has been restated and defended in our time by Neo-Thomists.[1] I shall describe the central claims of this natural law tradition and both internally critique it and attempt to show that a secular, humanistic ethic provides a more viable alternative. I shall then do a similar thing for the morality of Divine Commands, starting from the case for it made by the great contemporary Neo-Orthodox Protestant theologian Emil Brunner.[2]

II

Thomas Aquinas argues that all men have at least the potential ability to attain objective knowledge of good and evil. Moral knowledge, for him, did not rest on Divine revelation nor need we simply assume on *faith* that the ordinances of God are good. Aquinas would have us believe that we all have at least the capacity to know that there are certain fundamental things we should avoid and certain fundamental things we should seek.

If we will only note and then dwell on our most basic inclinations and the inclinations—the strivings and avoidings—of our fellow men, we will come to know what is good. This argument is almost like an argument that some anthropologists are inclined to make. The good is somehow the normal. We can discover what it is by noting what normal human beings strive for and avoid.[3]

Good is thus an objective concept and it is somehow in the very nature of things. But it is not in physical nature that one finds what is good. As the Neo-Thomist philosopher, Father C. B. Daly, puts it, "Catholic moralists . . . do not pronounce morally right whatever nature does; do not equate statistical averages of subhuman physical events with the moral good."[4] The good, the moral law that we can at least simply apprehend, is to be discovered in our own human natures. As "physico-spiritual" beings we find the rule of right within.

If we stopped at just this empirical strand in Aquinas's thinking—a strand that Jacques Maritain likes to stress when he is talking about relativism—Aquinas's theory would be a variety of ethical naturalism and his theory would be beset with the standard difficulties facing any ethical naturalism. "X is good" does not mean "I approve of X," "My culture approves of X," "People generally seek X," "Men desire X," or "Normal men seek X," for people may desire, approve of, or seek something that is bad. Indeed something could be widely approved of and still be evil. Most people at some time desire to commit adultery but that people have this desire does not *eo ipso* establish that adultery is good. It is equally true that the fact that my culture approves of something does not establish that it is a good thing to do. The Greeks of Plato's and Aristotle's time (like people in many other cultures) approved of infanticide. That this is so is established by anthropological investigation but this fact does not establish the truth of the moral statement "Infanticide is sometimes a good thing." What makes the anthropological statement true does not make the ethical statement true. Plato would not be contradicting himself if he said "My culture approves of infanticide but infanticide is evil"; and I would not be *contradicting* my self if I said "People generally disapprove of engaged couples sleeping together but there is in reality nothing wrong with it." I might in some way be mistaken if I were to assert that there is nothing wrong with it, but that in the present context, is beside the point. What is to the point is that I do not *contradict* myself, or say anything incoherent or conceptually out of order, in making that statement. We do *not eo ipso* establish that something is good by discovering that I or others approve of it, like it, desire it, strive for it, seek it and the like. A cross-cultural examination of what people desire is no doubt very important to a full understanding of what is good and what ends are worth seeking, but it is not enough to establish what ends are good or what ought to be.[5] Even when people desire something after careful reflection it does not follow that what they so desire is desirable. They might in various different ways be mistaken about what they desire or their moral thinking might in some way be defective. If we stress only this empirical strand of natural law morality we will encounter all of the traditional difficulties connected with ethical naturalism.

III

Aquinas's theory, it must be noted, is not simply an empirical theory. It has a metaphysical-theological strand as well. Father F. C. Copleston correctly remarks that we can only properly understand Aquinas's conception of the natural moral law if we place it against his doctrine of man as a creature of God in a rational, purposive universe. If we secularize the natural moral law we are, according to Jacques Maritain and Father C. G. Kossel, cutting out its very heart.[6] All men, whether they know it or not, are, Aquinas believes, seeking union with God. The *summum bonum* is in God's very essence. In this life we can not know what this essence is, but God, in His mercy, enables us in this life to understand *something* of His goodness. All lesser goods derive their goodness from God. Without God life could have no meaning or value, for in a Godless world nothing could, on Aquinas's view, be genuinely good. God tells us what is good by giving us laws. Laws, for Aquinas, are "ordinances of reason" promulgated "for the common good, by him who has care of the community."[7] There are rational precepts that are given to us to guide our conduct by authoritatively telling us what to do.

For Aquinas there are four basic kinds of law, though all laws must have the above mentioned features. There is Eternal Law. This is God's blueprint for the universe. It is an expression of God's Divine Subsisting Reason. It springs from God and it is promulgated in several ways for the good of God's creation. One of the ways it is promulgated is through Divine Law, which is that part of the eternal law that *man* cannot grasp with his reason but is given to man by God through Divine Revelation. The natural law, by contrast, is that part of the Eternal Law that man can grasp by the use of his reason, if his natural inclinations have not been "corrupted by vicious habits" or "darkened by passions and habits of sin."[8] As Aquinas puts it, "the communication of the Eternal Law to rational creatures . . . through their intellectual and rational powers . . . is called the Natural Law. . . ."[9] The natural law is simply the specifically rational moral way in which rational beings conform their conduct to the Eternal Law.

In addition to the above kinds of law there is what most people would ordinarily mean by "law," namely, "human law," though even here Aquinas gives it a meaning that might well disenfranchise some statutes that are called "laws," for human law, according to Aquinas, must be a precept devised by human reason for the common good. The important thing to remember about Aquinas' conception of human law is that in order to be genuine human laws the laws must *not* be incompatible with Natural Law. (Given this theory, one is committed to the extremely paradoxical contention that what ordinarily would be called "an evil or vile law" is not a law at all. Yet "The Nazi racial laws were vile laws" most certainly does not appear to be a contradiction, a logical oddity or a deviation from a linguistic regularity.)

There are, of course, different natural laws. There is first the primary (and what certainly seems to be the vacuous) first principle of the natural law. This primary precept—as it is called—is "Good is to be done and gone after and evil is to be avoided."[10] There are other less fundamental but substantive secondary precepts of the natural law. "Life ought to be preserved," "Men ought to know the truth about God," "Ignorance ought to be avoided" are examples of such natural moral laws.

While people can come to understand these natural laws through the use of their reason, it is important to understand, as Jacques Maritain in particular stresses, that man is not the measure of what are or are not natural laws. Man does not simply *resolve* to treat certain laws as crucial to his well-being and then correctly label them "natural laws." Rather, he apprehends—though sometimes rather dimly—these unalterable natural laws. Human beings do not create these laws and they cannot alter them by their collective decisions. They are not always self-evident *to* an individual or even to a whole society, but they are indeed *self-evident in themselves* and they serve as an absolute and unalterable foundation for correct moral decisions in our political, social, and personal lives.

IV

I am fully aware of the long and varied history of the natural moral law; and, I understand very well the strong ideological support that natural law conceptions have provided for the morally perplexed from the Greeks until the present, but as emotionally comforting as these conceptions are they do not constitute an adequate foundation for morality. I shall limit myself here to four general criticisms of the Thomistic conception of the natural moral law.

1. We are told that natural moral laws are self-evident, absolute, rational laws. They are certain and can be known without any doubt at all to be true. This sounds very reassuring for it promises to give us the kind of objective knowledge of good and evil that we very much desire. But there is here no genuine surcease from our perplexities about an objective justification of moral beliefs. It would be a mistake to believe that advocates of natural law are claiming that honest, non-evasive, intelligent reflection will necessarily make it clear to impartial and informed examiners that there are natural moral laws and that the laws generally claimed to be natural laws are indeed natural laws.[11] Since the natural laws are only *self-evident in themselves* and not necessarily self-evident to us, what could it *mean* to say that they are certain and that we can justifiably claim to be certain of them? For such a certain knowledge of good and evil, we require moral principles that can be seen to be self-evident to us or natural moral laws of whose truths we can be certain. But since natural moral laws are only self-evident in themselves (assuming we know what that means) and since it is God's reason and not man's that is the source of the moral law, we poor mortals can have no rational certitude that the precepts claimed to be natural laws are really natural laws. Beyond this it is surely a mistake to claim that laws or anything else are self-evident in themselves, where it is impossible to know or have grounds for asserting that they are self-evident. If a law or proposition *P* is such that we could never, even in principle, be in a position to justifiably claim that it either is or is not self-evident, since we mortals have and can have no grounds for claiming that it is self-evident, then it is senseless to assert or deny that *P* is self-evident in itself. If human beings can have no grounds for asserting that something is self-evident, they can have no grounds at all for asserting it is self-evident in itself. "What we don't know we don't know" is a significant tautology.

2. We find out what man *ought* to be, natural theorists claim, by finding out what are the specific rational ways in which he is to conform to the Eternal Law, by finding out what man is, by discovering man's *essential nature*. (They claim these things come to the

same thing.) As one natural law moralist put it, "Morality is man's knowledge that he ought to become what he is; that he ought to become a man by conduct becoming to a man."[12] In order to know how men should live and die we must understand man's essential nature.

But to this it can be objected that from the point of view of science man has *no* essential human nature. Men are not artifacts with an assigned function. It is both linguistically odd and cosmologically question-begging to ask what men are for—assuming by this very question that they are Divine artifacts rather than persons in their own right.[13] Science does not ask what men are for; it does not know how to inquire or even what it is to inquire into man's essential nature, where this is something human beings must achieve or hold in order to become or remain genuinely human.[14] Science has no such conception. For the Thomist to speak of man's essential nature requires the background assumption that a human being is a creature of God. But that human beings are creatures of God is not part of the corpus of any science. In fact it is a completely unverifiable statement whose very *factual* intelligibility is seriously in question.[15] But unless we can establish the factual significance of such an utterance we have no grounds at all for saying man has, in the requisite sense, an essential nature. If we have no grounds for saying man has an essential nature then we have no grounds for claiming there are natural moral laws. (In refusing to speak *in such a manner,* of "the essential nature of man," we are not denying that it *may* be discovered that there are certain characteristics that all men and only men as a matter *of fact* have, but these empirically discoverable properties—if such there are—do not prove or in any way establish that there is something a man *must* have in order properly to be called a man. It does not establish or even suggest that there is something man was made to be.)

3. The first principle of the natural moral law is a tautology (if you will, a truism) and is thus not a substantive moral proposition.[16] It is compatible with a completely relativistic view of morals, for it does not tell us *what* is good or *what* is evil but it only makes explicit what is already implicit in the use of the words "good" an "evil," namely, that if something is good it is, everything else being equal, to be sought and if it is evil it is, everything else being equal, to be avoided. But it does not and cannot tell us *what* is to be sought and *what* is to be avoided.

To discover this we must turn to the substantive secondary precepts of the natural moral law. But some of these run afoul of the facts concerning moral relativity, for some of them are not always even assented to, much less are they always accepted as self-evident by all people. If we say (as Aquinas does) that all people whose natural inclinations are not "corrupted by vicious habits" and "darkened by passions and habits of sin" acknowledge these natural laws, we can ask, in turn, where do we get our criteria for deciding whose habits are vicious and sinful and whose are not? To rule out some natural inclinations as corrupt or sinful indicates that we are using a criterion in moral appraisal that is distinct from the natural law criterion of basing man's moral conceptions on his natural inclinations. What actually happens is that those moral beliefs that are incompatible with Catholic doctrine, and as a result are called corrupt and sinful, are simply arbitrarily labelled as "unnatural" and "abnormal." (I will illustrate this in a moment.) But to do this is not to base morality squarely on natural law conceptions. We have here the application of moral criteria that in reality are not based on natural law conceptions. Without such an application—an application drawn from religious doctrine and not from what we learn about human nature or from what we can derive from the first principle of the natural law—natural law conceptions could not overcome the moral relativity they were designed to transcend. (Indeed, they do not anyway, for the tacit appeal to Church doctrine is surely an appeal to something that is culturally relative.)

If in defense of such natural law conceptions, it is replied: "We do not claim that all people and all cultures always acknowledge these laws, but the crucial thing is that most of them do," we make another egregious error, for, if we argue in this way, we have now presupposed that moral issues can be settled by statistics or by some cross-cultural Gallup Poll. But Aquinas would surely not wish to say that moral issues are "vote issues." As Father Daly puts it, "Catholic moralists . . . do not equate moral right with statistical averages."[17] To argue that what most people value is valuable is to assume rather simple democratic standards and by assuming them we again have a standard that is (a) *not* self-evident and (b) *independent* of the natural law. To avoid ethical relativism the natural law theorist must incorporate into his theory moral conceptions that are not based on the natural moral law and are questionable in their own right.

4. Natural moral law theorists confuse talking about what is the case with talking about what ought to be the case. They confuse *de jure* statements with *de facto* statements. A statement about what people or what normal people seek, strive for or desire is a factual, non-normative statement. From this statement or from any conjunction of such statements alone no normative (*de jure*) conclusions can be validly deduced except in such trivial cases as from "He wears black shoes" one can deduce "He wears black shoes or he ought to be a priest."[18] But this simply follows from the conventions governing the disjunction "or." Moreover, because it is a disjunction it is not actually action-guiding; it is not actually normative. To discover what our natural inclinations are is simply to discover a fact about ourselves; to discover

what purposes we have is simply to discover another fact about ourselves, but that we ought to have these inclinations or purposes or that
it is desirable that we have them does not follow from statements asserting that people have such and such inclinations or purposes. These
statements can very well be true but no moral or normative conclusions follow from them.

V

Natural law theorists and religious moralists generally feel that without a belief in God and His moral order an objective rational morality
is impossible. This seems to me a complete mistake. Smerdyakov is
wrong. The choice is not between nihilism or God.[19]
 I view morality as a practical (i.e., action-guiding, attitude-molding,
rule-governed activity, whose central function it is to adjudicate the
conflicting desires and interests of everyone involved in some human
conflict in an impartial and fair manner. In morality we are most fundamentally concerned with the reasoned pursuit of what is in everyone's best interest. How do we decide what is in anyone's best interest
let alone what is the best interests of everyone? In talking about a person's best interests we are talking about her most extensive welfare
and well-being and in talking about the best interests of everyone we
are talking about the most extensive welfare or well-being possible for
all in a given situation. This, of course, is not a pellucid notion, but it is
also not the case that we are unable to say anything reasonable about
it. It is this, though not only this, that morality tries to further. The concepts of well-being or welfare are indeed vague but not so vague for it
to fail to be evident that social practices could not be in our welfare if
they drastically frustrated our normal needs for sleep, food, sex, drink,
elimination and the like. And it is not just these mundane matters that
are a part of the very conception of human welfare or well-being. Any
way of life that denigrated personal affection, integrity, conscientious-
ness, knowledge, and the contemplation of beautiful things would be
an impoverished way of life, for to do any of these things is to strike a
blow at our very well-being. Similarly a community could not be a community whose social practices served human welfare or well-being if
those social practices pointlessly diminished self-respect, appreciation
and concern for others, creative employment, play, and diversion. Such
a community, if that is the right word for it, could not be a good
community.
 So while "welfare" and "well-being" are defeasible, context-
dependent terms, they are *not* so vague that they fail to exclude many
social systems both possible and actual—e.g., the Nazis, the Dobuans

or the Aztecs—as not furthering the welfare or well-being of their members. Those societies could not be truly human societies.

In morality we are concerned with the practical tasks of guiding conduct and altering behavior in such a way as to harmonize conflicting desires and interests so as to maximize to the greatest extent possible the welfare and well-being of each person involved. (One of the reasons that John Rawls's principles of justice as fairness are so important is their stress not just on maximizing well-being but on a concern, as a crucial element of what it is to be fair, for the well-being *of everyone* alike.) Our moral rules as well as social practices and actions not covered by these rules should be judged by this standard; and individual actions, unambiguously governed by the moral practices that the agent or agents in question are committed to, are to be judged by whether or not they are in accordance with the moral practice or practices in question. To act in accordance with them, when one sees that they are so related to such practices, is to act on principle: to act as a morally good man and not just a man of good morals.

Using this general conception of the function of morality, we can make appraisals of many practical moral issues. The natural law moralist can do this as well. But using my theoretical framework, I can do it more reasonably and with greater objectivity and internal consistency than can advocates of the natural moral law.

VI

I shall illustrate that this is so and how it is so by turning to some specific moral issues that often divide religious moralists and secular humanists. Consider the issue of miscegenation and the moral issues that have emerged around the use of contraceptives. (I could make similar points with reference to adultery, abortion, artificial insemination, and euthanasia.) I pick these two issues because on the first I suspected that by now, between religious moralists and secularists, there is often practical agreement over what is right and what is wrong, while on the second there is no such agreement. (The disagreement is not as deep as it is over abortion but it is there.) By airing the respective grounds for making one claim rather than another, we can gain some idea of both the differences and the respective merits and deficiencies of the contrasting orientations to morality.

Miscegenation is the mixture of races through marriage or other sexual contact. It remains illegal in South Africa and, until recently, it was legally impossible in many southern states of the United States for whites and blacks to marry each other. Such a law and the moral attitude behind it is plainly immoral and should be strenuously fought against. But that is not the natural inclination or the considered judgment of everyone or even of the majority of people in all societies.

A natural law theorist might well argue that laws or rules forbidding marriage between people of different races is evil because it is contrary to the natural moral law. I think it would be difficult for him to make such a case. It seems to me that it is, as a matter of fact, a quite natural inclination. It is very natural for human beings to make sharp and discriminatory distinctions between their own kind and those who have different pigmentation, physique, language, religion or mores. It took a Papal bull to make the conquistadores regard the Peruvian Indians as human beings with immortal souls. People who are very different from us are quite naturally regarded with distrust and aversion. It is unfortunate that we are naturally ethnocentric. It is natural for us to regard ourselves and our special mores and physical traits as being intrinsically superior to those of others. Most of us are quite naturally endogamous. It seems to me that we can only overcome these quite natural inclinations by a good bit of cultural education, including some *hard moral thinking*. If, on the one hand, we turn to man's primitive, immediate, unrehearsed inclinations and strivings—the strivings and inclinations of "raw human nature"—we could hardly find a ground for the condemnation of the moral belief that there should be no mixture of the races. If, on the other hand, we take only the inclinations that withstand reflection and examination—careful moral and factual scrutiny—we have already imported into morality principles that are not simply derived from or based on human inclinations. Rather, we are speaking of considered judgments that would not be extinguished when they faced the tribunal of wide reflective equilibrium.[20] That is to say, they are the moral convictions that would remain when they were seen to square with our considered judgments and those of other people (including people in other cultures) after we had made a careful comparison of the full range of moral theories humankind possesses and when they were seen firmly to square with our best sociological, sociopsychological, and other social scientific knowledge. But by making such an appeal we go beyond a natural law morality that tries to discover what we ought to do—on their account what God wills for us—by taking careful note of our natural inclinations.

On the humanist view of morality, which I outlined, we have, by contrast, a clear and unequivocal basis for opposing the belief that it is wrong for the races to intermarry. Biological and anthropological studies have made it abundantly clear that no one race is biologically inferior to another. They have also made it perfectly clear that no biological harm could come from such marriages. If anything it might make for a certain hybrid vigor. But the serious point is that ther are no rational grounds for being against them. This removes one supposed major impediment to such marriages. Culturally speaking it would cause distress to some people but this distress has no basis in reason, or indeed in morality, and it could be slowly alleviated by proper education and time. After all, it rests on pure prejudice. This distress, in turn, is plainly outweighed by the continued feelings of inferiority or racial tension that such irrational and discriminatory laws engender. Moreover, it is not enough for morality simply to consider the welfare and well-being of the majority; it must consider the welfare and well-being of *everyone* involved. Sometimes, in tragic situations, an individual's interests must be sacrificed but they can only be sacrificed on nonarbitrary grounds (say in the protection of the interests of the vast majority of people in a war); but in the miscegenation case nothing like this is even remotely at issue. What we have are the prejudices (and nothing else) of a goodly number of people and the welfare and well-being of the people who love each other and wish to marry. If people's prejudices are not catered to, their welfare is not being sacrificed, but the welfare of those who wish to marry is being sacrificed by such laws, even though this is not necessary for the fullest and fairest extension of human welfare and well-being for everyone involved. Interests deserve protection but not prejudices—the two are not the same.

Let us now consider the use of contraceptives as devices for birth control. I think contraceptives are something that people with normal sexual desires ought to use in many circumstances of their lives. The need and desire to make love is normal and natural. It should go without saying that it is one of the most intensely pleasurable experiences that we humans can have. When accompanied by deep affection, complete acceptance, and understanding, it can help us to experience a feeling of oneness and union that is precious in a world where human beings so often feel alienated and alone. These are positive values of sex that have nothing to do with the reproductive function of intercourse and there is no reason to inhibit their expression by forbidding all sexual activity not intended to function in the service of procreation. (In James Joyce's famous words "no recreation without procreation.")

The Catholic (but not the Anglican) version of the natural law position says that the use of artificial contraceptive methods is always wrong. It is unnatural, for in the words of Father Daly, it places an artificial substance between the lovers that obstructs the natural function of sex. It represents—we are told by Father Daly—both a psychological and a physical withdrawal. It is a variety of onanism, a species of withdrawal. In his immortal words: "Every contraceptive appliance or device is a 'hard wall of the ego' (or two egos) refusing to be two-in-one-flesh, refusing to be two-in-one-task."[21]

It seems to me that this argument—if that is the proper word for it—is utterly without merit. Few would deny that sexual experience without contraceptives was, until the age of the pill, usually a fuller, more enjoyable experience. But given modern oral contraceptives this very slight disadvantage of contraceptives completely disappears. And the positive values of contraception completely outweigh their very slight disvalue. The only serious question about them should be the purely medical one whether their prolonged use is harmful to the health of women. Women who ought not to have children at a given time or perhaps at all can now come to bed with their men without the fear and anxiety that makes a complete union between them impossible.

More fundamentally still, if we are going to say "Sexual intercourse under such circumstances is wrong because it is unnatural since it interrupts a natural function," we should also say that shaving, cutting one's toenails or hair, removing cancerous growths, wearing glasses, having an appendectomy, giving blood, or being circumcised are also immoral because unnatural. But part of the human animal's glory and creativeness lies in his ability to transform nature, including human nature, and not simply to be a frail reed completely at the mercy of his animal ancestry. There are no grounds for arguing that something is wrong because it is unnatural.

It is the case that there are good reasons—urgently good reasons—for controlling population growth. Throughout the world people die each day of starvation. Indeed approximately ten thousand of us die each day from malnutrition.[22] It may be that we are sufficiently inventive to prevent our planet from becoming a "plundered planet" without the institution of artificial birth control techniques, but it is still a very grave risk to take and overpopulation is at present causing severe misery in many parts of the world. But through the use of contraceptives and family planning, we could control our population very simply in a way that would further the welfare of all. It seems to me that a continued adherence to a dogmatic theology prevents us from adopting this humane and rational measure. Is it really that by "looking carefully into our hearts," by carefully monitoring our natural inclinations, we apprehend or come to appreciate that the use of contraceptives is unnatural and wrong? That is very implausible. Is it not rather that those religious people who judge it to be wrong do so simply because their church tells them that it is wrong? Do they really have any coherent independent reason for thinking it wrong? Talk of what is or is not "unnatural" is simply a dodge here.

It is not only considerations of overpopulation that count in favor of the use of contraceptives but also more personal considerations of human welfare and well-being. Where contraception is not practiced, children are frequently born to parents who do not want them or cannot afford to have them. It is a deep and permanently wounding blow to a child to be made to feel that he is not wanted, not loved. Mothers in families that do not practice contraception frequently have children in too rapid succession. Their physical and psychological health is often badly shaken, they suffer and as a result their children and husbands suffer as well. Lastly, for various financial or medical reasons, some couples cannot risk having children. Under these circumstances it is positively irrational and immoral to deny these couples the pleasure and sense of oneness they would gain from sexual union. It is bad enough that they cannot have children without adding to their suffering by denying them the closeness and joy that love-making could bring them.

By his very creativeness man has distinguished himself from the other primates. He has the distinctive capacity for culture and the correlated ability to transform his environment rather than being subject to it. The Catholic "natural moral law" doctrine on contraception in effect overrides and denies this distinctive human gift. It would in effect make man subject to blind forces that he could otherwise rationally control. This seems to me deeply immoral and it is time that people unhesitatingly say so. Let us never forget Sophocles' praise to the wonders of man.

VII

It is not unnatural to ask "Given the Decalogue [the Ten Commandments] why the natural law?" Natural law moralists reply: "Because what the Decalogue commands us to do is also discoverable by reason and not everyone has heard the word." Indeed, as Father Victor White puts it: "A Christian cannot and will not judge the Decalogue in the light of natural law; but he will find in the Decalogue the divine approbation of the intrinsic, though limited, rightness of natural law."[23] Attractive as this claim is, if my argument in the last two sections has been in the main correct, we can see that such a Thomistic conception of the natural law is thoroughly mythical and cannot serve as a sound foundation for our moral beliefs. But we still have the Decalogue and, what is called by religious people, the Revealed Word of God. Let us now look at those radical reformationist claims that contend that this is all that we have to rely on or rather that this is all we have and all that we need to give significance and direction to our moral lives.

The distinguished Protestant theologian Emil Brunner argues that we cannot discover any sound abstract principles of right action or good conduct under which we could subsume particular moral statements that concretely direct us to do this or that.[24] *Genuine human good is found only in the unconditional, unquestioned obedience of man to God.* Human conduct is good—that is, we are doing what we ought to be doing—when God Himself acts in it, through the Holy Spirit.

The religious person's obedience is not, Brunner would have us understand, obedience to a law or a principle "but only to the free sovereign will of God." The will of God cannot be summed up under any principle. We do not know what God is or what love is by apprehending a principle. We do not even understand these conceptions unless, quite concretely—existentially if you will—"we learn to know God in His action, in faith." All ethical thought and moral understanding is rooted in an existential knowledge of God; and "really good Christian conduct" needs to have the whole of the Revealed existential Christian knowledge of God behind it. This *Deus Absconditus,* this God that we should love and fear, is manifested solely in His Revelation.

We do indeed long for something that goes beyond Revelation. We long for something we can rationalize, for something that can give us a rationally justifiable standard in accordance with which we can live, but, natural law theorists to the contrary notwithstanding, *we human beings have no natural knowledge of good and evil.* We have not been able, for all our Faustian drives, for all our intelligence and knowledge, to seize the tree of knowledge of good and evil. The truth of the Judeo-Christian claim that God is the Perfect Good and obedience to God's command is the sole desirable ultimate end of human action is not "a truth of reason" or a truth that is objectively verifiable or in any way objectively establishable. Only the man of *faith* can know or even understand it. But it nonetheless remains true that this Christian ethic has universal validity. As Brunner puts it:

> But this does not mean that the Christian ethic makes no claim to universal validity. Whatever God demands can be universal, that is, valid for all men, even if those who do not hear this demand do not admit this validity and indeed do not even understand the claim to universal validity. The believer alone clearly perceives that the Good, as it is recognized in faith, is the sole Good, and that all that is otherwise called good cannot lay claim to this title, at least not in the ultimate sense of the word. It is precisely faith and faith alone which knows this: that alone is good which God does; and, indeed, faith really consists in the fact that man knows this—and that he knows it in such a way as it alone can be known, namely, in the recognition of faith. But once man does know this he also knows the unlimited unconditional validity of this conception and of the divine command. . . .

Since we cannot rely on abstract principles, we can never, as the natural law tradition claims, know beforehand what God requires. Rather, God commands, and whatever it is He commands, we must obey. Therein lies our sole good, for "The Good is simply what God wills that we should do on the basis of a principle of love." It is indeed true that God wills our true happiness; but *He* wills it, and He wills it in such a way that no one else knows what His will is. If we try to stick to the use of our own reason and to a sense of our own most fundamental inclinations or considered judgments, we will "never know what is right for us, nor what is the best for the other person." Here, as children of faith, we must simply and humbly rely on God. Doing the right thing is simply obeying God's commands. We go astray when we think that we can deduce our moral obligations "from some principle or another, or from some experience. . . ." This casuistry, this reasoning by cases and principles, Brunner contends, is legalistic thinking in the very worst sense of that term. Our very conception of God and his Divine Love is distorted if we think that we can know what God ought to will for us in accordance with His love. What His love is, what He would judge to be for our own good, is too utterly far from us to allow us this judgment. "But of one thing we may be quite sure: His will is love, even when we do not understand it—when He commands as well as when He gives." But it is a complete mistake to think that we can measure it, take the measure of it, by our ideas of love. God's love is beyond that.

Yet, Brunner argues, "God's will is expressed by His sanctions, by His rewards and punishments." God holds the keys to the Kingdom. Like Pascal, Brunner believes that man is lost, damned, without God but blest with Him.

> God alone gives life: to be with Him is life, to resist Him is ruin. It is impossible to exist apart from God; it is impossible to be neutral towards Him. He who is not for Him is against Him. God's Command means eternal life and good means nothing else than this. He is Love. But His will is utterly serious; it is the will of the Lord of Life and Death. Anyone who—finally—resists Him, will only dash himself to pieces against the rock of His Being. This is the holiness of the love of God. As the divine love cannot be separated from His gift of life, so the Holiness of God cannot be separated from His judicial wrath, the denial and destruction of life. To have a share in the will of God, in the sense of union with His will, means salvation; to resist Him spells utter disaster.

Many people, including Kantians, have complained that a morally good man (as distinct from a man who is only a man of good morals) does what is good because it is good, not because of what he will get out of it or because he will be damned or punished if he fails to act. The truly moral man, Kant argues, requires no such sanctions, no such pricks to his own intent. To require them is a perversion of moral endeavor. It is—in the Kantian phrase—to make morality heteronomous. We ought instead to do the good simply for the sake of the good.

Brunner rejects this Kantian approach. He argues that such a critique of the morality of Divine Commands fails to realize "that the Good is done for the sake of the Good when it is done for the sake of God, in obedience to the Divine Command."

> We ought to obey God because He commands it, not because obedience means happiness and disobedience means unhappines. Faith would not be faith, obedience would not be obedience, if things were otherwise. But obedience would not be obedience towards God, did we not know that His Command means life and His prohibition death. The primary concern is not that which refers to my Ego, to my life; no, the primary concern is this: that it is God's will, the will of Him to whom my life belongs. But that which refers to me, that which refers to my life, is the necessary second element for it concerns the will of Him who Himself is life—even my life. Obedience would be impure if this second element were made the first. But it would be unreal, and indeed impossible, if this second element, as the second, were not combined with the first. We cannot do anything good which has no significance for life, and we cannot avoid anything evil, unless at the same time we know it to be harmful. It is not the question whether all morality is not mingled with self-interest—without self-interest nothing would concern us at all—but the question is this: is this self-interest regarded as founded in God or in myself? To do the Good for the sake of the Good is only a pale reflection of the genuine Good; to do the Good for the sake of God means to do the Good not because my moral dignity requires it, but because it is that which is commanded by God.

VIII

We have here, starkly contrasting with the traditional Thomistic conception of the natural moral law, a powerful and classical expression of the morality of Divine Commands, a conception of morality that has been a very central one in the Protestant tradition.

To start to look at it critically, let us first ask again this ancient question: "Is something good because God wills it or commands it or does God command it because it is good?" Let us consider the alternatives we can take here. If we say God commands it because it is good, this implies that something can be good *independently* of God. Why? Because "God commands it *because* it is good" implies that God apprehends it to be good and then tells us to do it. But if God does this then it is at least *logically* possible for us to see or in some way know or come to appreciate that it is good without God's telling us to do it or informing us that it is good.

This last point needs explanation and justification. The above clearly implies that good is not a creation of God but it is rather something apprehended by God or known by God. If this is so, it is *in some way* there to be apprehended or known and thus it is logically possible for us to apprehend it or know it without knowing anything of God. Furthermore, since God apprehends it to be good, since it does not become good simply because he wills it or commands it, it is not unreasonable to believe that there can be this goodness even in a Godless world. Translated into the concrete, this means that it would be correct to assert that even in a world without God, killing little children just for the fun of it is wrong and caring for them is good.

Someone might grant that there is this *logical* independence of morality from religion, but still argue that, given man's corrupt and vicious nature (the sin of the Old Adam), he, as a matter of fact, needs God's help to understand what is good and to know what he ought to do. Man is pervasively sinful and there is and always will be much corruption in the palace of justice.

Such a response is confused. With or without a belief in God we can recognize such corruption. In some concrete situations at least, we understand perfectly well what is good or what we ought to do. The "corruption" religious apologists have noted does not lie here. The corruption comes not in our knowledge but in "our weakness of will." We find it in our inability to do, what in a "cool hour," we acknowledge to be good—"the good I would do that I do not." Religion—for some people at any rate—may be of value in putting their *hearts* into virtue, but that for *some* it is necessary in this way does not show us how it can provide us with a knowledge of good and evil by providing an ultimate standard of goodness.[25]

Suppose we say instead—as Brunner surely would—that an action or attitude is right or good simply because God *wills* it or *commands* it. Its goodness arises from Divine *fiat. God makes something good simply by commanding it.* (That, of course, is the course a consistent Divine Command theorist should take.)

Can *anything* be good or become good simply by being commanded or willed? Can a fiat, command or ban create goodness or moral obligation? I do not think so. But again I need to justify my thinking that it cannot. As a first step in seeing that it cannot, consider two ordinary, mundane examples of ordering or commanding.

Suppose you are in a course and the professor tells you "You must get a loose leaf notebook for this class." His commanding it, his telling you to do it, does not *eo ipso* make it something you *ought* to do or even make doing it good, though it might, given your circumstance, make it a prudent thing to do. But, whether or not it is prudent for you to do it, given his position of authority, and your dependence on him, it is, if there are no reasons for getting that particular type of notebook or any notebook at all, other than those consequent on his telling you to do it, all the same a perfectly arbitrary injunction on his part and not something that could properly be said to be good. Commanding it does not make it either good or obligatory.

Suppose a mother says to her college-age daughter: "You ought not go to class dressed like that." Her statement to her daughter does not *eo ipso* make it a bad thing and her order not to go to class dressed as her daughter is does not make it the case that the daughter ought not to go to class dressed like that. For the mother to be right here she must be able to give reasons for her judgment that her daughter ought not to dress as she does.

More generally speaking, the following are all perfectly intelligible.

(1) He wills Y but should I do it?
(2) X commands it but is it good?
(3) X told me to do it, but all the same I ought not to do it.
(4) X proclaimed it but all the same what he proclaimed is evil.

That is to say, (3) and (4) are not contradictions and (1) and (2) are not senseless, self-answering questions like "Is a wife a married woman?" This clearly indicates that the moral concepts "should," "good," and "ought" are, in their actual usage, not identified with the willing of something, the commanding or the proclaiming of something, or even with simply telling someone to do something. Even if moral utterances characteristically tell us to do something, not all "tellings to" are moral utterances. Among other things, "moral tellings to" are "tellings to" that must be supportable by *reasons* and for which it is always logically in order to ask for reasons. But this is not true for simple commands or imperatives. As a mere inspection of usage reveals, moral utterances are not identifiable with commands.

To this it will surely be replied: "It is true that these moral concepts cannot be identified with any old commands but *Divine* commands make all the difference. It is *God's* willing it, *God's* telling us to do it, that makes it good."

It is indeed true that, for the believer at least, it's being *God* who commands it, who wills it, that makes all the difference. This is so because believers assume that God is good. But now, it should be asked, *how* does the believer *know*, or indeed *does* he know, that God is good, except by what is in the end his own quite fallible moral judgment that God is good? Must he not appeal to his own considered judgments, his own moral sense here? Is there any escaping that?

It would seem not. To know that God is good we must see or come to appreciate that His acts, His revelation, His commands, are good. It is through the majesty and the goodness of His Revelation revealed in the Scriptures that we come to understand that God is good, that God supposedly is the ultimate criterion for all our moral actions and attitudes. But this, of course, rests on our own capacity to make moral assessments. It presupposes our own ability to make moral judgments and to recognize or appreciate the difference between right and wrong.

It could, of course, be denied that *all* the commands, all the attitudes, exhibited in the Bible are of the highest moral quality. The behavior of Lot's daughters and the damnation of unbelievers are cases in point. But let us assume what in reality should not be so lightly assumed: that the moral insights revealed in our Scriptures are of the very highest and that through His acts God reveals His goodness to us. However, if a believer so reasons, he has shown by that very line of reasoning, that he thinks, inconsistently with his own proclamations, that he has some knowledge of good and evil, and that knowledge has no logical dependence on its being willed by God.

We can see from the very structure of this argumentation that we must use our own moral insight to decide whether God's acts are good. We finally must judge the moral quality of the revelation; or, more accurately and less misleadingly, it is finally by what is no doubt fallible human insight that we must judge whether what *purports* to be Revelation is *indeed* Revelation. We must finally use our own moral understanding, if we are ever to know that God is good or, again more accurately, that there is a reality of such goodness that we should call that reality "God." Fallible or not, our own moral understanding is *logically* prior to our religious understanding.

The believer should indeed concede that if we start to inquire into, to deliberate about, the goodness of God, we cannot, if we reason accurately, but end up saying something very much like what I have just said. But our mistake, he could argue, is in ever starting this line of inquiry. Who is man to inquire into, to question, the goodness of God? That is utter blasphemy. No *genuine believer* thinks for one moment that he can question God's goodness. That God is good, indeed the Perfect Good, is *a given* for the believer. "God is good" or "God is the perfect God" are, in the technical jargon of philosophy, tautological or analytic. Given the believer's usage, it makes no sense to ask if what God commands is good, or if God is good. Any being who was not good could not properly be called "God"; nor would we call anything that was not perfectly good God. A person who seriously queried "Should I do what God ordains?" could not possibly be a believer. Indeed Jews and Christians do not mean by "He should do X," "God ordains X";

and "One should do what God ordains" is not equivalent to "What God ordains God ordains" but not all tautologies or analytic statements are statements of identity. It is not only blasphemy but it is, logically speaking, *senseless to question* the goodness of God.

Whence then, one might ask, emerges the ancient problem of evil? But let us assume, what it is reasonable to assume, namely, that in some way "God is good," "God is the Perfect Good" are tautologies or "truths of reason," it still remains true that we can only come to know that anything is good or evil through our own moral insight. Let us see how this is so. First it is important to see that "God is good" is not an identity statement, e.g., "God" is not equivalent to "good." "God spoke to Moses" makes sense. "Good spoke to Moses" is not even English. "The steak is good" and "Kennedy's act against big steel was good" are both standard English sentences; but if "God" replaces "good" as the last word in these sentences we have gibberish. But, as I have just said, not all tautologies are statements of identity. "Wives are women," "Triangles are three-sided" are not statements of identity, but they are clear cases of tautologies. It is reasonable to argue "God is good" has the same status, but, even if it does, we still must independently understand what is meant by "Good" and the criterion of goodness remains *independent* of God.[26]

As we could not apply the predicate "women" to wives, if we did not first understand what women are, and the predicate "three-sided" to triangles if we did not understand what it was for something to be three-sided, so we could not apply the predicate "good" to God unless we already understood what it meant to say that something was good and had some criterion of goodness. Furthermore we can and do meaningfully apply the predicate "good" to many things and attitudes that can be understood by a man who knows nothing of God. Even in a Godless world, to relieve suffering would still be good.

But is not "God is the Perfect Good" an identity statement? Do not "God" and "the Perfect Good" refer to and/or mean the same thing? The meaning of both of these terms is so very indefinite that it is hard to be sure, but it is plain enough that a believer cannot question "God is the Perfect Good." But granting that, we still must have a criterion for good that is indepedent of religion, that is independent of a belief in God, for clearly we could not judge anything to be *perfectly* good, until we could judge that it was good and we have already seen that our criterion for goodness must be independent of God.

Someone still might say: "Look, something must have gone wrong somewhere. No believer thinks he can question or presume to *judge* God. A devoutly religious person simply must use God as his ultimate criterion for moral behavior. If God wills it, he, as a 'knight of faith,' just does it!"

Surely this is in a way so, but it is perfectly compatible with everything I have said. "God" by *definition* is "a being worthy of worship," "wholly good," "a being upon whom we are completely dependent." These phrases, partially define the God of Judaism and Christianity. This being so, it makes no sense at all to speak of *judging* God or deciding that God is good or worthy of worship. But the crucial point here is this: before we can make any judgments at all that any conceivable being, force, Ground of Being, transcendental reality, Person or what not could be *worthy* of worship, could be properly called "good" and even "the Perfect Good," we must have a logically prior understanding of goodness. That we could call anything or any foundation of anything "God," presupposes that we have a moral understanding, an ability to discern what would be *worthy* of worship, perfectly good. Morality does not presuppose religion; religion presupposes morality. Feuerbach was at least partially right: our very concept of God seems, in an essential part at least, a logical product of our moral categories.

In *sum* then we can say this: a radically Reformationist ethic, divorcing itself from natural moral law conceptions, breaks down because something's being commanded cannot *eo ipso* make something good. Jews and Christians think it can because they take God be good and to be a being who always wills what is good. "God is good" no doubt has the status of a tautology in Christian thought, but if so "God is good" still is not a statement of identity and we must first understand what "good" means (including what criteria it has) before we can properly use "God is good" and "God is Perfectly Good." Finally, we must judge of *any command* whatever whether it ought to be obeyed; and we must use, whether we like it or not, our own moral insight and wisdom, defective though it undoubtedly is, to judge of *anything whatever whether* it is good, Perfectly Good, and whether anything could possibly be so perfectly good that it is *worthy* of worship.

If this be arrogance, it is inescapable, for it is built into the logic of our language about God. We cannot base our morality on our conception of God. Rather, our ability to have the concept of God we do have presupposes a reasonably sophisticated, and independent, moral understanding on our part. Brunner, and the whole Divine Command tradition, has the matter topsy-turvy.

IX

Suppose someone argues that it is a matter of faith with him that what God commands is what he ought to do; it is a matter of faith with him that God's willing it is his ultimate criterion for something's being good. He might say "I see the force of your argument, but for me it remains a straight matter of faith that there can be no goodness without God. I do not *know* this is so; I cannot give *grounds* for believing that this is so; I simply and humbly accept it on faith that something is good simply because God says that it is. I have no independent moral criterion."

My answer to such a fideist—to fix him with a label—is that in the very way he reasons, in his very talk of God as a being *worthy* of worship, he shows that he in reality has such an independent criterion. His own generalizations *about* what he does notwithstanding, he shows in his very behavior, including his linguistic behavior, that something's being willed or commanded does not *eo ipso* make it good or make it something that he ought to do, but that its being willed by a being *he takes* to be superlatively *worthy* of worship does make it good. But we should also note that it is by his own reflective decisions, by his own honest avowals, that he takes some being or, if you will, some X to be so *worthy* of worship and thus, he shows in his behavior, including his linguistic behavior, though not in his *talk about* his behavior, that he does not even take anything to be properly designatable as "God" unless he has made a moral judgment about that being. He *says* that on faith he takes God as his ultimate criterion for good, but his actions speak louder than his words and he shows by them that even his God is in part a product of his moral sensibilities. Only if he had a moral awareness could he use the word "God,"as a Jew or a Christian uses it, so that his protestations notwithstanding, he clearly has a criterion for good and evil that is *logically* independent of his belief in God. His talk of faith will not at all alter that.

If the fideist replies: "Look, I take it on faith that your argument here or any argument here is wrong. I'll not trust you or any philospher or even *my* own reason against *my* church. I take my stand here on faith and I won't listen to anyone." If he takes his stand here, we must shift our argument. We can and should point out to him, and perhaps more importantly to others, that he is acting like a blind, fanatical irrationalist—a man suffering from a *total* ideology. Suppose he replies: "So what? Then I am an irrationalist!" We can then point out to him the painful consequences to himself and to others of his irrationalism. We can point out that even if for some unknown reason he is right in his claim that one ought to accept a religious morality, he is mistaken in accepting it on such irrationalist grounds. The consequences of irrationalism are such that anything goes and this, if really followed, would be disastrous for him and for others. It is like the fascist idea of "thinking with your blood." If he says so what, he does not care even about this. It seems to me that if we were to continue to reason with him, we would now have to, perhaps like a psychoanalytic sleuth, question his *motives* for so responding in such a way. He can no longer have any reasons for his claims and indeed he does not care about reasons. So argument or discussion with him is out of place, though we can inquire into what *makes* him take this absurd stance.

There is another objection that I need briefly to consider. Someone might say: "I am not so sure about all these fancy semantical arguments of yours. I confess I do not know what to say about them, but one thing is certain, if there is a God, then He is the author, the creator and the sustainer of everything. He created everything other than Himself. Nothing else could exist without God and in this fundamental way morality and everything else is totally dependent on God. Without God there could be nothing to which moral principles or moral claims could be applied. Thus, in one important respect, morality, logic, and everything else is dependent on God."

I would first like to argue that there is a strict sense in which even this at least *prima facie* plausible claim of the religionist is not so. When we talk about what is morally good or morally right, we are not talking about what, except incidentally, *is* the case but about what *ought* to be the case or about what *ought to exist*. Even if there was nothing at all, that is, if there were no objects, processes, relations or sentient creatures, it would still be correct to say that *if* there were sentient creatures, a world in which there was less pain, less suffering, than the present world has would be a better world than a world *like* ours. The truth of this is quite independent of the actual existence of either the world or of anything's existing, though indeed we would, in such a circumstance, still have to have an *idea* of what it would be like for there to be sentient life and thus a world. That its truth is so independent obtains for the perfectly trivial reason that the "we" would denote a contingently empty class. Though no one could announce this truth, since *ex hypothesi* there are no people, yet it still would be true that if there were a country like the United States and it had a president like President Kennedy, then it would be wrong to have killed him. To talk about what exists is one thing, to talk about what is good or about what ought to exist is another. God could create the world, but He could not—logically could not—create moral values. *Existence is one thing, value is another.*

If all this talk of what ought to be as being something independent of what is, is stuff of a too heady nature for you, consider this independent and supplementary argument against the theist's reply. To assert that nothing would be good or bad, right or wrong, if nothing existed, is not to deny that we can come to understand, without reference to God, that it was wrong to kill President Kennedy and that religious tolerance is a good thing. The religious moralist has not shown that such killing would not be wrong and that such tolerance would not be good even if the atheist were right and God did not exist. But the religious apologist must show that in a Godless world morality and moral values would be impossible, if his position is to be made out. If there is no reason to believe that torturing little children would cease to be evil in a Godless world, we have no reason to believe that, in any important sense, morality is dependent on religion. We can see that we have independent criteria for what is right and wrong or good and bad. God or no God, religion or no religion, it is still wrong to inflict pain on helpless infants when the inflicting of such pain is without point.[27] This, of course, is an extreme case, but it makes vivid how our moral categories are not religion-dependent. In more mundane situations this is also plainly the case. In a Godless world the practice of promise keeping would still have a rational point.

X

There is a further stage in the dialectic of the argument about religion and ethics. I have shown that in a purely logical sense moral notions cannot rest on the doctrinal cosmic claims of religion. In fact quite the reverse is the case, namely, that only if a man has a religiously independent concept of good and evil can he even have the Judeo-Christian-Islamic conception of Deity. In this very fundamental sense, it is not morality that rests on religion but religion that rests on morality.[28] Note that this argument could be made out, even if we grant the theist his metaphysical claims about what there is. That is to say, the claims I have hitherto made are quite independent of skeptical arguments about the reliability or even the intelligibility of claims to the effect that God exists.

Some defenders of the faith will grant that there is indeed such a fundamental independence of ethical belief from religious belief, though very few, if any, would accept my last argument about the dependence of religious belief on human moral understanding. They could accept my basic claim and still argue that to develop a *fully human* and *adequate normative* ethic one must make it a religious ethic. Here in the arguments, for and against, the intellectual reliability of religious claims will become relevant.

The claim that such a religious apologist wishes to make is that only with a God-centered morality could we get a morality that would be adequate, that would go beyond the relativities and formalisms of a nonreligious ethic.[29] Only a God-centered and perhaps only a Christ-centered morality could meet our most persistent moral demands. Human beings have certain desires and needs; they experience loneliness and despair; they create certain "images of excellence"; they seek happiness and love. If the human animal was not like this, if man were not this searching, anxiety-ridden creature with a thirst for happiness and with strong desires and aversions, there would be no good and evil, no morality at all. In short our moralities are relative to our human natures. And given the human nature that we in fact have, we cannot be satisfied with any purely secular ethic. Nothing "the world" can give us will finally satisfy us. We thirst for a Father who will protect us—who will not let life be just one damn thing after another until we die and rot; we long for a God who can offer us the promise of a blissful everlasting life with Him. We need to love and obey such a Father. Unless we can picture ourselves as creations of such a loving Sovereign, and really convince ourselves of the truth of our picture, our deepest moral expectations will be frustrated.

No purely secular ethic can offer such a hope to us, a hope that is perhaps built on an illusion, but still a hope that is worth the full risk of faith. Whatever the rationality of such a faith, our very human nature makes us long for such assurances. Without it our lives will be without significance, without moral sense; morality finds its psychologically realistic foundation in certain human purposes, but human life without God will be devoid of all purpose or at least devoid of everything but trivial purposes. Thus without a belief in God, there could be no humanly satisfying morality. Secular humanism is in reality inhuman.

It is true that a secular morality can offer no hope for a blissful immortality; it is also true that secular morality does not provide for a protecting, living Father or some overarching Purpose *to* Life. But we have to balance this against the fact that these religious concepts are myths. We human beings are helpless, utterly dependent creatures for years and years. Because of this there develops in us a deep psychological need for an all-protecting Father or, depending on what culture we are in, some other cosmic assurances. It is natural enough for human beings to thirst for such security, but there is not the slightest reason to think that there is such security. That we have *feelings* of dependence does not mean that there is something on which we can depend. That we have such needs most certainly does not give us any reason at all to think that there is such a Super-mundane prop for our feelings of dependence.

Furthermore, and more importantly, if there is no such architectonic Purpose *to* Life, as our religions claim, this does not mean that there is no purpose *in* Life—that there is no way of living that is ultimately satisfying and significant. It indeed appears to be true that all small purposes, if pursued too relentlessly and exclusively, leave us with a sense of emptiness. Even Mozart when listened to endlessly becomes boring, but a varied life lived with verve and with a variety of conscious aims can survive the destruction of Vallhala. That there is no Purpose *to* life does not imply that there is no purpose *in* life. Man may not have a function and, if this is so, then unlike a tape recorder or a pencil or even a kind of homunculus, he does not have a Purpose. There is nothing he was made for. But he can and does have purposes in the sense that he has aims, goals, and things he finds worth seeking and admiring. There are indeed things we prize and admire; the achievement of these things and the realization of our aims and desires, including those we are most deeply committed to, can and typically do, give significance and moral ambience to our lives. We do not need a God to *give* meaning to our lives by making us for His Sovereign Purpose and thereby arguably robbing us of our freedom. We, by our deliberate acts and commitments, give meaning to our own lives. Here man has the "dreadful freedom" that gives him human dignity; freedom will indeed bring him anxiety, but he will be the *rider* and not the *ridden,* and by being able to choose, he can seek out and sometimes realize the things he most deeply prizes and admires, and thus his life can take on a significance. A life lived without purpose is indeed a most dreadful life, but we do not need God or the gods to give purpose to our lives.

There are believers who would say that these purely human purposes, forged in freedom and anguish, are not sufficient to meet our deepest moral needs. Man needs very much to see himself as a creature with a Purpose in a Divinely Ordered Universe. He needs to find some cosmic significance for his ideals and commitments; he wants the protection and the certainty of having a function. As the Grand Inquisitor realized, some religionists argue, this is even more desirable than his freedom. He wants and needs to live and be guided by the utterly Sovereign Will of God. If that entails a sacrifice of his autonomy, so be it.

If a religious moralist really wants this and would continue to want it on careful reflection, after all the consequences of his view and the alternatives had been placed vividly before him, and after he had taken the matter to heart, we *may* finally get back to an ultimate disagreement in attitude. But before we get there, there is a good bit that can be said. How could his purposes really be *his* own purposes, if he were a creature made for God's Sovereign Purpose and under the Sovereign Will of God? His ends would not be something he had deliberately chosen but would simply be something that he could not help *realizing.* Moreover, is it really compatible with human dignity to be *made for* something? What are you *for* is an insult! Finally, is it not *infantile* to go on looking for some Father, some Order, that will lift all the burden of *decision* from you? Children follow rules blindly, but do we want to be children all our lives? Is it really *hubris* or arrogance or sin on our part to wish for a life where we make our own decisions, where we follow rules because we see the point of them and where we need not crucify our intellects by believing in some transcendental Purpose whose very intelligibility is seriously in question? *Perhaps* by saying this I am only exhibiting my own *hubris,* my own corruption of soul, but I cannot believe that to ask this question is to exhibit such arrogance. It seems to me that such a move is rather that of a dying religion, suffering a failure of nerve, in a world which, in Max Weber's conception, is becoming progressively demystified. The present task is not only to continue this process, but to make our world as well a truly human world. Religion cannot achieve that for us, but as long as we, by our own collective actions, do not achieve it for ourselves there will be churned from the conditions of our social life pitiful phenomena like that of "the moral majority."

NOTES

1. The basic texts are Thomas Aquinas, *Summa Theologiae* I-II, Qq. 90-108 and *Summa Contra Gentiles,* Book III. For Neo-Thomist accounts see Jacques Maritain, "Natural Law and Moral Law" in *Moral Principles of Action,* edited by R. N. Anshen (New York, 1952); Jacques Maritain, *Man and the State,* (Chicago, 1951); Jacques Maritain, *The Range of Reason,* (New York, 1951); F. C. Copleston S.J., *Aquinas,* (Baltimore, 1955), chapter 5; Clifford G. Kossel S.J., "The Moral View of Thomas Aquinas," *Encyclopedia of Morals,* edited by V. Ferm (New York, 1956), pp. 11-23; and C. B. Daly, "A Criminal Lawyer on the Sanctity of Life," *Irish Theological Quarterly* (October, 1958, January, 1959 and July 1959): 330-336, 23-55, and 231-272. The article by Daly is an out of the way gem that secular humanists will find very revelatory of underlying Catholic attitudes toward humanism. Germain G. Griesez argues in his "The First Principle of Practical Reason" in *Aquinas,* edited by A. Kenny (Garden City, New York, 1969) that Maritain's account here is not a correct interpretation of Aquinas and that I too closely follow Maritain here. But the essential points I argue here do not rest, in any essential way, on Maritain's readings of Aquinas, so even if Maritain's account of Aquinas should be mistaken, it does not touch my criticisms of the natural moral law. See my "Examination of the Thomistic Theory of Natural Moral Law," *Natural Law Forum* 4 (1959) and my "The Myth of Natural Law" in Sidney Hook (ed.), *Law and Philosophy,* (New York, 1964). See also, for a Catholic defense, Eric D'Arcy " 'Worthy of Worship': A Catholic Contribution," Gene Outka and John P. Reeder (eds.), *Religion and Morality,* (Garden City, New York, 1973).

2. Emil Brunner, *The Divine Imperative* (Philadelphia, 1947). See also the collection edited by Janine Marie Idziak, *Divine Command Morality,* (New York, 1979).

3. Ruth Benedict, "Anthropology and the Abnormal" in Rodger Beehler and Alan R. Drengson (eds.), *The Philosophy of Society* (London, 1978), pp. 279-288.

224   **Atheism & Philosophy**

4. C. B. Daly, op cit., pp. 340-1.

5. Kai Nielsen, "Ethical Relativism and the Facts of Cultural Relativity," *Social Research* 33 (1966): 531-551.

6. See the references to Maritain and Kossel in note 1.

7. Aquinas, *Summa Theologiae,* I-II, Q. 90, art. I and I V.

8. Ibid.

9. Ibid.

10. Ibid.

11. This is particularly clear in the work of Maritain.

12. Daly, p. cit., p. 342.

13. See the articles by Kurt Baier and Kai Nielsen in E. D. Klemke (ed.) *The Meaning of Life* (New York: Oxford University Press, 1981).

14. Ibid.

15. Kai Nielsen, *Contemporary Critiques of Religion* (London, 1971) and Kai Nielsen, *Scepticism* (London, 1973).

16. Aquinas, *Summa Theologiae,* I-II, Q. 94, art ii.

17. Daly, op. cit.

18. Kai Nielsen, "On Deriving an Ought From an Is," *Review of Metaphysics* XXXII (March, 1979): 488-515.

19. I have argued that in some detail in my *Reason and Practice* (New York, 1971), pp. 243-319 and in my *Ethics Without God* (Buffalo: Prometheus Books, 1973).

20. Norman Daniels, "Wide Reflective Equilibrium and Theory Acceptance in Ethics," *Journal of Philosophy* 76 (1979) and his "Reflective Equilibrium and Archimedean Points," *Canadian Journal of Philosophy* (March, 1980): 83-103.

21. Daly, op cit., p. 359. Note his further remark on the same page: "Antiprocreative sexual unions represent a 'regression' towards infantile and specifically narcissistic sexuality. There is strict psychological justification for speaking of 'mutual masturbation.' "

22. William Aiken and Hugh La Follette (eds.) *World Hunger and Moral Obligation,* (Englewood Cliffs, New Jersey, 1977), p. 1.

23. Victor White, "Word of God and Natural Law" in *Writers on Ethics,* edited by Joseph Katz et al. (Princeton, New Jersey, (1962), p. 486.

24. Emil Brunner, *The Divine Imperative,* Section III. All the quotations from Brunner in VII of this article are from Section III of his book.

25. Stephen Toulmin, *The Place of Reason in Ethics,* (Cambridge, England, 1950), pp. 202-221.

26. Patterson Brown in his "God and the Good," *Religious Studies* (April, 1967) has argued that the understanding of what is meant by "good," but not the criteria of good, are, for the believer, independent of God's will. I have argued, in my *Reason and Practice,* pp. 251-253, that his claim rests on a mistake.

27. A. C. Ewing, "The Autonomy of Ethics," *Prospects for Metaphysics,* edited by I. T. Ramsey (London, 1961), p. 49.

28. See my *Ethics Without God,* chapters one and two and my "God and the Good: Does Morality Need Religion?" in Karsten J. Struhl and Paul Rothenberg (eds.), *Ethics in Perspective,* (New York, 1975), pp. 78-83.

29. See the essay by H. Richard Niebuhr in *Moral Principles of Action,* edited by R. N. Anshen, (New York, 1952).

10

Religion and Rationality

Introduction

It is not unnatural to wonder if reason is wanton. Much talk of what is reasonable and what is rational is not itself very rational. Often, people use such talk as a club to beat down those they oppose. Even when there is sensitivity toward such ideological employments of talk of rationality, it is still anything but evident that there are objective criteria of rationality that are sufficiently strong to enable impartial, well-informed people who are capable of exact reasoning to achieve a reflective consensus on the comparative rationality/irrationality of various social institutions and social practices, to say nothing of whole ways of life or societies. I am ambivalently skeptical of this extensive skepticism about reason. I shall try here to give some of the grounds for my skepticism.

Often we are not able to make fine enough discriminations and, in such circumstances, we have no basis for rankings or judgments in terms of the rationality of the various practices, institutions or ways of life we are reflecting upon. But in some other circumstances it is plain enough what should be said. Before we judge reason to be wanton, we should be careful not to assimilate certain difficult cases to the more general run of things where what the rational or reasonable thing to do is often not that problematic. That reason cannot always tell us what we ought to do does not mean that it never can or even that it cannot often give us guidance in important areas of our lives.

I shall first set out a characterization of what is ordinarily meant by "rationality," followed by a characterization of criteria of rationality both instrumental and noninstrumental, followed in turn by some examination of the limits of our commitment to rationality. That

227

will be followed by what might be taken as a crucial test case: to wit whether Jewish or Christian belief for an educated twentieth-century person is a reasonable option. I shall attempt to show something of what must be done to answer this question and I shall end with an examination of a Wittgensteinian challenge, which claims that to attempt to make such global assessments of the rationality of whole belief-systems is to give reason a rationalistic task that is not genuinely its own.

I

In understanding rationality, dictionaries can give us a start. If we look up "rational" and "reasonable" in the Oxford English Dictionary (OED), we find such things as the following. To be rational is to be endowed with reason, to have the faculty of reasoning. It is also to exercise one's reason in a proper manner and to have sound judgment and to be sensible and sane. Rational beliefs or rational principles of action are those that pertain to or relate to reason or are based on or derived from reason or reasoning. They are beliefs and principles that are "agreeable to reason" and thus are "reasonable, sensible, not foolish, absurd or extravagant." If we turn to the closely related term "reasonable," we are told that to be reasonable is to have sound judgment, to be sensible, sane.[1] We are also told that it sometimes means, curiously enough, "not to ask for too much." And in former times, but now only rarely, when an individual speaks of someone being reasonable, he means that this person is "endowed with reason." Moreover, something that is reasonable—say a consideration, claim or argument—is something that is agreeable to reason, not irrational, absurd or ridiculous. And there is in the OED, as well, the somewhat surprising claim that being reasonable is "not going beyond the limits assigned."

I think philosophers would be ill-advised to make sport of these notions. They give us a sense of the terrain we are concerned with and we might even be somewhat skeptical whether in such a specification we philosophers have done much better. But all the same, if we are perplexed about rationality, these dictionary definitions are not going to do much to help us. We surely are going to be puzzled about this "faculty of reason" or about being "endowed with reason." And we are going to be suspicious about talk of "being agreeable to reason." What is this reason that we are or may be endowed with? If it is only the faculty of speech and the ability to think and argue (set out an argument) that is being talked about, then it should be remarked that thoroughly irrational people have that ability too and thoroughly irrational claims have been expressed in nondeviant English, French, German, and other languages. Moreover, extravagant and irrational claims have had valid arguments as their vehicles. Validity is but a crucial necessary condition for sound and rational argumentation. So, if being "endowed with reason" or having the "faculty of reason" is only understood as being able to speak, to think, and to be able to form valid arguments, it will not be sufficient to give us an understanding of rationality.

Alternatively, we need to ask whether being endowed with reason or being agreeable to reason is simply its being the case that what is agreeable to reason is established or establishable by sound arguments, namely, valid arguments with true premises. If it is, then we are at least on familiar and in a way on unproblematic terrain. The problem becomes that of determining when arguments are valid and when statements are true or probably true. While this is surely part of the task of determining what is rationality, it is not all of it, for there are principles of action that are at least said to be rational and attitudes of which the same thing is said. Yet, concerning both principles and attitudes, it is not clear that the notions of truth or falsity have any determinate and/or unproblematic meaning. Moreover, we do not, in some instances at least, seem to be talking about knowledge claims here. But then why should the lack of a knowledge claim rule out rationality? Finally, in this context, and to make a quite different point, it is also the case that not everything that is reasonably believed is believed for a reason or (arguably) because it is known to be true or probably true. So, while reason is perhaps not wanton, it is, on such a characterization, still perplexing.

We are, if we are perplexed by rationality, also going to have trouble with the OED's characterizations of rationality in terms of "exercising one's reason in a *proper* manner" and "being *sensible, sane,* and of *sound* judgment," "not *foolish, absurd,* or *extravagant.*" And having trouble with those we are going to have still more trouble with such seemingly conservative ideological notions as "not asking for too much" or "not going beyond the limits assigned." The various notions cited above only have a determinate meaning in a contextual and culture-specific environment. Some of them are definitely ideological, some are normative terms with a definite emotive force (e.g., "foolish," "absurd," "extravagant") and "proper," "sensible," "sound," if not characteristically emotive in their force, are still normative and, as well, or at least, are terms with criteria that are contestable and perhaps even essentially contestable.[2] Manifestly rational and reasonable human beings—or at least intelligent and well-informed human beings capable of cool judgment—disagree about their criteria and about who is or is not of sound judgment, sensible, reasonable, and the like. When Henry Kissinger announces that such and such is a reasonable policy or that the parties in question are not being reasonable, I suspect a rather ideological, *persuasive* definition has been utilized; I realize that he and I do not, in some very important ways, agree about the criteria for rationality and reasonability. (Is that actually the right way of looking at it? Perhaps we do agree about *criteria* of rationality and reasonability but just very fundamentally and systematically disagree about *what* is rational or reasonable. Or is that, in this context, a distinction without a difference?) Whatever we might want to say about that parenthetical remark, the general thrust of the argument in this paragraph shows that the dictionary will not take us out of the woods, even if we use it sensibly.

II

Let me now look at some criteria that philosophers have set out for *rational belief* and *rational principles* of action to see if they are any improvement.[3] Presumably a rational human being will have rational *principles of action* and *rational beliefs*. Moreover, to have rational attitudes is at least to have attitudes that square with these principles and beliefs, and to be irrational is—though this perhaps is not all that it is—to not act in accordance with these principles and beliefs. But what are they? And are they as essentially contested and as indeterminate as the conceptions expressed in the dictionary entries?

Rational beliefs are typically beliefs that can withstand the scrutiny of people who are critical of their beliefs: that is to say, they are beliefs typically held open to refutation or modification by experience and/or by reflective examination. Rational beliefs—to spell out a little what is involved in the notion of reflective examination—are beliefs that must be capable of being held in such as way, *ceteris paribus,* as not to block or resist reflective inspection, namely, attempts to consider their assumptions, implications, and relations to other beliefs. Rational beliefs are also typically beliefs for which there is, or at least can be, good evidence or good reasons, or at least they are, *ceteris paribus,* beliefs for which such evidence or reasons, when the need arises, will be conscientiously and intelligently sought; and evidence or reasons (when available and utilizable) will not be ignored by people who hold such beliefs. Finally, rational beliefs are, *ceteris paribus,* beliefs for which it is reliably believed, or at least not implausible to assume, that there are good grounds for believing that they do not involve inconsistencies, contradictions or incoherencies. (The heavy reliance on *ceteris paribus* qualifications will no doubt cause unease. I address myself to that after I specify the rational principles of action.)

A rational person will also have rational principles of action and it will be irrational of him not to act in accordance with these principles. The following are at least plausible candidates:

1. The most efficient and effective means are to be taken, *ceteris paribus*, to achieve one's ends.
2. If one has several compatible ends, one, *ceteris paribus*, should take the means that will, as far as one can ascertain, most likely enable one to realize the greatest number of one's ends.
3. Of two ends, equally desired and equal in all other relevant respects, one is, *ceteris paribus*, to choose the end with the higher probability of being achieved.
4. If there are the same probabilities in two plans of action, which secure entirely different ends, that plan of action is to be chosen which, *ceteris paribus*, secures ends at least one of which is preferred to one of those secured by the other plan.
5. If one is unclear about what one's ends are or what they involve or how they are to be achieved, then it is usually wise to postpone making a choice among plans of action to secure those ends.
6. Those ends which form a dispassionate and informed point of view and which a person values absolutely higher than his other ends, are the ends which, *ceteris paribus*, he should try to realize. A rational agent will, *ceteris paribus*, seek plans of action which will satisfy those ends; and plans to satisfy his other ends will be adopted only in so far as they are compatible with the satisfaction of those ends he or she values most highly.[4]

A rational person will have rational beliefs, i.e., beliefs that satisfy the above criteria of rationality and rational principles of action, and he or she will in almost all circumstances act in accordance with them. (This does not mean he will constantly be calculating what is the rational thing to do. To act rationally will be in accordance with these principles but that does not mean he necessarily must be consciously following them.) However, with these principles of rationality as with the dictionary definitions, there are areas of indeterminateness.[5] Indeed, these areas were quite self-consciously introduced when the principles were stated. The *ceteris paribus* clause is essential as well as such qualifiers as "typically" or "usually," for without them the principles will surely fall to counterexamples: that is to say, there will be situations, real or plausibly imaginable, when it will be at least arguable that the reasonable thing to do in those situations will not be to act in accordance with one or another of the principles. In that way their function is guidance and "absoluteness" is closely analogous to the way in which *prima facie* duties work. To ask for anything more is unrealistic and perhaps even unreasonable.

However, even if something tighter is possible and is ultimately to be desired, a strong consideration for our discussion in favor of the principles of rationality I have set out above is that they are a good subset of the principles of rationality and, like *prima facie* duties, they *always usually hold*. That is to say, so as to make clear that I am not unsaying what I say here, it is always the case that these principles, where applicable, usually hold in a way quite analogous to the way that for everyone all of the time it is the case that promises, generally speaking, are to be kept.

III

The above characterization of rationality is a rather minimal one that might plausibly be thought to be normatively neutral. Jürgen Habermas, developing a conception of rationality that follows in the tradition of the Frankfurt School, gives us a much richer but normatively freighted conception of rationality.[6] It would, no doubt, contain the principles of rationality specified above and it, like those principles, goes beyond what is specified in the ordinary use of "rational" and "reasonable" and their German equivalences, but it is still, I believe, in the spirit of that use. At least it is plainly not in conflict with that use. It will be well, in trying to gain an understanding of rationality, to set alongside the principles of rationality that I have articulated those conceptions of Habermas's which are distinctively different. The ensemble or, perhaps better, the mélange should then be up for critical examination.

Habermas in a very considerable measure cashes out the concept of rationality in terms of an articulation of the concepts of enlightenment and emancipation.[7] A fully rational human being will be an emancipated, enlightened human being. Such people will have critical insight and an enlightened consciousness, i.e., a coherent total consciousness. They will have achieved a firm sense of self-identity and adult autonomy; they have an understanding of human needs and are liberated from the various illusions and dogmatisms that fetter humankind. Rationality, of course, admits of degrees and this conception is trying to capture that heuristic ideal, a fully rational person, but it is also, of course, an attempt to specify what we put into our conceptualization and indeed our ideal of full rationality or, perhaps, more in accordance with ordinary usage, full reasonability. This full reasonability will be coextensive with what it is to be enlightened and emancipated. Where enlightened and emancipated conditions obtain, and thus fully rational conditions (reasonable circumstances) obtain, people will be informed, perceptive, liberated, autonomous, self-controlled agents committed to developing their own distinctive powers and capacity for fairness, impartiality, and objectivity. They will be reflective about their ends, knowledgeable about the means for the efficient attainment of these ends, and they will be critical people not under the bondage of any ideology. Indeed, free from all self-imposed tutelage and indoctrination, they will see the world rightly. They will have identified the evils of the world and they will understand the conditions for surcease or amelioration of these evils and for the achievement of human community, to the extent that the community can be achieved at all.

IV

With both the specification in Part II of a minimal conception of rationality—an instrumental conception of rationality—and in Part III of a more ramified, noninstrumental conception of rationality before us, consider now whether we are ever justified in living according to commitments that we have cogent grounds, or at least very plausible grounds, for believing to involve the holding of irrational or thoroughly unreasonable beliefs? To get some purchase on this, let us examine one putative case..What we are looking for is whether there are any plausible examples of plainly irrational beliefs that are still beliefs, where the requisite self-deception is possible, which it would be reasonable to have. To show that there is such an example is to show that there can be justified irrational beliefs. To establish this, we need a paradigmatically irrational belief—a belief whose irrationality is unquestionable—a belief that is the ground for a justified commitment or reasonable mode of acting. In other words, can we give an airtight case of an action A—which is something, everything considered, we ought to do—which in turn is based on an irrational belief B, where it is better that we believe B and do A than either not believe B and do not -A or not believe B and not do or believe (B aside) anything about such matters at all?

Consider, for example, the case of a man with a terminal cancer, a plainly and unquestionably terminal cancer, on whom the medical experts have given up, where he knows they have given up on him. Moreover, he is also a man who knows that there is no reason at all to believe that in the two or three months he is expected to continue living that there will be a breakthrough in cancer research such that he can be cured after all. Yet, like most people, he wants very much to be cured; he does not want to go on suffering only to die in a couple of months. Suppose there is a man in Paraguay hounded out of the medical profession and almost certainly a quack who claims—in the face of the considered views of the medical profession and with no good evidence of his own—that he can cure cancers of this type, but it is essential for the working of the cure that the patient believes he will most certainly get well. Suppose further that this "doctor's" treatment will not shorten our terminal patient's life or cause him or anyone close to him anymore pain or distress than he or they would otherwise experience. Suppose the man goes to Paraguay, puts himself under the "doctor's" care, and in some way deceives himself into believing that he most certainly will get well. This belief that he most certainly will get well is a paradigmatically irrational or at least unreasonable belief, yet the act—in effect betting on a very long shot where he has everything to gain and nothing to lose—is, under the circumstances, not an irrational act but an act that requires a paradigmatically irrational or unreasonable belief about what is likely to happen. Yet it is at least arguable, to put it minimally, that the individual in question is justified in so acting and—as *ex hypothesi* he must to so act—in believing, if he can get himself to so believe, that he will most certainly get well. (Remember that "so acting" refers to the prescribed course of treatment; it is part of the prescribed cure that he believe that he will most certainly get well.) That is to say, in terms of what, everything considered, he is *justified* in doing, or at least can reasonably do, he is justified in having a belief that is plainly irrational or unreasonable. In this instance, it is the belief that he most certainly will get well. (How such a belief in such a circumstance can be stamped in is another question.)

Such cases are no doubt exceptional and the context is odd but they can occur. The lesson is that our very straining for such examples shows the close tie between justifiability and rationality and the exceptions show that, while the tie is very close, it is not so close that circumstances of a far-out sort cannot arise where we are justified in hoping that we will be able to deceive ourselves into having an irrational belief. We recognize that, if we can actually believe it, it would be a good thing if we could actually come to hold such an irrational belief.

What cases of this type show is that in certain circumstances we are justified, or at least not irrational, in acting in accordance with a particular irrational belief. Indeed, I think they even reveal something stronger, namely, that sometimes it is rational—in this context reasonable—deliberately to set ourselves on a course of action that will subsequently and in certain very circumscribed situations make it possible for us to act in accordance with a belief we *now* recognize to be irrational. (If, because of the power of the emotive force for "irrational," it seems too jarring to speak this way, substitute for "irrational," "utterly groundless," "utterly without warrant," or "utterly without rational warrant." Even with such substitutions, substantially the same point will be made.)

There is no paradox here if one reflects a moment, for it is, given the criteria and principles of rationality they jointly define, everything considered, the rational thing to do to act in such circumstances on such irrational beliefs. That is to say, the weight of reasons, justified by the principles of rationality, justify our acting on such an irrational belief.

The most crucial thing to see about such cases is that in so acting a human being is not acting "against reason" or "acting irrationally." Indeed, in so acting one is, everything considered, being guided by reason, being reasonable and is acting rationally or at least one is not acting irrationally.

V

So we can see that it is sometimes in accord with reason to act in certain circumstances, in accordance with an irrational or unreasonable belief. However, to say this is one thing, but it is another thing to say that someone would be, or even conceivably could be, justified in living according to a whole cluster of commitments that involve the holding of what she or he knows, or has very good grounds for believing, involve the holding of irrational or unreasonable beliefs. To make this clear take an extreme case. What would it be like to be justified in jettisoning all of the principles of rationality I have specified above? I shall argue that it is problematical whether this is something that can be intelligibly done. To try to ascertain whether this is so, let us consider whether we can describe what it would be like to do it and to be justified in doing it.

Our person who tries to reject rationality *tout court* would have to have beliefs that were not open to modification or refutation by experience. Thus, if he believes his lunch is in his briefcase but upon reaching for it does not find it in his briefcase, he would still perfectly well go on believing that it is in his briefcase. But, as most beliefs are not voluntary matters, it is doubtful whether he can actually go on believing that his lunch is in his briefcase in such a circumstance. Willy-nilly most of our beliefs—at least our mundane beliefs—do get modified by experience. In that limited way we cannot avoid being critical. Moreover, and even more centrally, people can not negotiate with the world, get around in the world and live with other human beings if their beliefs are not so modifiable by experience. If an agent has no concern with whether his beliefs involve inconsistencies, contradictions, or incoherencies and if he succeeds in being thoroughly incoherent and inconsistent, then there will come a point where he can not communicate with people and will not even understand himself so that he can believe what he tells himself and us that he believes.

Suppose Wayland is such a chap and he tells us that he is not concerned to be constrained in his beliefs by considerations of consistency or coherence, but that he believes—or so he proclaims—that he sleeps faster than Plumtree and yet at the same time, and in the same respect, Plumtree sleeps faster than he does. We point out to him, assuming first counterfactually that it is coherent, that his belief is contradictory—he believes p and not $-p$ and that, now dropping the assumption, it is incoherent as well, for it makes no sense to say, "X sleeps faster than Y" or "X sleeps slower than Y." He replies that—contradictory or not, coherent or not—he believes it all the same, for he is not constrained in his beliefs to what he takes to be coherent and consistent. But then the answer should be, in turn, that though he *says* he believes these things, he cannot possibly believe them, for, in uttering a contradiction, he unsays what he *apparently* says and in uttering something that is genuinely incoherent, *what* he believes cannot be specified or stated (asserted): his utterance lacks propositional content. Indeed, even he cannot do it for himself. He does not understand *what* it is that he is to believe. But if there is no saying or in any way specifying what is believed, then there is no belief. Wayland thinks he can believe such stark incoherencies and contradictions but he cannot. Moreover, just to have a disposition to act in a certain way is not enough to constitute a belief. So the man who sets out to have beliefs and commitments—things that involve beliefs but are not identical to them—cannot simply jettison rationality and still have beliefs and commitments. If a human being is to have any beliefs or commitments at all, there is no "rejecting rationality" in this *wholesale* manner, though this is not, of course, to show or claim that his beliefs and commitments must have all the earmarks of rational belief.

Where the attempt is not to put all the principles of rationality under the axe but only a few, *perhaps* some circumstances could arise in which someone might reasonably not act in accordance with some of them. But the closer one gets to anything like a wholesale or even extensive rejection of them, the closer what one does and says will be to a kind of utter incoherency. If we have a whole battery of diverse, unreasonable beliefs, our actions, if we try to act on those beliefs, will become utterly unreasonable. It is only in isolated, exceptional cases or perhaps (to be maximally liberal about possibilities here) closely interconnected cases where it can be reasonable to act on unreasonable beliefs.

VI

So in the above *crucial way* there is no *possible* alternative to rationality. Let us now ask as well if it is at least logically possible for a human being with rational beliefs simply to jettison rational principles of action in a similar wholesale way? Here it does, I believe, seem to be some kind of weak possibility, though hardly, and indeed by definition, a *rational* possibility. That is to say, we can, without vast tricks of the imagination, imagine situations in which we would understand what it would be like for an agent not to act on these principles. We are indeed *appalled* by such behavior, but we understand it: we can follow descriptions of what it would be like to so behave.

We can, I believe, understand a description of someone acting in such a way that he did not postpone acting on a matter that normally would be thought to be important and where there was no pressure to act immediately though he had no tolerably clear idea of the consequences in that circumstance of choosing to act one way rather than another, where he had no concern for which of his ends would have the greater likelihood of being achieved, where he did not care whether he satisfied a greater rather than a lesser number of his compatible ends, and where he did not even try to take the most effective means to achieve his ends. We might very well wonder just how all the compatible ends could be *his* ends when he was so indifferent about maximizing their achievement. But why should we not say that such perversity and irrationality is possible?

It is somewhat more questionable whether there really are alternatives to principles 4 and 6 stated in Part II. It might be thought that we could not choose to do, where this is a voluntary action, what we do not, everything considered, prefer most. But that is not so on a straightforward use of "prefer." I might prefer Chopin, and indeed even at a specific moment prefer Chopin, and still perversely, for no reason at all, listen to Brahms. In a similar vein—vis-à-vis principle 6—it might be said that if an individual did not try to achieve P or did *not* try to achieve it more than he tried to achieve S, R or Q, we would not, *ceteris paribus*, say that he valued it higher than those things. What one does not go after one does not value, unless there is some specific overriding reason for not going after it. This *may* be true. But it is not plainly and evidently true, and it seems at least to make nonsense out of what looks like the perceptive psychological remark that it is sometimes the case for some individuals that they do not do the good they would otherwise do. It at most shows that with principle 6, alone of the various rational principles of action, it may be impossible not to think in accordance with it. (If that were true, as I do not think it is, it would raise serious questions about the logical status of 6.)

The upshot of the above remarks is that while there is no possibility of rejecting at least certain of what I have called our criteria for rational belief, it does appear to be possible to reject the principles of rational action and to act quite irrationally and on a massive scale, though there is not a scintilla of a reason to believe that circumstances could arise in which these actions are justified. But, even if such circumstances could arise, if my arguments are correct, there still is no way of rejecting reason *en masse*.

VII

I have been concerned to show what rational beliefs are, what the principles of instrumental rationality are, and something of what noninstrumental conceptions of rationality come to. Together they give us some understanding of rationality, an understanding that goes beyond, yet is still compatible with, what can be garnered about rationality from an examination of the ordinary employments of the terms "rational" and "reasonable" in everyday contexts. I then try to show that even with such an understanding of reason there is a problem about coping with reason, namely, that our rationalistic expectations to the contrary notwithstanding, it may sometimes be the case that in the living of our lives it is, everything considered, reasonable to have unreasonable beliefs. But this fact, if it is indeed a fact, does not make reason wanton. It does not show that it is even possible, let alone justified, to reject reason, to abandon reason, or to not live one's life largely in accordance with the unproblematic elements in the concept of reason I have characterized. Even the most psychotic people, where they can in any way function at all, cannot quite pull off anything like that. It is indeed only by appealing to these principles of rationality that we can in some specific situation justify having an unreasonable belief or not following one or another of the principles of rationality. More generally, there is no alternative to acting in accordance with the principles of rationality. In that general way, there is no sense to the question "Why be rational?" though this does not show, or give to understand, that "cold reason"—hard, careful thinking—can by itself, or coupled with a knowledge of the facts, independently of our reflective sentiments or our deepest hopes, resolve for us how it is that we ought to live or show us that, in all circumstances, maximally reliable information is a *desideratum* for all human beings, no matter how they may be placed.[8]

VIII

Consider a specific religion such as Judaism or Christianity. Can we both understand it and believe it? Are our criteria of rationality and intelligibility such that it can be established that the core beliefs of Judaism and/or Christianity are irrational? Most fundamentally, what we—or at least many of us—want to know is whether Jewish or Christian belief in God is a rational belief or at least not an irrational belief. Note this is perfectly parallel to a question pursued by Evans-Pritchard, Winch, MacIntyre, Lukes, Hollis, and others: "Is the Zande belief in witches a rational belief?"[9]

What we are trying to ask, both in the Zande case and in the Jewish/Christian case, is whether in terms of a common notion of rationality, such as we have articulated in the previous sections, such beliefs can and indeed should be said to be rational or at least not irrational. For the nonce, we are assuming (what needs to be argued) that it is *not* the case that one standard of rationality applies to the Zande and another to us or one standard of intelligibililty applies to the Christian and another to the secularist. I will, that is, start by assuming a unitary conception of rationality and see where it leads us.[10]

In asking about the rationality of the Jewish and Christian belief in God, as well as in asking about the rationality of Zande belief in witchcraft, it is wise, I believe, to break down the question in the following way. (I shall do it first for the Zande.) "Is the Zande belief in witches a rational belief?" can be taken as either: (a) "Can we members of twentieth-century Western culture, with the rather full information and learning available to an educated member of our culture, rationally believe in witches as the Zande do?" or (b) "Are the Zande rational in believing in witches; have they acted reasonably and not disregarded evidence, reasoning, and information readily available to them in believing in witches?"

In talking about the Zande it is plainly evident that it is important to distinguish between these questions because what we have learned from social anthropology concerning other cultures should make us extremely loath to claim that the average Zande or the average member of any other tribe is irrational. But, given the pervasiveness and centrality of Zande belief in witchcraft, this is exactly what we should conclude if we answer (b) by claiming that the Zande are irrational in believing as they do. Yet, on the other hand, we do not want, in acknowledging that the Zande are not behaving irrationally in believing in witches, to give to understand that if we Westerners do not believe in witches we are being irrational. Hence the importance of distinguishing between (a) and (b).

I will maintain that it is important to make a parallel distinction in talking about the rationality of Christian and Jewish belief in God. However, since in speaking of Christian and Jewish belief we are talking intraculturally and not cross-culturally between radically different cultures, the importance of drawing that distinction is not so evident to us. (It may be perfectly evident to someone coming from another culture.)

Let me first draw this distinction with greater exactitude and then I shall try to show the importance of drawing it. "Is the Judeo-Christian belief in God a rational belief?" can be understood as: Can we members of the twentieth-century Western culture, with the rather full information and learning available to an educated member of our culture, rationally believe in the God of the mainstream Jewish and Christian traditions?" or (d) "Are Christians and Jews rational in believing in God; have they acted reasonably and not disregarded evidence, reasoning, and information readily available to them in believing in God?"

There is an important disanalogy between (a) and (b), on the one hand, and (c) and (d), on the other, that we should immediately note. There is no overlap in the class of persons referred to in (a) and (b), but there is in (c) and (d). There are plenty of Christians and Jews who are manifestly rational and are members of the class of twentieth-century persons who are highly educated and reflective. This is just a sociological fact that we should not allow any ideological or philosophical convictions to obscure or distort. If anyone is to answer (c) in the negative, as he or she presumably would answer (a) in the negative, he or she will need to make out a very good case for the claim that while there are some Christians and Jews who are reflective, well-educated, and manifestly rational, that nonetheless their belief in God is irrational and that, in living in accordance with that belief, they—though perhaps understandably enough—are being irrational. (This, of course, does not mean that in other respects they are being irrational.)

This is a strong and indeed an embarrassing claim to make in our tolerant and (in many respects) liberal ethos. However, it is just the claim that anyone who consistently supports (c) must make and, although radical, it is a claim, that I shall make. The important thing to see is whether it can be given a reasonable explication and a sound defense. There are many who believe that any such claim is thoroughly wrong-headed. T. M. Penelhum, for example, believes that while the claims of natural theology to give sound reasons for believing in God do not succeed, neither do the allegedly clinching arguments against religious belief, so that vis-à-vis Judaism and Christianity we are left in a stalemate.[11] He believes, along with many others, that reason—

human ratiocination and rationality—cannot settle the matter one way or another.

What we are asking (assuming we are members of the class of reasonably educated twentieth-century Westerners or are people who have gained a participant's understanding of that cultural background) is whether it is rational to believe in the God of the Jews and the Christians. We want to know whether such a belief is irrational for such people, i.e., educated Westerners or people who have gained a firm participant's grasp of Western culture. Just as there are Zande who reasonably believe in witches, given what they can readily know, so there are plenty of Jews and Christians who are neither scientifically nor philosophically educated, who, given what they know and what is readily available to them, reasonably believe in God. This is not at all a patronizing remark on my part for we all stand—and unavoidably so—in the same position *vis-à-vis* some beliefs. Hegel is right in asserting that we cannot overleap history. This note is not a form of relativism, but unless a certain relativism about rationality is true (and indeed sufficiently coherent so that it could be true), there is no obvious reason, and perhaps no sound reason at all, for thinking that it could not correctly be claimed that reasonable people can have some irrational beliefs and indeed some very fundamental ones at that. In recognizing that we all are in the same boat, that we all may very well have some irrational beliefs, I show that I am not being patronizing to Jews or Christians. (It could not, of course, be the case that we could knowingly hold what we regarded—everything considered—as an irrational belief and still remain fully rational. Recall also that rationality admits of degrees.)

IX

What synoptically should be said about the rationality/irrationality of beliefs is this: A belief (religious or otherwise) is in most circumstances irrational if the person holding it knows or has very good grounds for believing that it is either (1) inconsistent, (2) unintelligible (does not make sense), (3) incoherent or (4) false or very probably false. It is also something that is irrational for him to believe if (5) it is held by that person in such a way that no attention is given to considerations of evidence that might be relevant (directly or indirectly) to the holding of that belief, (6) the person in question knowingly ignores relevant evidence or grounds for his belief or (7) that the belief is held in such a way that the holder of the belief will not countenance the reflective inspection of its implications for other beliefs or practices. (It is tricky to state (6) without saying something false or misleading. Where there

is a well developed, firmly established theory that the evidence discon-
firms and there are no competing theories that can account for a given
theory's recalcitrant evidence, such evidence can be rightly ignored.
That is not ignoring evidence *full stop* but deliberately ignoring some
of it under very determinate constraints. For this practice to be understandable, there must be a standing presumption that evidence will
not be ignored. But, like a *prima facie* obligation, that presumption
can sometimes with reason be overridden.) A belief-system that at a
given time has many central beliefs that have achieved this status is
an irrational belief-system for people at that time and place, if they
have a reasonably good scientific and philosophical education.

In asking whether the Judeo-Christian belief in God is rational, or
at least not irrational, we are asking:

1. Is belief in such a God free of inconsistencies or contradictions?
2. Is belief in such a God intelligible? (Does such a belief make
   sense?)
3. Is belief in such a God a belief in a coherent conception? (Is
   such a belief incoherent?)
4. Is belief in such a God a belief in something that we have very
   good grounds to believe not to be the case?

If any of 1 through 3 obtain, then belief in such a God is irrational
for a man who recognizes any of these things or for a man who is
in a position where he could, but for self-deception, recognize these
things. If this is so, we can say derivatively that the beliefs are
irrational beliefs. Question 4 is somewhat more problematic. It attaining probability even makes the belief, everything considered, irrational.
But for Kierkegaardian reasons this is not entirely clear.

Questions 1 and 4, at least on the surface, are fairly straightforward and only careful examination of the appropriate strands of
religious discourse would give us good grounds for answering one way
or another. But 2 and 3 are more troublesome. What are we claiming
when we claim that such a religious belief is unintelligible or incoherent? What counts as "being unintelligible" or "being incoherent"
here and how can we ascertain when this condition obtains? It would
seem, from the above, that we are saying such beliefs are irrational
because they are unintelligible or incoherent. But it has also been
suggested that to say "a belief is irrational" is to say (among other
things) that it is inconsistent, incoherent, or unintelligible. But then
the "because" loses much of its force. Plainly, to make any headway
here we must gain some clarity concerning what we are talking about
when we claim that a religious belief is incoherent or unintelligible.[12]

X

With the issues posed as they were in the previous section, as is certainly characteristic of most philosophical questions, there will be those who will feel that in posing them in that way we have already gone down the garden path: we have unwittingly steered things in the wrong direction. There are, some will claim, no substantive norms or principles of rationality or criteria of reasonableness that afford us an Archimedean point in accordance with which we can make such sweeping judgments. We need to take to heart Wittgenstein's penetrating and unsettling realization that there are just a diverse, incommensurable number of language-games and forms-of-life, with their attendant world-pictures, with no possible objective ground—if that isn't a pleonasm—for ranking or choosing between them. We are simply taught some world-picture; we are unreflectively and matter-of-coursely drilled, indoctrinated or, if you will, socialized, with one such world-picture. With that we have a number of beliefs—indeed, a system of beliefs—that *stand fast* for us, that we, in our practices and actual judgments, feel certain of and assume in any genuine investigating, doubting, knowing or rational believing that we engage in. They are, if you will, our *vor Wissen* that we take as a matter of course in our diverse activities. They are the grounds or at least the essential background for what we rationally believe, but they themselves are ungrounded—and necessarily so.

Christians—say of the Middle Ages—have one such world-picture with its related language-games and forms-of-life, and Zande (at the time Evans-Pritchard visited them) and contemporary Western secularists (to take two different cases) have other importantly dissimilar world-pictures. It is in accordance with these world-pictures that we can say what rational/irrational or reasonable/unreasonable beliefs, practices, and institutions are. But we have no vantage point—and, indeed, can have no such vantage point—for making assessments of these diverse and incommensurable world-pictures themselves.

If this is so, then the questions I tried to ask—or so at least it seems—are in reality questions that cannot sensibly be asked. We have no possible way of answering them that would not involve the question-begging procedure of simply, in accordance with the norms of rationality of one world-picture, criticizing and judging the beliefs distinctive of an incommensurable world-picture. There is no way of sensibly asking whether Christian belief is irrational because it is incoherent or inconsistent or whatever. This can no more be made out than that English is inconsistent or German is incoherent or ordinary language is inconsistent. In all such talk the engine is idling.

So, at least some Wittgensteinians would say, we should not try straightforwardly to answer my questions, but we should first examine in this domain the adequacy of Wittgenstein's account—an account, which, if correct, shows the senselessness or at least the pointlessness of asking what I am trying to ask. However, it is also important to note that, whatever the results of that endeavor, Wittgenstein's account not only presents a challenge for arguments with a skeptical thrust such as my own, but it is also a challenge for a variety of theistic accounts. If one argues, as has been argued, that (a) the ontological argument, if sound, provides a rational ground for worship, and (b) that the ontological argument is sound, one runs afoul of the above Wittgensteinian questions about "rational ground." One faces a similar difficulty if one claims that we should believe in God because the theistic interpretation is the most rational explanation of human religious experience. And finally, if Wittgenstein's remarks about rationality and world-pictures are right, it is impossible to establish in any significant way that, as John Hick puts it, "faith-awareness of God is a mode of cognition which can properly be trusted and in terms of which it is rational to live."[13] Even if we do not balk at "faith-awareness" and a "mode of cognition," whether it is rational to place our trust here and so live is trivially "answered," if we accept Wittgenstein's account, in terms of the world-picture we were taught. If you were brought up with a Christian, Jewish or Islamic world-picture and the instruction and indoctrination took, it is rational for you to trust "faith-awareness." If you were brought up with a secular or Buddhist or Zande world-picture, it is not. And that is the end of it. There is no superior vantage point of reason.

There is, in short, if Wittgenstein is right, no vantage point from where we could make progress with the "question(s)" that many of us, including many who have no taste for metaphysics at all, in certain moods at least, very much want answered: to wit, and most centrally, which vantage-point or world-picture is "really rational" or even—coming down a bit—which vantage-point or world-picture is the more reasonable to accept and to live in accordance with? These are not—and cannot be—genuine questions if Wittgenstein's account is on the mark.

XI

We should, however, be cautious about drawing such severe relativistic conclusions. Language-games and forms-of-life are not compartmentalized. The criteria of rational appraisal I have described cuts across them. Very basic things like asserting, inquiring, questioning, hoping, concluding, and remonstrating are distinct language-games, but these can be done in a rational and in a not-so-rational way. If we think of larger activities such as the particular forms that science, religion, and law take in a particular society at a given time, there is no reason to think they are *sui generis* and uncriticizable. At the very least, questions can be raised about how the various practices and forms-of-life of a society fit together. If elements of the law or of religion conflict with well-grounded scientific claims or with plain and careful empirical observations of what is the case, then, given these conflicts, there is plainly a need to make adjustments somewhere in the belief-system of the society and, given the strong way in which the scientific claims in question and the common-sense empirical claims in question are warranted, there are good reasons in such a circumstance to abandon or radically to modify certain elements of the religious or legal claims.

Similarly, since the language-games in a given culture are not insulated from each other (they are not self-contained units), there is good reason to believe that the criteria of what it makes sense to say and believe are not utterly idiosyncratic to a particular language-game. Our conceptions of consistency, coherence, and evidence are not utterly language-game-dependent. "Not" does not function differently in religious, scientific, and legal discourse, though to what it will be applied may be in part domain-dependent.

Coherence criteria are more difficult, but if in one domain we are forced to use conceptions that are very different from our other conceptions and are conflicting or at least are apparently conflicting with conceptions in other domains of what it makes sense to say—conceptions we are indeed very confident of—we have good reason to be skeptical of the idiosyncratic conceptions. This is exactly the position that certain key religious conceptions appear to be heir to. Jews and Christians, for example, must believe that there is an infinite individual (indeed, a person) who is transcendent to the world yet standing in personal relations of caring and loving to the world. Yet it is anything but evident that such talk makes any coherent sense at all. How can we give to understand that an individual is both transcendent to the world and at the same time that very same individual stands in some personal relation to it? Here the theist surely seems at least to be unsaying what he has just said. It is only a thinly veiled way of saying that at time t some specified object S has property p and property *not-p*. Furthermore, it is anything but evident that we can understand talk of "a being transcendent to the world." If we are honest with ourselves, we should be very skeptical about whether such a conception has any coherent sense at all. And it is doubly impossible for an individual—indeed a person—to have such a characteristic. (If we say that all these terms are used metaphorically, then we still must be able to say in nonmetaphorical terms what they are metaphors of.)

Considerations concerning evidence are also not that language-game or form-of-life eccentric. It is true that theories are underdetermined by the evidence or the data. We know, for example, from archaeological evidence, that agricultural tools of a certain sort spread gradually into Europe over a certain period of time. The theory that they arrived with new invading peoples who pushed out the hunters and gatherers and the opposing theory that the hunters and gatherers themselves, through cultural borrowing, gradually took up their use are both plausible and equally compatible with the evidence. The evidence does not determine which, if either, theory to accept. We cannot simply read off our theories or overall accounts from the evidence. However, while this underdetermination thesis is true, it is also true that rationally acceptable theories still do require evidence. When we have well-elaborated and systematically coherent theories for which there is a paucity of evidence and equally well-elaborated and systematically coherent theories for which there is substantial evidence, the rational thing to do is to accept the theories for which there is substantial evidence. (Stated in just the way I have, Galileo's theory is not a disconfirming instance.)

While there *may* be some groundless beliefs that are still rationally believed, for which nothing like evidence is in order, e.g., "Every event has a cause," it is still the case that reasonable people will in almost all situations assume that if their beliefs are justified there is evidence for them and when their beliefs are not in accord with the evidence and others come up with a plausible set of beliefs that are in accord with the evidence, reasonable people will alter their beliefs in accordance with the evidence.[14] Such remarks are not scientistic remarks reflecting the hegemony of "the scientific attitude" but cut across the various forms-of-life and, in that crucial sense, are language-game-independent.

The upshot of this argument is to show that reason is not wanton. There are principles of rational belief and rational action that are universal, and there are general ways in which we can appraise institutions, practices, and forms-of-life with respect to their rationality without falling into ethnocentrism or some tendentious ideological stance. Judaism, Christianity, and Islam are such forms-of-life and they can be so appraised in the light of reason and experience.

The consistency, coherence, and evidential warrant of Jewish, Christian, and Islamic belief-systems are of a very low order indeed.[15] In terms of the conception of rationality I have articulated—a reasonably unproblematic conception, I believe—such belief-systems are not reasonably believed by a twentieth-century person with a good grounding in Western scientific and philosophical culture. It is not reasonable for such a person to believe in Zande witchcraft and it is not reasonable for such a person to believe in the belief-systems of Judaism, Christianity, and Islam either.

NOTES

1. Max Black and W. M. Sibley note some of the differences in usage between "reasonable" and "rational." I think that some of these differences can be significant, but for the considerations raised in this essay nothing turns on these differences. Max Black, "Reasonableness" in R. F. Dearden, et al., *Education and the Development of Reason* (London: Routledge & Kegan Paul, 1972), pp. 194–207; W. M. Sibley, "The Rational versus the Reasonable," *The Philosophical Review* XIII (October 1953): 554–560.

2. The conception is borrowed from W. B. Gallie and Alasdair MacIntyre. W. B. Gallie, *Philosophy and the Historical Understanding* (London: Chatto and Windus, 1964), pp. 157–191 and Alasdair MacIntyre, "The Essential Contestability of Some Social Concepts," *Ethics* 84 (October 1973): 1–9.

3. Something like this has been stated by, among others, John Rawls, *A Theory of Justice*, (Cambridge, MA: Harvard University Press, 1971), pp. 408–431, and more explicitly and in greater detail by David A. Richards, *A Theory of Reasons for Action* (Oxford: Clarendon Press, 1971), pp. 63–91.

4. These conceptions are extensively discussed in my "Principles of Rationality," *Philosophical Papers* III (October 1974); "The Embeddedness of Conceptual Relativism," *Dialogos* XI, (November 1977); "Rationality and Relativism," *Philosophy of the Social Sciences* 4 (December 1974); and "Rationality and Universality," *The Monist* 59 (July 1975).

5. See the references in the previous footnote.

6. Jürgen Habermas, *Toward a Rational Society,* translated by Jeremy J. Shapiro (Boston: Beacon Press 1970); Jürgen Habermas, *Theorie und Praxis* (Frankfurt am Main, Germany: Suhrkamp Verlag, fourth edition, 1971); Jürgen Habermas, *Erkenntnis und Interesse* (Frankfurt am Main, Germany: Suhrkamp Verlag, 1968).

7. Kai Nielsen "Can There Be an Emancipatory Rationality?" *Critica* VIII (December 1976) and Kai Nielsen, "Rationality, Needs and Politics," *Cultural Hermeneutics* 4 (1977).

8. These themes are developed in my "Reason and Sentiment" in *Rationality Today*, ed. by Theodore Geraets, (Ottawa, ON: Ottawa University Press, 1979).

9. E. E. Evans-Pritchard, "Levy-Bruhl's Theory of Primitive Mentality," *Bulletin of the Faculty of Arts* (Alexandria, Egypt) II (1934): 1–36 and his "The Intellectualist Interpretation of Magic," *Bulletin of the Faculty of Arts,* (Alexandria, Egypt) I (1933): 281–311; Peter Winch, "Understanding a Primitive Society," *American Philosophical Quarterly* I (1964): 307–24; Alasdair MacIntyre, "Is Understanding Religion Compatible with Believing?" in *Faith and the Philosophers,* ed. by John Hick (London: Macmillan, 1964); Steven Lukes "Some Problems About Rationality," in *Rationality,* ed. by Bryan R. Wilson (Oxford: Basil Blackwell Ltd., 1970), and Martin Hollis, "The Limits of

Irrationality," and "Reason and Ritual," both in *Rationality*.

10. What exactly this is is not unambiguous. What I have in mind is spelled out in the articles by Lukes and Hollis cited in footnote 9. Some of the ambiguities and difficulties in such accounts are discussed in the last two articles mentioned in footnote 4.

11. Terence Penelhum, *Problems of Religious Knowledge* (London: Macmillan, 1971) and *Religion and Rationality* (New York: Random House, 1971). I have tried to show what is essentially defective in Penelhum's account vis-á-vis the issues discussed in this essay in my "On the Rationality of Radical Theological Non-Naturalism," *Religious Studies* (1978).

12. I have tried to explicate, develop, and defend such an account in my two articles reprinted in Norbert O. Schedler (ed.), *Philosophy of Religion: Contemporary Perspectives* (New York: Macmillan Publishing Co., 1974), in my *Contemporary Critiques of Religion*, (New York: Herder and Herder, 1971) and in my *Scepticism*, (New York: St. Martin's Press, 1973).

13. John Hick, *The Existence of God* (New York: The Macmillan Co., 1964), p. 19.

14. Kai Nielsen, "On the Rationality of Groundless Believing," *Idealistic Studies* (1981).

15. I have argued that in my *Reason and Practice* (New York: Harper and Row, 1971), pp. 135–257.

11

The Embeddedness of Atheism

Things are difficult nowadays for both the simple believer and the simple atheist. If they are at all reflective, they are going to be perplexed when arguments about religion are encountered. Let me show how it might go with a simple atheist (since he is closer to my heart) but I could have started with the simple believer just as well and have drawn rather similar conclusions though by a rather different route. (I am not implying that the simple believer or the simple atheist is simple-minded, though he is likely to be either innocent of or dismissive about the intricacies of philosophical theology and the philosophy of religion.)

Let our simple atheist happen on some philosophy: Suppose he is directed by some well-meaning atheist friends to read the defenses of atheism given by two no-nonsense, tough-minded atheistic, analytical philosophers, N. R. Hanson and Michael Scriven.[1]

In reading them and reflecting on his reading, he comes to face the following core set of considerations. There is a fairly widespread, though utterly uncritical, belief that there is rough epistemic parity between theism and atheism. Hanson and Scriven rightly challenge this belief, which seems to be a comfort to some. Suppose a person tries to be an agnostic or fideist and claims that there is no positive evidence or any other epistemic ground for thinking that there is a God, or for that matter, for thinking there is not. That surely is, on the face of it at least, a not unreasonable position. None of the classical arguments for the existence of God are sound arguments and, after years and years of intense discussion, no new plausible candidates are in sight.[2] There is no empirical evidence for the existence of

God, and this means that there is no *evidence* for the existence of God, since "empirical *evidence*" is pleonastic and claims of direct acquaintance with God—to have encountered God—make no sense, for the God of developed theism is not, like an utterly anthropomorphic deity, the sort of reality you could bump into and get acquainted with.[3] After all, this putative reality is said to be an infinite person without body and to be, as well, while remaining a person, transcendent to the world.[4] Given such an arcane, utterly mysterious putative reality—a nonmysterious God would not be the God of Judaism, Christianity, or Islam—it would indeed be surprising if we could prove that there *is* such a reality. Attempted ontological disproofs of the existence of God are not as common as attempted ontological proofs but they have fared no better.[5] Some conceptualizations of God might very well be shown to be inconsistent, but to show that the very concept of God itself (as distinct from certain conceptualizations of God) is inconsistent, as distinct from being problematic, would take some showing.[6] And while we do not have any evidence for the existence of God, it is also the case that, given the kind of putative reality God is, we also do not understand what it would be like to have evidence for His existence or to have an "evidential awareness" or an experiential awareness of God. Given this, some might conclude, we can hardly speak of having good evidence that God does *not* exist. So it is often concluded that, at least cognitively speaking, agnosticism is the name of the game.

It is here where Hanson and Scriven enter on the atheist side with what looks to the simple atheist to be just plain good sense, though a nice philosophically sanitized version. According to Hanson, we cannot be in such a circumstance of epistemic parity where there is no good reason for believing one way or another, for, where we are making positive existence claims (as we most surely appear to be when we assert that there is a God), then "When there is no good reason for thinking a claim to be true, *that* in itself is good reason for thinking the claim to be false."[7] Where what we are talking about are positive existence claims—propositions that assert the existence of some object—"a 'proof,' " as Hanson puts it, "of X's nonexistence usually derives from the fact that there is no good reason for supposing that X does exist."[8] Scriven, in a way that should bring joy to the heart of the simple atheist, draws the following conclusion from this: "The proper alternative, when there is no evidence, is not mere suspension of belief; it is disbelief."[9] "Atheism," Scriven tells us, "is obligatory in the absence of any evidence for God's existence."[10]

A little translation into the concrete might help. I am sitting here in my study and I am relatively sober. Suppose someone tells me that there is a thousand dollars in my wallet, which is lying in the top drawer of my desk. I open my drawer with the chap standing there and we take a good look, but I only find a ten dollar bill. I have, in the relevant sense of "proof" here, disproved the claim that I have a thousand dollars in my wallet.[11] Perhaps as soon as I close the drawer the thousand dollars will pop into existence or pop back into existence in my wallet only to disappear as soon as I open my drawer; but that and a myriad of other logical possibilities or putative logical possibilities notwithstanding, I have no good reason here for thinking there is a thousand dollars in my wallet, and that fact in itself is, in such circumstances, tantamount to a proof that there is not a thousand dollars in my wallet. Or suppose someone tells me there is a Siberian wolf hound in my study. I don't see him or hear him barking or scratching nor do I smell him. My friend and I look around in the closets, behind the desk, and under the rug and the like. In such a circumstance agnosticism about there being such a dog in my study is not the proper stance. We are surely entitled to conclude, after such an examination, that there is no Siberian wolf hound in my study. This is how we do proceed in such a circumstance and we would conclude (and rightly so) that we had conclusively disproved that, then and there, there was a Siberian wolf hound in my study. There is no good reason to believe, Hanson and Scriven conclude, that things stand differently with God. After all "There is a God" is also a positive existence claim.

Reading all this, the simple atheist is reassured. He always thought there was something specious and evasive about agnosticism. Now he sees why. And he is doubly reassured in finding philosophers deploying good sturdy common sense without any philosophical hat tricks. Moreover, it is comforting for him to know that the absence of any evidence or any other positive epistemic grounds for there being a God will provide a decisive ground for atheism. Things are not as much up in the air, he now sees, as the traditional received opinion (at least among the literate) had led him to believe.

However, a philosophical friend tells him that unfortunately things are not quite that simple. There is a strange Christian chap around, Alvin Plantinga, who is a kind of reincarnation in this modern age of St. Anselm with some modal logic. This chap, his philosopher friend tells him, has a nifty argument against the Hanson-Scriven position.[12] It goes something like this: Consider the proposition "There is at least one human being who was not created by God"—a strange positive existence claim but all the same something that looks like such a claim. (It has that surface grammar.) Now, given the way statistically normal Christians talk, it is a necessary truth that if God exists He has created all the human beings there are. Since this is so then any evidence for the truth of the proposition that

252   **Atheism & Philosophy**

there is at least one human being who was not created by God will also have to contain an argument, Plantinga tells us, that there is no God. However, what if there is no good arugment against God's existence? Then, if that is so, we will have no good argument for "There was at least one human being who was not created by God." But then, given the Hanson-Scriven thesis, if we are going to be through and through rational, we must accept the proposition that all human beings are created by God. But that surely is not a conclusion to which Hanson and Scriven would like to be driven.

However, their troubles do not stop there. Plantinga asks us now to suppose that there is no good argument for God's existence, something that Hanson and Scriven do indeed firmly believe. But then, when considering the proposition "There is a God," we are obliged, given the Hanson-Scriven thesis, to come to believe there is no God. But then, Plantinga continues, assuming that there are no good arguments for or against the existence of God, we are forced, if we accept the Hanson-Scriven thesis, to the conclusion that there is no God and all human beings were created by God.

Faced with this *reductio* of the Hanson-Scriven thesis, the simple atheist is understandably both disheartened and perplexed. He thought, or at least hoped, the sturdy common sense of Hanson and Scriven would reinforce his considered judgments about the rationality of believing in God by giving him a sound philosophical rationale for his atheism. (It is analogous to faith in search of understanding.) But now it seems that Hanson and Scriven have led him down the garden path. But he also, since he is a sensible fellow, remains incredulous. Plantinga's argument has at least the smell of being valid but it also has the look of being the kind of hat trick that the simple atheist, from the sad experience of a philosophy course during his undergraduate days, has come to expect from philosophers. (He remembers with a sense of its appropriateness Hobbes's remark that there is nothing so absurd that some philosopher has not said it.) He had been pleasantly surprised in not finding Hanson and Scriven engaging in such philosophical antics. But now he is back in the soup. Still, he asks himself, what is wrong with Plantinga's argument? There must be something wrong, he suspects, if we end up deriving such absurdities form such a plausibility. Perhaps the exact way the Hanson-Scriven thesis is stated should be fiddled with or perhaps Plantinga makes some question-begging assumption.

Surely, given the conclusion, it is natural enough to suspect something like that. The simple atheist is likely to think, as his counterpart the simple believer is likely to think in analogous situations, that he should have stayed clear of philosophy in the first place. He should have followed his initial hunches after his philosophy course. Still he remains puzzled and slightly ill at ease. Being a reasonable chap, he cannot just shrug off an argument that seems at least to be tightly constructed.

But God is good and a Christian philosopher comes to his rescue. Thomas Morris, in the course of a fine article on Pascal's wager, argues that Plantinga does indeed beg the question.[13] In making his argument Plantinga assumes that there are no good arguments for or against the existence of God. But to make that assumption—an assumption he needs to make for his argument to go through—he does quite plainly beg the question against Hanson and Scriven, for on their thesis the proposition that Plantinga just assumes could never be true. The absence of any good argument *for* the existence of God would just itself provide us with a good argument *against* the existence of God.

However, Morris takes away with his right hand what he gives with his left, and here he does not do so by playing hat tricks (engaging in *eristic* if you want to be pedantic), but extends, for non-atheistic purposes, the sturdy common sense that the simple atheist had come to appreciate in Hanson and Scriven.

Morris notes an important problem about the scope of the Hanson-Scriven principle. The kinds of situations where the Hanson-Scriven principle squares well with our intuitions are those—as in my homely examples above—in which the person claims that, since he has no evidence for the truth of the proposition, he is then justified in denying that the proposition is true, are those situations, and only those in which he (a) rationally believes (where he is justified in believing) he is in a good epistemic position relative to the propositon he is denying and (b) where, in spite of being in this position, he in fact is in possession of no good evidence or any other epistemic ground for thinking the proposition in question is true. (To be in a good epistemic position to the proposition in question, the proposition must be such that if it were true, there would be positive epistemic considerations indicating or manifesting its truth.) Only where that is the situation is a person justified in believing that when there is no good reason for thinking a proposition to be true that that in itself is good reason for thinking the proposition to be false. If it is true that there is a Siberian wolf hound in my study, then there would be—to put it in pedantic philosophical jargon—positive epistemic considerations pointing to the truth of that proposition. If I am sitting in my study under good lighting conditions, I am reasonably rational, possess good sight and hearing, and am cold sober, then I am in a very good epistemic position to possess such evidence. Where I am in that position, and only where I am in that position, am I therefore justified in taking it that where there is no good reason for thinking a claim to be true, that in itself is a good reason for thinking it to be false.

I am in that position with respect to the thousand dollars and to the Siberian wolf hound, but I am not in that position with respect to a transcendent mysterious God. Here I am a token of the type which is humankind. For Siberian wolf hounds and the like, and then only under certain conditions, the Hanson-Scriven argument goes through, but it does not go through for belief in God.

The simple atheist has come to see that one initially attractive way to provide a rational ground for his atheism will not work. It is a short cut and short cuts, when it comes to assessing a pervasive belief-system that is so old and has been so extensively examined, start out, and quite rightly so, by being suspect. There is, in other words, a presumption against them. That the Hanson-Scriven tack should flounder, no matter how reasonable it sounds, should not be such a surprise to the simple atheist. On the other side, there is a similar moral to be learned by the simple believer about Christian philosophical one-liners. A Christian philosopher who has a short and snappy way with religious skepticism is not to be trusted. Philosophical skepticism—the creation of some metaphysicians and epistemologists—is another matter. That is hardly an old and firmly embedded belief.

However, the simple atheist still has intact what may have driven him in the direction of Hanson and Scriven in the first place. The philosophical situation vis-à-vis theistic religions looks like this. No one has been able to give a sound ontological proof or disproof of the existence of God, no cosmological or design-type arguments have been shown to be sound, and no other attempts to infer the existence of God from either evident or not-so-evident empirical facts (if that is not a pleonasm) have worked. The idea of seeing God or directly knowing or encountering God seems at least to be incoherent, and even if we assume coherence here there seems at least to be no reason to believe that anyone has actually seen, directly known—as in *knowledge by acquaintance*—or encountered God. Hovering over all this, and perhaps explaining but at least complicating the above considerations, is the fact that the concept of God, at least in developed Judaeo-Christian-Islamic traditions, is a very problematic concept, in a way that the concept of chair, dog, or even electron, is not. It is a necessary truth, for those who play Christian language games, that God is mysterious. It may even be a necessary truth that He is the Ultimate Mystery (whatever that means). Reflective believers, on the one hand, will acknowledge that anything that would count as the Christian God must be mysterious and, while continuing to trust in God, they will be perplexed about their central religious concept. They will recognize that the concept of God is in some way problematic. Many reflective skeptics (agnostics and atheists), on the other hand, will believe that what is to be taken to be "Ultimate Mystery" is in reality a disguised incoherence. So we know that our God-talk is not unproblematic; the question is whether our God-talk is sufficiently coherent so that certain key religious utterances do indeed make genuine truth claims, without a watering-down of the belief-system, or becoming a gross anthropomorphism.[14]

We have a situation in which there is no evidence or other epistemic grounds for the existence of God, where it is not the case that, evidence or no evidence, one must believe in God to make sense of one's life or to make sense of morality.[15] Moreover—and this is conceptually fundamental—the very concept of God is so problematic that its coherence is very much in doubt.[16]

In the teeth of all this—and sometimes even self-consciously so—there are plenty of knights of faith about and, as a sociological fact, in North America at least, and in spite of the intelligentsia, both Jewish and Christian belief-systems (often in very Neanderthal forms) are flourishing and the same holds for Islamic belief-systems in other parts of the world. Things, unfortunately, go that way in both Tehran and Dallas and, as well, in the ghettos of Jerusalem. Freud's expectations, rather than those of Engels seem, at least in the short run, to be winning out.[17] We are not seeing the withering away of religious belief-systems. Indeed, even the most barbaric ones hang on and in some places flourish.

Faced with such a situation, what kind of an attitude (if he has any choice in the matter) should the simple atheist and the simple believer have? We should also, in thinking about this, throw into the hopper the great diversity of religious belief-systems and with it, particularly given the situation as I have characterized it above, the question "How can I reasonably, in such a circumstance, believe that Christ is *The* Truth and *The* Way?"

I think the simple atheist—or any atheist or agnostic—can, and should, make a *burden of proof argument* here. Given the religious situation—the state of play for anyone touched by modernity in living religious or secular lives and thinking about belief and unbelief—the onus is now on the Jew, the Christian or the Moslem to give us reasons supporting the claim that we should be, or should continue to be, Jews, Christians, or Moslems. (Presumably, if we should be Jews or Christians at all, we should, in the exclusive sense of "or," either be Jews or Christians, for either a man became God or He did not. For a Jew no man could be God, and for a Christian Jesus—a man—must be God. But that is a fraternal religious dispute. The atheist is interested in more fundamental issues.)

On the surface, it appears irrational for a philosophically *and* scientifically educated person, who is part of the culture of modernity in the twentieth century, to believe in God, at least where God is construed in anything like an orthodox way. The God of Braithwaite and Hare can, of course, be accepted by anyone and does not threaten secular sensibilities or beliefs, though their conceptions might amuse the atheist a bit.[19] If nothing more is involved in the belief in God than what Braithwaite and Hare allow (to believe in God is to have a certain agapeistic attitude that we associate with certain stories, the truth of which we may or may not believe), then, as my colleague C. B. Martin said years ago, all unbelievers can be led gently into belief.[20] But where the concept of God is a serious one, the burden of proof is on the religious believer to show that appearances are deceiving by, on the one hand, showing that it is perfectly rational, or at least not irrational, to believe in God or, on the other hand, à la Kierkegaard and Hamann, to show that, though it is irrational, or cognitively speaking irrational, to believe in God, that that notwithstanding we should, or perhaps even must, believe in God to avoid sickness unto death.

II

Elsewhere I have looked at the Kierkegaardian option from a host of sides and I will concentrate on the *prima facie*, but only *prima facie*, more plausible non-Kierkegaardian response.[21]

Some Christian philosophers might accept the burden of proof and argue that Christian belief is no less a rational option than atheism.[22] A central argument in this tradition is that the world of our experience is systematically ambiguous sustaining both theistic and atheistic interpretations of our experience but lending decisive support to neither. Believing one way or another, for both atheist and theist, involves something like an act of faith. Moreover, religious beliefs, the claim goes, are in no worse shape than many of our fundamental everyday beliefs held by believers and atheists alike. We may not be able to prove that there is a God but, it has been argued, we cannot prove that there are other minds, that the sun will come up tomorrow, that time is real, that there are real causal powers, or that there is an external world. We are just as stuck with these evident realities as we are with God.

People arguing out of this tradition often invoke a kind of *parity argument*. The secularist, it is claimed, has to take a lot of things on faith, too.[23] If it is demonstration you are after, it has been said, you can no more demonstrate the existence of other minds, the presence of causes, the existence of the external world, or the reliability of your senses, than you can the existence of God. If it is irrational to believe in God because we cannot demonstrate His existence, then it is equally irrational to believe in other minds, induction, the external world, the reality of time, causal powers, and the like. If you say that it is irrational to doubt those things, even though you cannot prove (i.e., demonstrate) their existence, then why you do not also say that it is irrational to doubt the existence of God, or, at the very least, why do you not say that it is not irrational to believe in God, even though you cannot prove that God exists? If, on the other hand, you are a kind of romantic rationalist and you say that it is irrational to believe that there are these seemingly evident things (e.g., causal powers, time, the external world), then (if that is so) the atheist (simple or convoluted) is plainly in no better position than the theist. Science, the claim might go, rests just as much or just as little on faith as does religion.[24] Either we have very good reasons to be skeptical about both or we have good reasons not to be skeptical about either. If demonstration is our ideal—that is, if we are rationalists—we should be skeptical about both.[25] Neither will yield demonstrations. In any event, the religious person need not think that religious beliefs are any more epistemologically threatened than other key beliefs dear to the hearts of common-sense realists, "scientific realists," and fallibilistic empiricists alike. (G. E. Moore, David Armstrong, and J. L. Mackie, atheists all, are exemplifications in order of presentation of those positions.[26])

Though these arguments, in one form or another, are remarkably popular, they seem to me to have very little merit. Their defenders have (to first put the matter historically) never taken to heart lessons we have learned, or should have learned, from such diverse philosophers as Locke, Moore, Wittgenstein, and Austin. People who defend theism in the above way take bad rationalistic metaphysics far too seriously and have an utterly unrealistic conception of proof or, if you insist on taking proof in that "strict" way, an utterly unrealistic conception of its role in reasonable human deliberation. They are unaware of what Frederich Waismann once called the "irrational heart of rationalism."

Take the contrast between belief in God and belief in other minds. (I take other minds but I could have taken any of the other traditional metaphysical conundrums.) After listening with comprehension (or, for that matter, even without much comprehension) to a careful demonstration that we cannot know that other people have minds, the simple atheist, or indeed the simple believer, is surely justified in believing, no matter how good the metaphysical argument, that it is, after all, just an arcane academic conundrum devised by philosophers for their delectation. (Someone said, who was very much caught up in these little games, that a philosopher is someone who is fascinated by puzzles. But let us not confuse this with genuine inquiry. After all, we know with perfect certainty that Achilles can outrun the Tortoise.) The problem of whether God exists or whether we have a soul (which is quite different than whether we have a mind) is of a very different sort from the problem of other minds or the problem of the external world. Whether God exists or whether we have a soul are real perplexities of ours about what there is or perhaps can be and not just perplexities about the limits of demonstration or about what we mean when we say certain things or how we can most perspicuously display what we know. For other minds, the problem is simply *how* we know, not *that* we know, that others have minds. A successful analysis will have to show us how we can know that there are other minds. If it fails to do that, it is not a successful analysis. The correct outcome of the puzzle is not in the slightest in dispute or in doubt. After all, the chap in philosophical perplexity about other minds (the skeptical philosopher chap) is addressing his argument to others whom he assumes have—or at least some of them have—the brains to understand it and assess it and who will come, if his argument is sound, to believe that we do not know *how* there can be other minds. But there is something *Erzatz* about his skepticism, for that he, like all of us, believes, without the slightest doubt, that there are other minds is evident from the very fact that he directs his argument to others for their comprehension and assessment. His doubt is not a first-order doubt about what we know but a second-order doubt about *how* we can know what we most *certainly do know.* Our doubts about whether God exists or whether we have souls are not at all like that, they are first-order doubts about what exists or *can* exist. They pose conceptual puzzles as well, but the outcome of the puzzle about what there is or can be is genuinely in doubt. We have, as Peirce stressed, real doubts here, not mere Cartesian doubts parading as genuine doubts. (This is not anti-intellectualism but seriousness about inquiry.)

Even if someone, caught up in an absurd kind of romantic rationalism, did not accept the above line of reasoning, there is a modification of a familiar argument of G. E. Moore's that we can deploy. If some philosopher gives us a cleverly-constructed, seemingly airtight argument that we cannot know that there are other minds or an external world, it is always more reasonable to believe that somewhere there has been a flaw in the argument, either in the lines of inference or in the premises accepted or in the reading given to the premises, than to believe that we do not really know that there are other minds or that there is an external world. The greater miracle must be in accepting the skeptical arguments. (Remember that it is sound arguments we want here and not just valid arguments.)

The force of this Moorean argument is enhanced if we take to heart the truism that proofs require premises and that in any proof there must be a utilization, at some level, of premisses that themselves are not proved in that argument. Moreover, all justification is not by way of deductive arguments or, for that matter, by way of induction and we must not take proof and demonstration to be identical with justification.[27]

Finally, even if all of that were rejected by someone, the parity argument would still be a bad one for it would only show, for someone who could bring himself to such levels of fancy, that religious belief is not uniquely irrational or the only set of beliefs that are irrational, not that it may not be or is not itself irrational.[28] Perhaps—so fancy heats the imagination—the atheist, who believes that there are other minds or that the sun will come up tomorrow or that he has a pair of hands, has beliefs that are as irrational as those of the theist, who believes there is a God, because the atheist, without proof (i.e., demonstration), believes these things as does the theist as well who *also* believes, and again all around without proof, that there is a God. However, even if we accept all this fanciful stuff for the sake of the argument, this does not at all show that the theist is not being irrational both in believing in God and in believing that there is a God. Moreover, even here, after making all these implausible assumptions, we still would have to say that the theist was even more irrational than the atheist, for he not only has all the atheist's irrational beliefs, he has some additional ones as well of a very strange sort—beliefs that Ockham's razor would justify us in shaving away. The other "irrational beliefs" he *shares* with the atheist are not so shaveable, for they, humanly speaking, as both theist and atheist acknowledge, are not beliefs they can do without. But his theistic beliefs are not so indispensable. By sticking to them, he exhibits an even greater irrationality than does the atheist. We should resist playing this game in the first place. However, if for the sake of continuing the argument we do play, the atheist still comes out better than the theist.

III

I have appropriated for my own purposes what I take to be certain Moorean or Wittgensteinian insights. A certain kind of Wittgensteinian (Norman Malcolm is a paradigm case) might turn this way of viewing things back on me.[29] Wittgenstein said: "The difficulty is to realize the groundlessness of our believing. At the foundation of well-founded belief lies belief that is not well founded."[30] Religious belief is like that, the Wittgensteinian claim goes, but so is scientific belief, moral belief, and the whole battery of common-sense beliefs about how to navigate in our world and how in both practical and not so

.ctical ways to conceptualize it. The idea that rational persons hold
.eir beliefs or even could come to hold their beliefs solely on the basis
of evidence is an empiricist myth of a pre-fallibilist empiricist vintage.
(It is not the fallibilistic empiricism of John Dewey or John Mackie.)

"Religion," as one of Wittgenstein's disciples puts it, "is a form of
life; it is language embedded in action—what Wittgenstein calls a
'language game.' Science is another. Neither stands in need of justification, the one no more than the other."[31] It is, it has been argued,
one of the primary pathologies of philosophy to believe that we must
justify our language games or forms of life. There is nothing to be
grounded here—nothing that is either well-grounded or ill-grounded.
We should not be concerned with trying to prove the existence of God
or with giving evidence or other epistemological considerations for
believing that He exists. It is just these traditional philosphical tasks—
central endeavors of the philosophy of religion—that are so mistaken.
To so proceed just assumes, quite uncritically, as Norman Malcolm
puts it, "that in order for religious belief to be intellectually respectable
it *ought* to have an intellectual justification."[32] Working with that
assumption, philosophers have then went out to look for that rational
justification—that rational foundation—and, where they have been
clear-sighted, they have come back empty-handed. Indeed, they have
come back empty-handed in any event. But that has not been apparent
to all such God-seekers.

Malcolm—following Wittgenstein—says that the mistake is in engaging in that *endeavor* and to make that assumption in the first
place. Thinking that our fundamental religious beliefs require justification is, Malcolm tells us, like having the "idea that we are not
justified in relying on memory until memory has been proved reliable."[33] Philosophers have an irrational fear of groundless beliefs.
Only when we have come to see, and to take to heart, how pervasive
they are in all domains of life, how necessary and both how ineradic-
able and how benign most of them are, will we free ourselves from this
pointless fear, from this rationalist prejudice that we must have a
reason for everything, that everything we reasonably believe we must
believe for a reason. (When it is put so bluntly most of us would back
away from it. But where we do not put it to ourselves so crudely, most
of us, if we are philosophers, seem unself-consciously to assume something like that. It is the rationalistic prejudice of philosophers, whether
they be rationalist or nonrationalist.)

Many of these groundless beliefs are quite diverse over cultural
space and historical time; and they, not infrequently—or so the claim
goes—form into belief-systems that are incommensurable.[34] These different belief-systems, these different forms of life, have different framework beliefs, fundamental propositions appealed to in justifying beliefs

within the belief-system but, though they are so centrally placed in the belief-system, they are still beliefs concerning which no coherent question of their justification can arise. Our (Jewish, Christian, Islamic) fundamental religious beliefs—including our very belief in God—fall into this category. They are beliefs that contrast with a purely secular way of looking at things as well as with a Buddhist, Confucian, or Hindu way of looking at things.

I have only sketched such a Wittgensteinian account. I have not been able to convey its subtlety and its power.[35] I have tried in various places to do that and to show both how it should be queried and challenged.[36] But I have tried as well to show how it should not be so easily dismissed as many rationalistic philosophers (philosophers with unrealistic expectations from philosophy) are wont to do, though I should also remark that in my last series of essays about this Wittgensteinianism I have, in trying to convey its power, made too many concessions to it and I did not sufficiently see how a Peirceian-Deweyan pragmatism (a fallibilistic empiricism or naturalism) while sharing some of its important insights, overcomes central difficulties of that view of the world.[37]

What I want to do here, very briefly, is to show that, even if we do succeed in establishing that such a Wittgensteinian view of things is the right one, we also, in that very stroke, utterly undermine Christianity in anything even approximating the Christian form or forms of life we have known historically. Christian beliefs become the beliefs of a form of life, not capable of being justified, but also not coherently claimable as being superior to other sometimes quite different and sometimes at least apparently conflicting forms of life, religious and nonreligious. But then the proud and assured claims to Revealed Truth and to the belief that Christ is *The* Truth and *The* Way undergo an undermining sea-change. Christianity could not be what it purports to be, for anyone who is even close to Christian orthodoxy, if such a Wittgensteinian conception of things is on the mark. But this is not a problem for the atheist who happens also to be a Wittgensteinian. It is, however, a problem for the religious believer, for, on that Wittgensteinian conception, Christianity becomes but one form of life among many—a form of life that cannot be shown to have any superior rationality, authenticity, or justifiability to other incommensurable forms of life. But that is precisely what anyone who regards himself as a Christian, in any tolerably orthodox sense, cannot accept.

I do not regard such a Wittgensteinian view of things as correct, but if it is, the intentions of some Wittgensteinians to the contrary notwithstanding, it yields an utterly devastating view for Christianity. (In that way philosophy doesn't leave everything as it is. Or does it only not do so because it is bad philosophy?) That kind of bailout from the difficulties I raised in the earlier sections is no bailout at all. With such Wittgensteinian friends, the Christian philosopher might remark, who needs enemies.[38]

IV

I want to end on a different note, the concision of which may give it an unintended dogmatic sound. Why—deliberately to commit the fallacy of the complex question—is the philosophy of religion so boring? I think the reason—or at least a principal reason—is that the case for atheism is so strong that it is difficult to work up much enthusiasm for the topic. (This strength of atheism or at least nonbelief is something that philosophers and other intellectuals in our era have their educated hunches about *before* they get into the intricacies of the philosophy of religion. These hunches are not just arbitrary cultural artifacts but have behind them the thrust of the development of our intellectual culture since the Enlightenment.) There is really not much of a contest anymore in the dispute between belief and unbelief. Since the Enlightenment religion has been on the run and on the abstract side; two major figures of the Enlightenment, Hume and Kant, have dealt a death blow to arguments for the existence of God. There are some philosophers who make new little twists and turns here that require a little fixing up, but basically the work here was done. Contemporary atheistic arguments here, such as J. L. Mackie's splendid *The Miracle of Theism,* are mopping up operations after the Enlightenment. (The puzzles in the philosophy of logic generated along the way by the contemporary argument are best examined independently of philosophical theology. It is significant that Saul Kripke, Michael Dummett, and Bas van Fraassen, major philosophers of logic and sophisticated philosophers, who are also very orthodox religious believers, have not come to the defense of the Faith. The reason is clearly not indifference or general diffidence.)

It is very difficult, after all this history, to suppress a yawn when someone comes up, yet again, with a new version of the ontological argument, some new cosmological argument, another argument for design or one supporting knowledge of God from religious experience or from moral values. It would be consoling but utterly naive for the atheist to believe that after Mackie's book such philosophcial activity would subside. Mackie's book may for the time being be the best of that sort going but in the history of the debate there have been plenty of similar books.

Much perceptive religious thought in the nineteenth and twentieth centuries saw that the game was up with natural theology and tried some variant of fideism, but such accounts (and they were varied) turned out on the sociological and psychological side to be vulnerable to the criticisms (again varied) of Feuerbach, Marx, Nietzsche, Freud, Weber, Durkheim, and Fromm as well as to the study of comparative religion and particularly to an anthropological study of religion.[39] It is very difficult for a reasonable person informed by modernity to accept the Christian Bible (or indeed any other sacred text) as the revealed word of God, as a rock-bottom philosophically unsupplemented appeal, when he knows (1) that putative revelations are many and often conflicting—anthropologically speaking there are thousands of religions (faiths)—and (2) when he also well understands that we are debarred, with such a rock-bottom appeal to the Bible, from appealing to any philosophical or scientific argument or set of considerations or to any other non-question-begging argument or set of considerations for determining which, if any, of these putative revelations is genuine (if Christianity can allow such a thing). (Talk of "higher" and "lower" religions, if all we have to go on is revelation, is going to be question-begging. There is no less and no more reason for following the belief-system of the Akuna of New Guinea than the Anglicans of Ontario.) When we add to these empirical criticisms of such broadly speaking fideist turns, the varied but often penetrating philosophical critiques of Brand Blanshard, Walter Kaufmann, C. B. Martin, Paul Edwards, Sidney Hook, Ronald Hepburn, Antony Flew, Michael Durrant, Axel Hägerström, and Ingemar Hedenius among others, the situation for Judaism, Christianity, and Islam looks very bleak indeed.[40] There is reason, *pace* Malcolm, to worry about the intellectual respectability, and thus the respectability, of those religions. And it also looks as if there were more interesting and/or more humanly pressing things for philosophers to do than to keep warming up this old stew.[41]

It is true that there are fascinating and vital things about religion that remain after its claims to legitimacy have been criticized to death, but they have nothing to do with claims to true religious beliefs or with claims that in some other way religious beliefs are justifiable or even sufficiently coherent so that they may be reasonably believed. And they have nothing to do with arguments for accepting religious authority. What remains is what Bernard Williams alludes to at the end of a sensitive and sympathetic review of Mackie's *The Miracle of Theism*.[42] Williams remarks "as soon as one sees religion, as Mackie rightly does, as a purely human phenomenon, it becomes a matter of great importance what human phenomenon it is and which of these explanations [explanations like those of Feuerbach, Marx and Freud], if any, are true."[43] It is particularly crucial to ascertain, if we can, whether the content of religion (particularly "its more unnerving and antihumanist content") is best understood "as something alien to

humanity and its needs" or whether it is best understood "as expressing needs that will have to be expressed in some form when belief in
God has disappeared."[44]

However, this, as Williams recognizes, doesn't leave any room for
the philosophy of religion. The concern of philosophy of religion is
with the truth, justifiability, and coherence of religious beliefs. If philosophy establishes the coherence of theism, it then can go on to try to
establish its truth, probable truth, or (otherwise construed) its rationality and authority.[45] These are the distinctive tasks of a Jewish,
Christian, or Islamic philosopher.

A philosopher who, in Axel Hägerström's phrase, is a neutral observer of the actual (if such there be), is simply concerned to sort out
those arguments along with the arguments of the atheistic and agnostic opposition. (John Wisdom and D. Z. Phillips believe that in their
philosophical activities they are such neutral chaps. But reading a
reasonable chunk of their work will reveal this to be pure self-deception.) The atheist philosopher, by contrast, is concerned to show either
the incoherence of theistic belief, its falsity or probable falsity, or
otherwise its lack of rational warrant or moral requiredness. These
tasks complete the tasks of the philosophy of religion and they are all
prior to and distinct from Williams's very pressing question. As Williams remarks, Mackie might have put it himself, "after the issues of
truth and argument have been laid aside, there is no philosophy of
religion, but only anthropology or another social science to help us, or
perhaps the imaginative powers of literature."[46] Williams opines that
"still philosophy in the guise of moral philosophy and philosophy in
its reflections about society and about the mind" may be of help here
in our gaining a reasonable undersanding of and our coming to have
the best attitude toward (if there is a "best attitude" here) the needs
that religion has served and their new role in the Godless world of
increasingly secularized societies. (Here we should keep in mind Max
Weber on the de-mystification of the world.)

I am rather more skeptical than is Williams about whether moral
philosophy, social philosophy, and most strikingly the philosophy of
mind, particularly as those things are practiced in our dominant
Anglo-Saxon and Scandinavian tradition, is likely to be of much help.
It is also not terribly evident that much help will come from elsewhere:
the Continent or the East. (Perhaps Gilbert Ryle was not just being
ethnocentric when he was reported to have said that the only light
that comes from the East is the sun.) Perhaps philosophy radically
reconstructed in some Marxian, Deweyan, or Habermasian way, or
combination thereof, might be of help. But the proof of this pudding is
in the eating. But, be that as it may, Williams's question about the
needs religion answers to is the crucial question to ask if it is the case,

as it surely appears to be, that there is no longer any point in talking about religious claims being true. But whether or not, there is room here for some kind of *philosophical* work (itself a comparatively trivial question), there surely is a new agenda here for a reflective examination of religion, given the demise of natural theology, revealed theology, and the philosophy of religion.

NOTES

1. N. R. Hanson, *What I Do Not Believe and Other Essays* (Dordrecht, Holland: D. Reidel, 1972), p. 323; and Michael Scriven, *Primary Philosophy,* (New York: McGraw Hill, 1966), p. 103.

2. This is recently powerfully argued, and in considerable detail, by J. L. Mackie, *The Miracle of Theism* (Oxford, England: Clarendon Press, 1982). Similar results are achieved, though not quite so penetratingly, in Wallace I. Matson, *The Existence of God* (Ithaca, New York: Cornell University Press, 1965); and by Terence Penelhum, *Religion and Rationality* (New York: Random House, 1971).

3. C. B. Martin, *Religious Belief* (Ithaca, NY: Cornell University Press, 1965), pp. 64-93; Ronald Hepburn, *Christianity and Paradox* (New York, NY: Humanities Press, 1958), pp. 24-59; and Kai Nielsen, *Scepticism* (New York: St. Martin's Press, 1973), pp. 41-59.

4. One of the weaknesses of Mackie's otherwise excellent book is that, following Richard Swinburne, Mackie too easily takes such God-talk as unproblematic. Mackie and Swinburne think they understand it well enough and just wonder whether if what it says is true. But the meaning of God-talk is far more problematical than they acknowledge. Swinburne, at least, tries to argue the case and show that such talk is, after all, perfectly coherent. Mackie just assumes that it is. For some reasons for thinking Swinburne's case for the coherence of theism is unsteady at best, see Antony Flew, "The Burden of Proof," *Boston Studies in the Philosophy of Religion,* forthcoming. The book by Swinburne I refer to is his *The Coherence of Theism* (Oxford, England: Clarendon Press, 1977). These worries about the coherence of God-talk may be coherently held by someone who does not believe that we have available to us a general theory of meaning.

5. The best known, relatively recent, such attempted disproof is J. N. Findlay's "Can God's Existence Be Disproved?" *New Essays in Philosophical Theology,* Anthony Flew and Alasdair MacIntyre (eds.), (New York: The Macmillan Company, 1955), pp. 47-56 and 71-75. The standard sort of criticism of it is given by John Hick, "God as Necessary Being," *Journal of Philosophy* 57 (1960). Findlay came to see the error of his ways in his "Reflections on Necessary Existence," in *Process and Divinity,* William L. Reese and Eugene Freeman (eds.), (Lasalle, IL: Open Court Publishing Company, 1964), pp. 515-528. See also here William Kennick, "On Proving that God Exists," in Sidney Hook (ed.) *Religious Experience and Truth* (New York: New York University Press, 1961), pp. 261-269.

6. For the distinction between concepts and conceptualizations see John Rawls, *A Theory of Justice* (Cambridge, MA: Harvard University Press, 1971), pp. 5-6; and H. L. A. Hart, *The Concept of Law* (Oxford, England: The Clarendon Press, 1961), pp. 155-159.

7. Hanson, op. cit., p. 323.

8. Ibid.

9. Scriven, op. cit., p. 103.

10. Ibid.

11. To think it is not a disproof for Popperian reasons is only to reveal how unrealistic and how narrow a sense of 'proof' Popper has. That Popper's alleged fallibilism is no fallibilism at all but a disguised form of skepticism and how he in reality is a romantic rationalist with an unrealistic and narrow conception of proof and a similarly narrow and unrealistic conception of science and scientific method is shown by Ernest Nagel, *Teleology Revisited* (New York: Columbia University Press, 1979), pp. 64-77 and Jonathan Lieberson, "The Romantic Rationalist," *The New York Review of Books* XXIX (November 1982): 51-53. See also his exchange with David Miller, "The Karl Popper Problem," *The New York Review of Books* XXXI (March 15, 1984): 43-4.

12. Alvin Plantinga, "Reason and Belief in God," in *Faith and Rationality*, A. Plantinga and N. Wolterstorff (eds.), (Notre Dame, IN: The University of Notre Dame Press, 1983), pp. 27-29.

13. Thomas Morris, "Pascalian Wagering," *Canadian Journal of Philosophy*, forthcoming.

14. Hanson, Scriven and Mackie all easily, and without argument, assume that it is. But a not inconsiderable amount of skeptical reflection on religion in the twentieth century, starting with Hägerström, Carnap and Ayer, has forcefully argued that God-talk is deeply problematic. It is anything but clear what we are talking about when we speak of God. One cannot just side-step that problem with a few philosophical one-liners.

15. Kai Nielsen, "Linguistic Philosophy and 'The Meaning of Life'," in E. D. Klemke (ed.) *The Meaning of Life* (New York: Oxford University Press, 1981), pp. 177-204; Kai Nielsen, "Linguistic Philosophy and Beliefs," in *Philosophy Today* No. 2, J. H. Gill (ed.), (New York: The Macmillan Company, 1969); and Kai Nielsen, *Ethics Without God* (Buffalo, NY: Prometheus Books, 1973).

16. Kai Nielsen, "God Talk," in *Sophia* III (April 1964); Kai Nielsen, "On Speaking of God," *Theoria* XXVIII (1962), Part 2; Kai Nielsen, *Contemporary Critiques of Religion* (New York: Herder and Herder, 1971); Kai Nielsen, *Scepticism* (New York: St. Martin's Press, 1973); and Kai Nielsen, *An Introduction to the Philosophy of Religion* (London, England: The Macmillan Press, 1982).

17. See Alasdair MacIntyre's remarks about Engels in his *Secularization and Moral Change* (London, England: Oxford University Press, 1967).

18. Some think, rather simple-mindedly, that religious diversity should no more count against religious truth than diversity in moral beliefs should count against ethical objectivity. But in neither case is that the heart of the matter. As Edward Westermarck powerfully argued, it is diversity in moral belief

together with the failure of ethical objectivists to provide an adequate rationale for ethical objectivism that counts in favor of ethical relativity. See Edward Westermarck, *Ethical Relativity* (Paterson, NJ: Littlefield, Adams and Company, 1960); Kai Nielsen, "Problems for Westermarck's Subjectivism," in Timothy Stroup (ed.), *Edward Westermarck: Essays on His Life and Works* (Helsinki, Finland: Societas Philosophica Fenica, 1982); and Timothy Stroup, *Westermarck's Ethics* (Abo, Finland: Abo Akademi, 1982). A parallel argument works in the religious case. It is the diversity of religious faiths in conjunction with the failure of natural theology and the like which counts so powerfully in favor of religious skepticism. Without such religious diversity we might learn to live with the failure of natural theology. Without this diversity, fideism would be in a stronger position.

19. See my discussion of Braithwaite and Hare in my "Christian Empiricism," in *The Journal of Religion* 61 (April, 1981).

20. C. B. Martin, op. cit., chapter one.

21. Kai Nielsen, "Can Faith Validate God-talk," *Theology Today* (July 1963); Kai Nielsen, "Faith and Authority," *The Southern Journal of Philosophy* III (Winter 1965); Kai Nielsen, "Religious Perplexity and Faith," *Crane Review* VIII (Fall 1965); the citations given in footnote 15 and my *Scepticism*, chapter 2.

22. John Hick, *Faith and Knowledge;* John Hick, *God and the Universe of Faiths;* Basil Mitchell, *The Justification of Religious Belief;* and Terence Penelhum, *God and Scepticism.*

23. It is revealing to contrast here Raphael Demos, "Religious Faith and Scientific Faith" and Arthur C. Danto, "Faith, Language and Religious Experience: A Dialogue," both in Sidney Hook (ed.) *Religious Experience and Truth* (New York: New York University Press, 1961), pp. 130-149. See also Demos's "Naturalism and Values" in John A. Clark (ed.) *The Student Seeks an Answer,* (Waterville, MN: Colby College Press, 1960), pp. 163-179.

24. See the references in the previous footnote to Demos and as well his "Are Religious Dogmas Cognitive and Meaningful?" in Mortin White (ed.) *Academic Freedom, Logic and Religion,* (Philadelphia, PA: University of Pennsylvania Press, 1953), pp. 71-87.

25. Stephen Toulmin's by now nearly forgotten critique of such an 'analytical ideal' needs bringing to mind here. Stephen Toulmin, *The Uses of Argument,* (Cambridge, England: Cambridge University Press, 1958).

26. For G. E. Moore's defense of atheism see his "The Value of Religion," *Ethics* 12 (October 1901), pp. 81-98 and his review of James Ward's "Naturalism and Agnosticism," in *Cambridge Review* XXI (1899): 57.

27. John Rawls, *A Theory of Justice,* pp. 577-587. Ernest Nagel, *Teleology Revisited,* pp. 64-83; Gilbert Ryle, *Collected Papers,* (London, England: Hutchinson of London, 1971), pp. 319-325 and 194-211.

28. I owe some of this to Shabbir Akhtar.

29. Norman Malcolm, "The Groundlessness of Belief" in his *Thought and Knowledge* (Ithaca, NY: Cornell University Press, 1977). See here as well my "On the Rationality of Groundless Believing," *Idealistic Studies* XI (September 1981): 215-229.

30. Ludwig Wittgenstein, *On Certainty;* (Oxford, England: Basil Blackwell,

1969), paragraph 559. See also paragraphs 167 and 217.

31. Malcolm, op. cit., p. 212.

32. Ibid., p. 211.

33. Ibid.

34. Powerful challenges to such incommensurability claims have come from the pragmatist tradition and from Donald Davidson. See Isaac Levi, "Escape from Boredom: Edification According to Rorty," *Canadian Journal of Philosophy* XI (December 1981): 589-601; and Ian Hacking "On the Frontier," *The New York Review of Books* XXXI (December 28, 1984): 54-58.

35. I have tried to do so in the following: "On the Rationality of Groundless Believing," op. cit.; "Rationality and Universality," *The Monist* 59 (July 1975); "Reasonable Belief Without Justification," in *Body, Mind and Method: Essays in Honor of Virgil Aldrich*, D. Gustafson (ed.), (Dordrecht, Holland: D. Reidel, 1978); "The Embeddedness of Conceptual Relativism," *Dialogos* (1977); "Wisdom and Dilman and the Reality of God," *Religious Studies* Vol. 26 (1980); "Wisdom and Dilman on the Scope of Religion," *Philosophical Investigations* 3 (Fall 1980); "Religion and Groundless Believing," in the *Autonomy of Religious Belief* in F. Grosson (ed.) (Notre Dame, IN: University of Notre Dame Press, 1981); and "Rationality and Relativism," *Philosophy of the Social Sciences* 4 (December 1974).

36. Kai Nielsen, *Contemporary Critiques of Religion* (New York, NY: Herder and Herder, 1971); *Scepticism* (New York: St. Martin's Press, 1973), Kai Nielsen, *An Introduction to the Philosophy of Religion* (London, England: The Macmillan Press, 1982).

37. This is particularly true in my "On the Rationality of Groundless Believing," *Idealistic Studies* XI (September 1981): 215-229. I am indebted to Sidney Hook for forcing this realization on me.

38. Nothing I have said here in criticism of such Wittgensteinian fideism (if that is the right phrase for it) should be taken as a criticism of Wittgenstein and particularly of his ways of doing philosophy. As Ian Hacking has nicely displayed, Wittgenstein, in contrast with our latest philosophical hero, Donald Davidson, thought that our various language games make it clear that we should not seek a single model for language. They show us the *disunity* of language. This contrasts interestingly not only with Michael Dummett but also with Donald Davidson's opposite vision. Hacking well conveys the power of both Wittgenstein's and Davidson's visions in his two popular perceptive discussions—discussions which make two philosophers who are not readily accessible to non-philosophers more accessible. Ian Hacking, "Wittgenstein the Psychologist," *The New York Review of Books* XXIX (April 1, 1982): 42-44 and Ian Hacking, "On the Frontier," *The New Review of Books* XXXI (December 20, 1984): 54-58. In contrasting Wittgenstein and Davidson, we might do well to reflect on Hacking's remark: Philosophers such as Donald Davidson and Michael Dummett have "fallen prey to the idea that there could be such a thing as a 'theory of meaning' in general, and that there could be a general theory of the conditions under which what we say is true. I think that Wittgenstein's theme of the disunity of life, reason, and language runs counter even to Dummett, let alone Davidson. Neither of these men, nor their students, will be much moved by the disunity of *Remarks on the Philosophy of Psy-*

chology, but in the end Wittgenstein's little guerrilla army of unlike examples may begin to tell against the big guns." "Wittgenstein the Psychologist," p. 44. However, in thinking about religion in a Wittgensteinian way one really needs to face the sort of considerations raised by John W. Cook, "Magic, Witchcraft and Science," *Philosophical Investigations* 6 (January 1983): 2-36.

39. Something of the range and subtlety of that debate is well conveyed in B. M. G. Reardon's splendidly conceived anthology, *Religious Thought in the Nineteenth Century,* (Cambridge, England: Cambridge University Press, 1966).

40. Brand Blanshard, *Reason and Belief,* (New Haven, CT: Yale University Press, 1975); C. B. Martin, *Religious Belief,* (Ithaca, NY: Cornell University Press, 1959); Paul Edwards, "Difficulties in the Idea of God," in *The Idea of God,* Edward H. Madden et al. (eds.), (Springfield, IL: Charles E. Thomas, 1968), pp. 43-77; Sidney Hook, *The Quest for Being,* (New York: St. Martin's Press, 1961); Antony Flew, *God and Philosophy,* (London, England: Hutchinson of London, 1966), and *The Presumption of Atheism* (New York: Barnes and Noble, 1976); Michael Durrant, *The Logical Status of 'God'* (New York: St. Martin's Press, 1973); Ronald Hepburn, *Christianity and Paradox,* (London, England: C. A. Watts, 1958); Axel Hägerström, *Philosophy and Religion,* (London, England: George Allen and Unwin, Ltd., 1964); and see the collection edited by Peter Angeles, *Critiques of God,* (Buffalo, NY: Prometheus Books, 1976).

41. I have tried to give some sense of what they are and a hint of a direction to explore, after we have taken to heart Richard Rorty's critique of philosophy, in my "Challenging Analytic Philosophy," *Free Inquiry* 4 (Fall 1984): 52-53; "On Finding One's Feet in Philosophy: From Wittgenstein to Marx," *Meta-philosophy* 16 (January 1985); and "How to Be Skeptical About Philosophy," *Philosophy,* forthcoming.

42. Barnard Williams, "Review of *The Miracle of Theism,*" *Times Literary Supplement* (March 11, 1983): 231.

43. Ibid.

44. Ibid.

45. It is this sort of thing that is Swinburne's project, a project subverted at different stages by Flew and Mackie. R. Swinburne, *The Coherence of Theism, The Existence of God,* and *Faith and Reason.*

46. Williams, op. cit.